PAWNS

IN THE GAME

By William Guy Carr

DAUPHIN
PUBLICATIONS

CONTENTS

TITLE   page

Pawns In The Game

Here is a TRUE story of international intrigue, romances, corruption, graft, and political assassinations, the like of which has never been written before. It is the story of how different groups or atheistic- materialistic men have played in an international chess tournament to decide which group would win ultimate control of the wealth, natural resources, and man- power of the entire world. It is explained how the game has reached the final stage. The International Communists, and the International Capitalists, (both of whom have totalitarian ambitions) have temporarily joined hands to defeat Christian-democracy. The cover design shows that all moves made by the International Conspirators are directed by Satan and while the situation is decidedly serious it is definitely not hopeless. The solution is to end the game the International Conspirators have been playing right now before one or another totalitarian-minded group imposes their ideas on the rest of mankind. The story is sensational and shocking, but it is educational because it is the TRUTH. The author offers practical solutions to problems so many people consider insoluble.

INSIGNIA OF THE ORDER OF ILLUMINATI WHICH IS THE REVERSE OF THE U.S. SEAL AND APPEARS ON U.S. $1.00 BILLS

The insignia of the Order of Illuminati was adopted by Weishaupt at the time he founded the Order, on May 1, 1776. It is that event that is memorialized by the MDCCLXXVI at the base of the pyramid, and not the date of the signing of the Declaration of Independence, as the uninformed have supposed.

The significance of the design is as follows : the pyramid represents the conspiracy for destruction of the Catholic (Universal Christian) Church, and establishment of a "One World", or UN dictatorship, the "secret" of the Order; the eye radiating in all directions, is the "all-spying eye" that symbolizes the terroristic, Gestapo-like, espionage agency that Weishaupt set up under the name of "Insinuating Brethren", to guard the "secret" of the Order and to terrorize the populace into acceptance of its rule. This "Ogpu" had its first workout in the Reign of Terror of the French Revolution, which it was Instrumental in organizing. It is a source of amazement that the electorate tolerates the continuance of use of this insignia as part of the Great Seal of the U.S.

"ANNUIT COEPTIS" means "our enterprise (conspiracy) has been crowned with success". Below, "NOVUS ORDO SECLORUM" explains the nature of the enterprise: and it means "a New Social Order", or "New Deal". It should be noted that this insignia acquired Masonic significance only after merger of that Order with Order of Illuminati at the Congress of Wilhelmsbad, in 1782.

Benjamin Franklin, John Adams (Roosevelt kinsman) and Thomas Jefferson, ardent Illuminist, proposed the above as the reverse of the seal, on the face of which was the eagle symbol, to Congress, which adopted it on June 20, 1782. On adoption of the Constitution, Congress decreed, by Act of September 15, 1789, its retention as seal of the United States. It is stated however, by the State Department in its latest publication on the subject (2860), that "the reverse has never been cut and used as a seal", and that only the observed, bearing the eagle symbol has been used as official seal and coat of arms. It first was published on the left of the reverse of the dollar bills at the beginning of the New Deal, 1933 by order of President F.D. Roosevelt.

What is the meaning of the publication at the outset of the New Deal of this "Gestapo" symbol that had been so carefully suppressed up to that date that few Americana knew of its existence, other than as a Masonic symbol?

It can only mean that with the advent of the New Deal the Illuminist-Socialist-Communist conspirators, followers of Professor Weishaupt, regarded their efforts as beginning to be crowned with success.

In effect this seal proclaims to the One Worlders that the entire power of the U.S. Government is now controlled by the Illuminati's agents and is persuaded or forced to adopt policies which further the secret plans of the conspirators to undermine and destroy it together with the remaining governments of the so-called 'Free World', ALL existing religions, etc., etc., so that the Synagogue of Satan will be able to usurp the powers of the first world government to be established and then impose a Luciferian totalitarian dictatorship upon what remains of the Human Race.

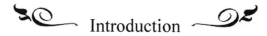

Introduction

If what I reveal surprises and shocks the reader, please don't develop an inferiority complex because I am frank to admit that although I have worked since 1911, trying to find out *why the Human Race can't live in peace and enjoy the bounties and blessing God provides for our use and benefit in such abundance?* It was 1950 before I penetrated the secret that the wars and revolutions which scourge our lives, and the chaotic conditions that prevail, are nothing more or less than the effects of the continuing Luciferian conspiracy. It started in that part of the universe we call heaven when Lucifer challenged The Right of God to exercise supreme authority. The Holy Scriptures tell us how the Luciferian conspiracy was transferred to this world in the Garden of Eden. Until I realized that our struggle is not with flesh and blood, but with the spiritual forces of darkness who control all those in high places on this earth (Eph. 6:12) the pieces of evidence gathered all over this world just didn't fit together and make sense. (I am not ashamed to admit that the "Bible" provided the "Key" which enabled me to obtain an answer to the question quoted above.)

Very few people seem able to appreciate that Lucifer is the brightest and most intelligent of the heavenly host and, because he is a pure spirit, he is indestructible. The scriptures tell us his power is such that he caused one-third of the most intelligent of the heavenly host to defect from God, and join him, because he claimed God's Plan for the rule of the universe is weak and impractical because it is based on the premise that lesser beings can be taught to know, love, and wish to serve him voluntarily out of respect for his own infinite perfections. The Luciferian ideology states might is right. It claims beings of proven superior intelligence have the right to rule those less gifted because the masses don't know what is best for them. The Luciferian ideology is what we call totalitarianism today.

The Old Testament is simply the history of how Satan became prince of the world, and caused our first parents to defect from God. It relates how the synagogue of Satan was established on this earth; it tells how it has worked since to prevent God's Plan for the rule of the universe being established on this earth. Christ came to earth when the conspiracy reached the stage that, to use his own words, Satan controlled all those in high places. He exposed the synagogue of Satan (Rev. 2:9; 3:9) he denounced those who belonged to it as sons of the devil (Lucifer), whom he castigated as the father of lies (John 8:44) and the prince of deceit (2 Cor. 11:14). He was specific in his statement that those who comprised the synagogue of Satan were those who called themselves Jews, but were not, and did lie (Rev. 2:9; 3:9). He identified the Money-Changers (Bankers) the Scribes, and the Pharisees as the Illuminati of his day. What so many people seem to forget is the fact that Christ came on earth to release us from the bonds of Satan with which we were being bound tighter and tighter as the years rolled by. Christ gave us the solution to our problem when he told us we must go forth and teach the truth, regarding this conspiracy (John

8. 31:59), to all people of all nations. He promised that if we did this, knowledge of the truth would set us free (Matt. 28:19). The Luciferian Conspiracy has developed until it is in its semi-final stage (Matt. 24: 15:34), simply because we have failed to put the mandate Christ gave us into effect.

In 1784 "An Act of God" placed the Bavarian government in possession of evidence which proved the existence of the continuing Luciferian Conspiracy. Adam Weishaupt, a Jesuit- trained professor of canon law, defected from Christianity, and embraced the Luciferian ideology while teaching in Ingoldstadt University. In 1770 the money lenders (who had recently organized the House of Rothschild), retained him to revise and modernize the age-old 'protocols' designed to give the Synagogue of Satan ultimate world domination so they can impose the Luciferian ideology upon what remains of the Human Race, after the final social cataclysm, by use of satanic despotism. Weishaupt completed his task May 1st, 1776.

The plan required the destruction of ALL existing governments and religions. This objective was to be reached by dividing the masses, which he termed Goyim (meaning human cattle) into opposing camps in ever increasing numbers on political, racial, social, economic and other issues. The opposing sides were then to be armed and an 'incident' provided which would cause them to fight and weaken themselves as they destroyed National Governments and Religious Institutions.

In 1776 Weishaupt organized the Illuminati to put the plot into execution. The word Illuminati is derived from Lucifer, and means 'holders of the light'. Using the lie that his objective was to bring about a one world government to enable men with proven mental ability to govern the world, he recruited about two thousand followers. These included the most intelligent men in the field of arts and letters, education, the sciences, finance and industry. He then established Lodges of the Grand Orient to be their secret headquarters.

Weishaupt's revised plan required his Illuminati to do the following things to help them accomplish their purpose:

1. Use monetary and sex bribery to obtain control of people already occupying positions in high places in the various levels of ALL governments and other fields of human endeavor. Once an influential person had fallen for the lies, deceits, and temptations of the Illuminati they were to be held in bondage by application of political and other forms of blackmail and threats of financial ruin, public exposure, and physical harm and even death to themselves and their loved ones.

2. Illuminati on the faculties of colleges and universities were to recommend students possessing exceptional mental ability belonging to well-bred families with international leanings for special training in internationalism. This

training was to be provided by granting scholarships to those selected. They were to be educated (indoctrinated) into accepting the 'Idea' that only a One World Government can put an end to recurring wars and tribulations. They were to be at first persuaded and then convinced that men of special ability and brains had the RIGHT to rule those less gifted, because the Goyim (masses of the people) don't know what is best for them physically, mentally and spiritually. Today three such special schools are located in Gordonstoun in Scotland; Salem in Germany; and Anavryta in Greece. Prince Phillip, the husband of Queen Elizabeth of England, was educated at Gordonstoun at the instigation of Lord Louis Mountbatten, his Uncle, who became Britain's Admiral of the Fleet after World War Two ended.

3. Influential people trapped into coming under the control of the Illuminati, and students who had been specially educated and trained were to be used as agents and placed behind the scenes of ALL governments as "Experts" and "Specialists" so they could advise the top executives to adopt policies which would in the long run, serve the secret plans of the One Worlders and bring about the ultimate destruction of the governments and religions they were elected or appointed to serve.

4. The Illuminati were to obtain control of the Press and all other agencies which distribute information to the public. News and information was to be slanted so that the Goyim would come to believe that a One World Government is the ONLY solution to our many and varied problems.

Because Britain and France were the two greatest powers at the end of the 18th Century, Weishaupt ordered the Illuminati to foment the Colonial Wars to weaken the British Empire and organize the Great Revolution to weaken the French Empire. The latter he scheduled should start in 1789.

A German author named Zwack put Weishaupt's revised version of the age-old conspiracy into book form and named it "Einige Original-Scripten." In 1784 a copy of this document was sent to the Illuminists Weishaupt had delegated to foment the French revolution. The courier was struck dead by lightning as he rode through Ratisbon on his way from Frankfurt to Paris. The police found the subversive documents on his body and turned them over to the proper government authorities.

After careful study of the plot the Bavarian Government ordered the police to raid Weishaupt's newly organized lodges of the Grand Orient and the homes of some of his most influential associates, including the castle of Baron Bassus-in-Sandersdorf. Additional evidence thus obtained convinced the authorities the documents were a genuine copy of a conspiracy by which the synagogue of Satan, who controlled the Illuminati AT THE TOP, planned to use wars and revolutions to bring about the establishment of one kind or another of a One World Government, the powers of which they intended to usurp as soon as it was established.

In 1785, the Bavarian Government outlawed the Illuminati and closed the lodges of the Grand Orient. In 1786, they published the details of the conspiracy. The English title is "The Original Writings of the Order and Sect of The Illuminati". Copies of the conspiracy were sent to the heads of church and state. The power of the Illuminati was so great that this warning was ignored, as were the warnings Christ had given the world.

The Illuminati went underground. Weishaupt instructed his Illuminists to infiltrate into the lodges of Blue Masonry and form a secret society within secret societies.

Only masons who proved themselves Internationalists, and those whose conduct proved they had defected from God, are initiated into the Illuminati. Thus the conspirators used the cloak of philanthropy to hide their revolutionary and subversive activities. In order to infiltrate into masonic lodges in Britain Illuminists invited John Robison over to Europe. He was a high degree mason in the Scottish Rite: Professor of natural philosophy at Edinburgh University; and Secretary of The Royal Society of Edinburgh. John Robison did not fall for the lie that the objective of the one worlders was to form a benevolent dictatorship. He kept his reactions to himself however, and was entrusted with a copy of Weishaupt's Revised Conspiracy for study and safe keeping.

Because the heads of church and state in France were advised to ignore the warnings given them the revolution broke out in 1789. In order to alert other governments to their danger, in 1798 John Robison published a book, entitled "Proof of a Conspiracy to Destroy All Governments and Religions". But his warnings have been ignored, as were the others.

Thomas Jefferson had become a student of Weishaupt's. He was one of his strongest defenders when he was outlawed by his government. Jefferson infiltrated the Illuminati into the newly organized Lodges of The Scottish Rite in New England. Realizing this information will shock many Americans I wish to record the following facts:

In 1789, John Robison warned masonic leaders the Illuminati had infiltrated into their lodges. On July 19th, 1798, David Pappen, President of Harvard University, issued the same warning to the graduating class and lectured them on the influence illuminism was having on American politics and religion.

John Quincy Adams had organized the New England Masonic Lodges. In 1800 he decided to oppose Jefferson for the presidency. He wrote three letters to Colonel Wm. L. Stone exposing how Jefferson was using masonic lodges for subversive purposes. The information contained in these letters is credited with winning Adams the election. The letters are in Rittenburg Square Library, in

Philadelphia.

In 1826 Captain Wm. Morgan decided it was his duty to inform other Masons and the general public what the TRUTH is regarding the Illuminati, their secret plans and intended purpose. The Illuminati obtained the services of Richard Howard, an English Illuminist, to carry out their sentence "That Morgan be EXECUTED as a traitor. Captain Morgan was warned of his danger. He tried to escape to Canada but Howard caught up with him near the border. He was murdered near the Niagara Gorge. Research proved that one Avery Allyn made a sworn affidavit in the City of New York to the effect that he heard Richard Howard report to a meeting of Knights Templars in St. John's Hall, New York, how he had 'Executed' Morgan. He told how arrangements had then been made to ship Howard back to England

Very few people to-day know that general disapproval and disgust over this incident caused nearly 40% of Masons belonging to the Northern Jurisdiction of the United States to secede. I have copies of minutes of a meeting held to discuss this particular matter. The power of those who direct the Luciferian conspiracy against God and Man can be realized by the ability of their agents to prevent such outstanding events of history being taught in our public schools.

In 1829, the Illuminati held a meeting in New York which was addressed by a British Illuminist named Wright. Those in attendance were informed that the Illuminati intended to unite the Nihilist and Atheist groups with all other subversive organizations into an international organization to be known as Communism. This destructive force was to be used to enable the Illuminati to foment future wars and revolutions. Clinton Roosevelt (a direct ancestor of F.D. R.) Horace Greeley and Chas. Dana were appointed a committee to raise funds for this new venture. The fund they raised financed Karl Marx and Engels when they wrote "Das Capital" and "The Communist Manifesto" in Soho, England.

In 1830, Weishaupt died. He carried the deception that the Illuminati were dead to his own death- bed where, to convince his spiritual advisers, he pretended to repent and rejoin the Church.

According to Weishaupt's revised version of the Age-Old conspiracy the Illuminati were to organize, finance, direct and control ALL international organizations and groups by working their agents into executive positions AT THE TOP. Thus it was that while Karl Marx was writing the Communist Manifesto under direction of one group of Illuminists, Professor Karl Ritter of Frankfurt University was writing the antithesis under direction of another group, so that those who direct the conspiracy AT THE TOP could use the differences in these two ideologies to start dividing larger and larger numbers of the Human Race into opposing camps so they could be armed and then made to fight and destroy each other, together with their political and religious institutions. The work Ritter started was continued by the German so-called philosopher Friedrich Wilhelm Nietzsche (1844-1900) who founded Nietzscheism.

Nietzscheism was developed into Fascism and later into Nazism and used to enable the agents of the Illuminati to foment World Wars One and Two.

In 1834 the Italian revolutionary leader Gussepi Mazzini was selected by the Illuminati to be director of their revolutionary program throughout the world. He held this post until he died in 1872.

In 1840, General Albert Pike was brought under the influence of Mazzini because he became a disgruntled officer when President Jefferson Davis disbanded his auxiliary Indian troops on the grounds they had committed atrocities under the cloak of legitimate warfare. Pike accepted the idea of a one world government and ultimately became head of the Luciferian Priesthood. Between 1859, and 1871, he worked out the details of a military blue-print, for three world wars, and three major revolutions which he considered would further the conspiracy to its final stage during the twentieth century.

Most of his work was done in the 13 room mansion he built in Little Rock, Arkansas, in 1840. When the Illuminati, and the lodges of the Grand Orient, became suspect, because of Mazzini's revolutionary activities in Europe, Pike organized the New and Reformed Palladian Rite. He established three supreme councils; one in Charleston, S.C., another in Rome, Italy and another in Berlin, Germany. He had Mazzini establish twenty three subordinate councils in strategic locations throughout the world. These have been the secret headquarters of the world revolutionary movement ever since. Long before Marconi invented wireless (Radio), the scientists who were of the Illuminati had made it possible for Pike and the Heads of his councils to communicate secretly. It was the discovery of this secret that enabled intelligence officers to understand how apparently unrelated 'incidents' took place simultaneously throughout the world which aggravated a situation and developed into a war or revolution.

Pike's plan was as simple as it has proved effective. He required that Communism, Nazism, Political Zionism, and other International movements be organized and used to foment the three global wars and three major revolutions. The first world war was to be fought so as to enable the Illuminati to overthrow the powers of the Tzars in Russia and turn that country into the stronghold of Atheistic-Communism. The differences stirred up by agents of the Illuminati between the British and German Empires were to be used to foment this war. After the war ended, Communism was to be built up and used to destroy other governments and weaken religions.

World War Two was to be fomented by using the differences between Fascists and Political Zionists. This war was to be fought so that Nazism would be destroyed and the power of Political Zionism increased so that the sovereign state of Israel could be established in Palestine. During world war two International Communism was to be built up until it equaled in strength that of united Christendom. At this point it was to be contained and kept in check until required for the final social cataclysm. Can any informed person deny

Roosevelt and Churchill did not put this policy into effect?

World War Three is to be fomented by using the differences the agents of the Illuminati stir up between Political Zionists and the leaders of the Moslem world. The war is to be directed in such a manner that Islam (the Arab World including Mohammedanism) and Political Zionism (including the State of Israel) will destroy themselves while at the same time the remaining nations, once more divided against each other on this issue, will be forced to fight themselves into a state of complete exhaustion physically, mentally, spiritually and economically. Can any unbiased and reasoning person deny that the intrigue now going on in the Near, Middle, and Far East isn't designed to accomplish this devilish purpose?

On August 15, 1871, Pike told Mazzini that after World War Three is ended, those who aspire to undisputed world domination will provoke the greatest social cataclysm the world has ever known. We quote his own written words (taken from the letter catalogued in the British Museum Library, London, Eng.):

"We shall unleash the Nihilists and Atheists, and we shall provoke a formidable social cataclysm which in all its horror will show clearly to the nations the effect of absolute atheism, origin of savagery and of the bloodiest turmoil. Then everywhere, the citizens, obliged to defend themselves against the world minority of revolutionaries, will exterminate those destroyers of civilization, and the multitude, disillusioned with Christianity, whose deistic spirits will be from that moment without compass (direction), anxious for an ideal, but without knowing where to render its adoration, will receive the true light through the universal manifestation of the pure doctrine of Lucifer brought finally out in the public view, a manifestation which will result from the general reactionary movement which will follow the destruction of Christianity and atheism, both conquered and exterminated at the same time."

When Mazzini died in 1872, Pike made another Italian revolutionary leader, named Adriano Lemmi, his successor. Lemmi was later succeeded by Lenin and Trotsky. The revolutionary activities of all these men were financed by British, French, German, and American international bankers. The reader must remember that the International Bankers of to-day, like the Money-Changers of Christ's day, are only tools or agents of the Illuminati.

While the general public has been lead to believe that Communism is a movement of the workers (soviets) to destroy Capitalism, Pawns In The Game and The Red Fog Over America prove that both British and American Intelligence Officers obtained authentic documentary evidence which proved that internationalist capitalists operating through their international banking houses had financed both sides in every war and revolution fought since 1776. Those who to-day comprise The Synagogue of Satan direct our governments, whom they hold in usury, to fight the wars and revolutions so they further Pike's plans to bring the world to that stage of the conspiracy when Atheistic-Communism and the whole of Christendom can be forced into an all-out war within each remaining nation as well as on an international scale.

There is plenty of documentary evidence to prove that Pike, like Weishaupt, was head of the Luciferian Priesthood in his day. In addition to the letter he wrote Mazzini in 1871, another he wrote to the heads of his Palladian Councils July 14th, 1889 fell into hands other than intended. It was written to explain the Luciferian dogma, concerning worship of Satan and worship of Lucifer. In it, he said in part:

"That which we say to the crowd is 'we worship God'. But it is the God that one worships without superstition. The religion should be, by all us initiates of the high degrees, maintained in the purity of the Luciferian doctrine ... Yes! Lucifer is God. And unfortunately Adonay (the name given by Luciferians to the God we worship) is God also ... for the absolute can only exist as two gods. Thus, the doctrine of Satanism is a heresy: and the true and pure philosophical religion is the belief in Lucifer, the equal of Adonay: but Lucifer, God of Light, and God of Good, is struggling for humanity against Adonay the God of Darkness and Evil."

Propaganda put out by those who direct the Luciferian conspiracy has caused the general public to believe all who oppose Christianity are Atheists. This is a deliberate lie circulated to hide the secret plans of the High Priests of the Luciferian Creed who direct the Synagogue of Satan so that the human race still find it impossible to establish on this earth God's plan for the rule of the universe, as he explained it to our first parents in the Garden of Eden, told in Genesis. The High Priests of the Luciferian Creed work from the darkness. They remain behind the scenes. They keep their identity and true purpose secret, even from the vast majority of those they deceive into doing their will and furthering their secret plans and ambitions. They know that the final success of their conspiracy to usurp the powers of world government depends upon their ability to keep their identity and TRUE purpose secret until no cunning or power can prevent them crowning THEIR leader King-despot of the entire world. The Holy Scriptures predicted what Weishaupt and Pike planned would be put into effect until the Spiritual forces of evil controlled this earth. Rev. 20 tells us how, after these things we relate have come to pass, Satan will be bound for a thousand years. What the term a thousand years means in measure of time as we know it I don't pretend to know. As far as I am concerned study of the Luciferian conspiracy, in the light of knowledge contained in the Holy Scriptures, has convinced me that the binding of Satan and the containment of Satanic forces upon this earth can be brought about more speedily if the WHOLE TRUTH concerning the existence of the continuing Luciferian conspiracy is made known as quickly as possible to ALL the people of ALL remaining nations.

Research dug up letters from Mazzini which revealed how the High Priests of the Luciferian Creed keep their identity and true purpose secret. In a letter Mazzini wrote to his revolutionary associate, Dr. Breidenstine, only a few years before he died he said "We form an association of brothers in all points of the globe. We wish to break every yoke. Yet, there is one unseen that can be hardly felt, yet it weighs on us. Whence comes it? Where is it? No one knows ... or at least no one tells. This association is secret even to us the veterans of secret societies."

In 1925 his Eminence Cardinal Caro y Rodriguez, Archbishop of Santiago, Chile, published a book "The Mystery of Freemasonry Unveiled", to expose how the Illuminati, the Satanists, and the Luciferians had imposed a secret society upon a secret society. He produces a great deal of documentary evidence to prove that not even 32nd and 33rd degree Masons know what goes on in the Lodges of the Grand Orient and Pike's New and Reformed Palladian Rite and the affiliated Lodges of Adoption in which female members of the conspiracy are initiated. On page 108 he quotes the authority Margiotta to prove that before Pike selected Lemmi to succeed Mazzini as Director of the World Revolutionary Movement Lemmi was a rabid and confirmed Satanist. But after he had been selected he was initiated into the Luciferian ideology.

The fact that the High Priests of the Luciferian Creed on this earth introduced the worship of Satan in the lower degrees of both Grand Orient Lodges and the councils of the Palladian Rite and then initiated selected individuals to the FULL SECRET that Lucifer is God the equal of Adonay, has puzzled many historians and research workers. The Holy Scriptures mention Lucifer only a few times — Isa. 14; Luke 10:18; Rev. 9:1-11. The Luciferian Doctrine however states definitely that Lucifer led the Heavenly revolt; that Satan is the oldest son of God (Adonay) and the brother of St. Michael who defeated the Luciferian conspiracy in Heaven. The Luciferian teachings also claim that St. Michael came on earth in the person of Jesus Christ to try to repeat what he had done in Heaven ... and failed. Because Lucifer, Satan, the Devil — call him what you may — is the father of lies, it would appear that those spiritual forces of darkness deceive as many as possible so called intellectuals into doing their will here as they did in heaven.

Without getting into controversy it should be easy for the average Christian to realize that there are TWO supernatural powers. One we refer to as God to whom the Scriptures give many names; and the other, the Devil, who also seems to have many names. The important thing to remember is that according to Revelations there is to be a final judgment. Satan will break or be released from the bonds with which he is bound for a thousand years. He will again create chaos on this earth. Then Christ will intervene on behalf of the elect and God will divide the Sheep from the Goats. We are told that those who defect from God will be ruled in utter chaos and confusion by Lucifer, Satan, or the Devil, for all eternity and will hate their ruler, themselves, and each other because they will realize they were deceived into defecting from God and losing his love and friendship forever.

Once a person reads *Pawns In The Game* and *The Red Fog Over America* it will be easy to realize that the struggle going on is NOT of a worldly or temporal nature. It originated in that part of the universe we designate "The Celestial World"; its purpose is to win the souls of men away from God Almighty.

Learned theologians have stated that Lucifer, Satan, or call the head of the Forces of Evil simply "The Devil" knows he did wrong and knows that he was wrong. He is a pure spirit and therefore indestructible. Knowing he is wrong he still is determined to drag as many souls as possible into hell with him to share his misery. This being a fact our duty is clear : We have to make known the TRUTH in this regard to as many others as quickly as possible so they can avoid the snares and pit-falls set by those who serve the devil's purpose and penetrate the lies and deceits of those who wander about the world seeking the ruin of souls. Wars and revolutions give the devil his greatest harvests of human souls, because "so many are called and so few are chosen" Matt. 20; 16; 22: 14. We so often hear what is going on in the world to-day referred to as "A war for the minds of men". That is only a half truth and is worse than a whole lie. Weishaupt's plot requires:

1. Abolition of ALL ordered national governments.
2. Abolition of inheritance.
3. Abolition of private property.
4. Abolition of patriotism.
5. Abolition of the individual home and family life as the cell from which all civilizations have stemmed.
6. Abolition of ALL religions established and existing so that the Luciferian ideology of totalitarianism may be imposed on mankind

The headquarters of the conspiracy in the late 1700s was in Frankfurt, Germany, where the House of Rothschild had been established and linked together other international financiers who had literally "Sold their souls to the devil". After the Bavarian Government's exposure in 1786, the High Priests of the Luciferian Creed established their headquarters in Switzerland; since World War Two the headquarters have been in the Harold Pratt Building New York. The Rockefellers have replaced the Rothschilds as far as the manipulation of finances is concerned.

In the final phase of the conspiracy the government will consist of the king-despot, the Synagogue of Satan, and a few millionaires, economists, and scientists who have proved their devotion to the Luciferian cause. All others are to be integrated into a vast conglomeration of mongrelized humanity, by artificial insemination practiced on an international scale. On pages 49-51 "The impact of Science on Society" Bertrand Russell says that ultimately less than 30 percent of the female population and 5 percent of the male population will be used for breeding purposes. Reproduction will be strictly limited to the type and numbers required to fill the needs of the state.

Because the rulings of the courts are so much in the public mind to-day, I will conclude my introduction by quoting from a lecture given to the members of the Grand Orient Lodge of Paris, France, by a top executive of Pike's Palladian Rite, at the turn of the present century. He said:

"Under our influence the execution of the laws of the Goyim has been reduced to a minimum. The prestige of the law has been exploded by the liberal interpretations introduced into this sphere. In the most important and fundamental affairs and questions judges decide as we dictate to them: see matters in the light where with we enfold them for the administration of the Goyim, of course through persons who are our tools though we do not appear to have anything in common with them. Even Senators and the higher administration accept our council..."

This should explain the "Little Rock" incident, which took place a half century later.

Can any thinking person deny that the conspiracy as revised by Weishaupt in the latter 1700s, and the plans drawn up by Pike in the latter 1800s, haven't matured exactly as intended? The empires of Russia and Germany have been destroyed. Those of Britain and France reduced to third class powers. The crowned heads have fallen like over-ripe fruit. The world's population has twice been divided into opposing camps as the result of propaganda put out by the Illuminati. Two world wars have seen Christians kill each other off efficiently by the tens of millions without any person engaged having the slightest personal animosity towards the other. Two of the major revolutions, those of Russia and China, are accomplished facts. Communism has been built up until it is equal in strength to the whole of Christendom. Intrigue now going on in the East and Middle East is fomenting World War Three. After that, unless stopped right now by sheer weight of informed public opinion, will come the final social cataclysm; then absolute physical, mental, and spiritual slavery will follow.

Can any informed person deny that Communism is being tolerated in the remaining so-called free countries? The British special branch of intelligence; the Canadian R.C.M.P., and the U.S. F.B.I. could arrest every Communist leader within twenty four hours of the order being given, but they are not allowed to act. WHY? The answer is simple. Communism is being 'Contained' on the national and international levels of government on the 'ADVICE' of the Illuminati's agents who give a great many utterly unconvincing excuses for the present policy of Britain, Canada, and the United States towards national and international Communism. If the F.B.I. or the R.C.M.P. act then the Judges of the Supreme Courts of both countries find reason in law why those arrested should be set free. Such action would be utterly ridiculous if Communism wasn't being contained for use in the final social cataclysm.

Is it not time Christians woke up to the realization of their danger? Is it not time parents refused to allow their children to be used as cannon fodder to serve the Luciferian cause? Is it not time we became "Doers" of the WORD of God instead of "Hearers" only?

The Federation of Christian Laymen, of which I have the honor to be president, has made available all the knowledge obtained to date dealing with the various aspects of the conspiracy. We have published Pawns In The Game and Red Fog Over America in book form, and other pamphlets. We keep those who have read our books up to date concerning the progress of the conspiracy by publishing a monthly newsletter, entitled News Behind The News. Our predictions of forthcoming events are based on our knowledge of the continuing conspiracy. They have come true to such an amazing extent that we have aroused the interest of thinking people throughout the world. We invite you to join us. Make yourselves fully acquainted with the various aspects of the conspiracy, then pass that knowledge on to others. Do this and the power of informed public opinion will become the greatest power on earth.

I urge you to organize Christian Civic Leagues or similar groups. Use them as study groups. Use them to elect men who are loyal citizens. But before you select a candidate for public office, make sure he is fully informed regarding all aspects of the International Conspiracy on the municipal, state, and federal levels of government. All one worlders won't serve the Synagogue of Satan, knowingly. It is our duty to make them acquainted with the truth. Christian civic leagues should be non-partisan, and non-denominational. Their purpose should be to put God back into politics so we may establish government in accordance with His Plan for the rule of the universe as explained to us in The Scriptures and by God's only Son Jesus Christ. Only then will his will be done here as it is in heaven. In my humble opinion, not until this is done will God intervene on our behalf and the words of The Lord's Prayer be accomplished.

Signed: *William Guy Carr*
Clearwater Fla.
Oct. 13th, 1958.

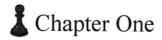

Chapter One

The World Revolutionary Movement (W.R.M.)

In order to understand the Causes in the past, which have produced the *Effects* we experience to- day, especially in regard to the unsatisfactory state of national and international affairs, history must be studied because history does repeat itself. History repeats itself because there has been perfect continuity of purpose in the struggle which has been going on since the beginning of Time between the forces of *Good* and *Evil* to decide whether the Rule of Almighty God, shall prevail, or whether the world shall literally go to the Devil. The issue is just as simple as that.

It is a fact that both the forces for *Good*, and the forces for *Evil*, have been divided and split into factions. These factions often oppose each other in an effort to reach a common goal — this makes a study of the subject complicated. These differences in opinion have been produced by propaganda which is used more often for spreading lies and half-truths, than it is used as a medium for telling the plain unvarnished truth regarding any given event or subject.

War-mongers have used propaganda to divide human beings into opposing camps on political, social, economic and religious issues so they could stir them up into such a state of emotionalism that they will fight and kill each other. In order to discover the causes which have produced the effects we experience to-day all available evidence must be studied carefully. Truths must be separated from falsehoods, and fiction from fact. Past events must be studied to see how they have affected and influenced conditions existing today.

The human race is divided into two main camps as far as religion is concerned. Those in one camp believe in the existence of a God. Those in the other camp deny the existence of a Supreme Being of any kind. This fact is of major importance, because it will be proved that all wars and revolutions have been the result of one group or another trying to force their ideologies upon the people of the entire world.

The conception of GOD varies with different sects. Theism teaches that God is a personal being and the author and ruler of the universe. Pantheism identifies God with the universe but not as a personal Being. Pantheists believe in the doctrine of the universal Presence of the Divine Spirit in nature. A kind of Pantheism has found its way into many religious and philosophical systems — Buddhism and Hinduism both partake of this doctrine. Belief in a personal God includes belief in a celestial world, belief in the soul and life in the celestial world after the death of our mortal bodies. People who believe in a personal God must of necessity believe in the existence of Satan — a personal Devil.

A study of comparative religions proves that, as far as it is possible to probe back, even the members of isolated tribes have always had a religious instinct which caused them to discuss and ponder the questions: "Why were we born?" "For what purpose do we live?" "What ends do we serve?" "Whither do we go when we die?" Even the most backward tribes of Central Africa and Australia seem to have had no doubts regarding the existence of God, a spiritual world and another existence for their own souls, after the death of their mortal bodies.

A study of comparative religions also indicates that most, if not all, religions (which teach belief in a Supreme Being) started out on a more or less uniformly high level in which the worship and love of Almighty God, respect for our elders and parents, love for our neighbors, i.e. benefactors, and the offering of prayers for deceased relatives and friends formed the basic principle. Evil men, actuated by motives of selfishness and greed and the desire for power, caused nearly all religions to deteriorate to the levels we find at them to-day. Some religions deteriorated as far as having priests sacrifice human beings as their offerings to God. Even Christianity, which is one of the most recent religions, deteriorated. Christianity has been split up into many factions (denominations) and it would require a great deal of imagination to picture the vast majority, who profess to be Christians today, as true soldiers, or followers, of Jesus Christ.

Generally speaking, Christianity has deteriorated in regard to the practice of good works. This becomes a matter of major importance when we study the struggle going on between the forces of Good and Evil today, because the practice of good works created neighborliness, and brought about unity in the Christian Fold. The real definition of the word 'neighbor' is a person who has proved himself your benefactor; a person upon whom you can rely; a person, who you are certain, wouldn't do you any harm under any circumstances; that man or woman is your neighbor. The Scriptures tell us we must love our neighbor as ourselves for God's sake. The only way to make good neighbors is to perform good works unselfishly. Lack of individual good works means lack of unity and lack of the proper community spirit. Today we have adopted the cold checkbook type of doing good works. We leave the performance to professional Social Welfare Workers. This has justified the use of the term "As cold as professional charity". It is well to remember that even government Social Security legislation does not relieve individuals of the duties of neighborliness. Prayer without good works avails a man nothing. In Christian weakness and disunity lies the atheistic strength.

For one reason or another many Christian denominations are fast losing their hold upon the youth of the so-called Free Nations. Each person lost to the Christian belief usually turns to secularism and often ends up as a "Fellow Traveler" in one or another of the atheistic ideologies of Communism or Nazism. [1]

The vast majority of professed Christians are not real "Soldiers of Jesus Christ" whereas every card-bearing member of either the Communist or Nazi parties must swear to give unlimited obedience to the leaders; to devote every waking hour to the furtherance of the Cause; and contribute one tenth of his, or

2

her, income, towards financing the party's activities.

While Christians are hopelessly divided into approximately 400 denominations, Communists and Nazis are all solidly united as anti-Christians. A continuation of this state of affairs cannot help but enable the leaders of one or another atheistic group winning world domination. When they do so they will enslave body, soul and mind, all who refuse to accept their heathen ideology. The Illuminati will then impose the despotism of Satan.

There is a great similarity in the beliefs of those who worship a Supreme Being, regarding the origin of Man. The majority believes that "The Great Father" peopled this world for the purpose of giving the less culpable of those who followed Lucifer during the heavenly revolution another chance to decide, of their own free will, whether they will accept God's authority, and give Him unlimited obedience or, literally, go to the Devil. It is such beliefs that sustain such despised sects as Doukhobors in their passive resistance to man-made laws which they consider are contrary to God's Divine Laws. It is well to remember that the name Lucifer means Holder of the Light — a very brilliant being, the "Brightest" of the Angels. Notwithstanding these special gifts and privileges, he revolted against the supremacy of Almighty God.

Most people, other than Atheists and Darwinists, accept the story of the Creation. There are however, a great many different opinions regarding the story of Adam and Eve and the Garden of Eden. Many students of Comparative Religion argue that it is likely God created many worlds, and many Adams and Eves, and placed them in locations where they could reproduce their kind and populate the planets upon which they lived.

The fact that human beings are placed on this earth by a method and process of birth, which prevents them having any knowledge of a previous existence, fits in with this theory. All we know, regarding the period before Creation, is what has been revealed to us as told in the Scriptures. It really doesn't matter a great deal if there was one or many Adams and Eves. The important thing to remember is the fact that all human beings have been given a Free Will and must decide for themselves whether they believe in a God and a Devil, or if they believe in the atheistic-materialistic ideology. Each and every human being must make up his, or her, mind one way or the other. If a person believes there is a God and a Devil, then that person must decide which he is going to serve. An Atheist, if he joins either of the totalitarian ideologies serves the Party and the State. He must give unlimited obedience to the head of the Party and the State. The penalty for diversion is suffering, imprisonment, and possibly death.

Belief in the existence of God automatically includes belief in supernaturally good and evil Spirits which can influence men's minds for good or evil purposes. It is the struggle going on for the possession of men's souls that causes the conditions which prevail upon this earth to- day. The power of the Devil was dramatically emphasized when he tempted Christ himself, while he was in the desert preparing himself for his ministry.

3

Atheists, on the other hand, do not believe in the existence of Supernatural Beings. They argue that God has never been proved to exist. There are many groups of Atheists. True Communists, Grand Orient Masons, Free Thinkers, Members of the League of the Godless, Illuminatists, Nihilists, Anarchists, True Nazi, [2] and the Mafia. Many Godless people subscribe to various forms of Secularism, even if they fight shy of becoming active in the Atheistic Communists and Nazi groups. [3]

Most Atheists base their beliefs on the principle that there is only one reality — MATTER — That the blind forces of MATTER (sometimes referred to as ENERGY) evolve into vegetable, animal, and man. They deny the existence of a soul, and the possibility of life, in another world, after the death of our mortal bodies.

Evidence will be produced to prove that Modern Communism was organized in the year 1773 by a group of International Money-Barons who have used it since, as their manual of action, to further their secret plans to bring about a Totalitarian Godless State. Lenin made this clear in his book Left Wing Communism. On page 53, he said: "Our theory (Communism) is not a dogma (Settled Doctrine); it is a manual of action". Many modern leaders have said and done the same things as Lucifer did during the heavenly revolution. There is no appreciable difference between Red and Black Atheism. The only difference is in the plans used by the opposing leaders to ultimately win undisputed control of the world's resources, and bring into being their ideas for a Totalitarian, Godless, Dictatorship.

Karl Marx (1818-1883) was a German of Jewish descent. He was expelled from Germany, and afterwards from France, for his revolutionary activities. He was given asylum in England. In 1848 he published the Communist Manifesto. Marx admitted this long range plan, to turn the world into an International of Soviet Socialist Republics, may take centuries to accomplish.

Karl Ritter (1779-1859) was a German Professor of History and Geopolitical science. He wrote the anti-thesis to Karl Marx's Communist Manifesto. He also drew up a plan by which he maintained the Aryan Race could first dominate Europe and then the entire world. Certain Atheistic leaders of the Aryan Group adopted Karl Ritter's plan. They organized Nazism to further their secret ambitions to obtain ultimate control of the World and turn it into a Godless State, under their conception of a totalitarian dictatorship. This small group of men knew they must either join up with, or destroy, the power and influence of the International Bankers. It is doubtful if more than a mere handful of the top level leaders of the Communist and Fascist movements know their organizations are being used to further the secret ambitions of the Illuminati which are the High Priests of Satanism.

According to the leaders of both atheistic groups the State must be Supreme. This being so the Head of the State is God on Earth. This belief brings into actual practice the deification of man.

Much more is generally known about Karl Marx and Communism than about Karl Ritter and Nazism. Ritter was for many years Professor of History at Frankfort University, Germany. Afterwards he taught Geography at the Berlin University. In educational circles he was considered one of the greatest authorities on History, Geography, and Geopolitical Science. Because the "Aims and Objects" of the Leaders of the Aryan Party have always been kept secret, Karl Ritter's connection with the Leaders and Nazism is very little known. Intelligence Officers connected with the British Government unearthed his connection with the Aryan War Lords when studying Political Economy; Geopolitical Science; and Comparative Religions, in German universities. [4] This information was passed on to the proper authorities but, as so often happens, political leaders and diplomats, either failed to realize the significance of what they were told or wished to ignore it.[5]

Karl Ritter's study of History convinced him that a very small group of wealthy, and influential, international Bankers, who gave allegiance to no country but meddled in the affairs of all, had, in 1773 organized Grand Orient Freemasonry for the purpose of using The World Revolutionary Movement to further their secret ambitions. Their Long Range Plan was for their group to gain ultimate control of the wealth, natural resources, and man-power of the entire world. Their ultimate objective was to form a Totalitarian Dictatorship based on their theories of Atheistic dialectical and historical materialism. Ritter claimed that most of, if not all, the International Bankers were of Jewish descent, regardless of whether or not they practiced the Jewish faith.

In his anti-thesis to Karl Marx's Communist Manifesto he dealt with the dangers to be faced if this group of men were allowed to continue to control and direct the policies of International Communism. He offered the German Aryan War-Lords very concrete and practical suggestions for defeating the conspiracy of the International Money-Barons. [6] Professor Ritter gave the Aryan War-Lords an alternative Long Range Plan by which they could gain ultimate control of the world's resources for the Aryan races.

To offset the plans of the International Money-Barons, Karl Ritter advised the Leaders of the Aryan Groups to organize Nazism and use Fascism i.e. National Socialism, as their manual of action to further their secret ambitions, for world conquest. Professor Ritter also pointed out that because the International Bankers intended to use all phases of Semitism to further their plans, the Aryan Leaders should use all phases of anti-Semitism to further their Cause.

Karl Ritter's Long Range Plan for ultimate world conquest included the following suggestions:

1. The subjugation of all European countries by Germany. To achieve this end he suggested the German military Junkers be encouraged and assisted to obtain control of the Government so they could engage in a series of Military Adventures, interspersed with economic wars. The objective being to weaken the economy and manpower of the European nations to be subjugated. [7] Karl Ritter stated that it was NOT absolutely essential, to

5

the success of his Long Range Plan, that each Military Adventure end in a clear cut victory, provided the other nations involved, were left in such a weakened condition that their recovery economically; and in strength of man-power, took longer than that of Germany. Karl Ritter stressed the importance of convincing the German people that they were physically and mentally superior to the Semitic races. From this thought Aryan propagandists developed the idea of The German Master Race. They did this to counter the Propaganda of the International Bankers which claimed the Semitic Race is to be God's Chosen People and Divinely chosen to inherit the earth. The Aryan leaders promulgated the doctrine that "Their Race" was The Master Race on this Earth. Thus millions of people were divided into opposing camps.

2. Karl Ritter recommended a financial policy which would prevent the International Bankers obtaining control of the economy of Germany, and her Satellite States as they had obtained economic control in England, France, and America.

3. He recommended the organization of a Nazi 5th Column to counteract the Communist Underground organization. Its objective was to persuade the upper and middle classes, of the countries they planned to subjugate, to accept Fascism as the only antidote to Communism. German 5th Columnists were to condition people in other countries to welcome the German Armies as their Military Protectors against threatened Communist aggression. Karl Ritter warned the leaders of the Aryan Group that a Military Invasion of another country should NEVER be undertaken until the 5th Column, and propaganda machines, had thoroughly paved the way, and convinced the majority of the people to accept their armed intervention as the act of Saviors or Crusaders, and not as aggressors.[8]

4. Karl Ritter cold-bloodedly recommended the total destruction of Communism and the extermination of the Jewish Race as essential to obtaining ultimate control of International Affairs by the Aryan Leaders. He justified this drastic stipulation on the facts of history which he claimed proved Communism was being used by the International Jewish Bankers to further their own selfish materialistic ambitions.

There were many more items making up the over-all Long Range Plan but in this chapter it is sufficient to produce enough evidence to unlock the door, behind which the Secret plans of two small groups of totalitarian-minded, atheistic-materialistic men were hidden. The study of Comparative Religions, Geo-political Science, and Political Economy, and years of intensive research, revealed the truth that many millions of human beings have been used as Pawns in the Game by the leaders of the two atheistic totalitarian-minded groups who will continue playing their hideous game of International Chess until one or the other is eliminated. Evidence will be produced to show how this game has been conducted in the past, and what moves are likely to be made in the near future, to enable one group to win the game.

The followers of all religions, that teach the existence of God, and life in a hereafter, believe in the love and worship of God, and charity towards all men of good will. Sincere believers will suffer any hardship, and make any sacrifice, in order to ensure their eternal salvation. The followers of Atheism are taught to HATE all who refuse to accept their materialistic creed. The determination of the leaders of both Atheist groups, to achieve world domination, permits them to conceive the most diabolical conspiracies, and perpetrate all kinds of crime, from individual assassinations to genocide. They foment wars in order to weaken nations they still have to subjugate.

The study of Comparative Religions shows also that Communism and Nazism are utterly incompatible with all religions that believe in the existence of an Almighty God. Experience, and history, proves that those who believe in God, and those who deny His existence, are in such contradiction that neither can survive the triumph of the other. Atheistic leaders in subjugated countries may, for a time, tolerate religions which teach belief in God but they only allow the priests to function on the social periphery. They take good care that the priests do not have the opportunity to influence the social and political behavior of their congregations. Evidence proves that the ULTIMATE objective of both major Atheistic Ideologies is to obliterate from the minds of mankind, by persecution, and a systematically applied program of continuous brain-washing, all knowledge of a Supreme Being; the existence of a soul; and hope of life in a hereafter. These being facts, any talk of co-existence is either utter non-sense or propaganda.

The trouble today is the continuation of the Heavenly Revolution. If God has placed human beings on this earth so they may know Him; love Him; and serve Him in this life in order to be happy with Him forever in the next world, then it is logical to reason that the only way in which Lucifer could hope to win back the souls in dispute would be to inoculate them with the doctrine of Atheistic-Materialism.

Undoubtedly many people will ask "But how could the Devil inoculate the minds of men with Atheistic and other evil ideas?" That question can be answered in this way, If HUMAN Beings call establish radio, and television stations, from which one individual can influence millions of others by broadcasting his opinions on any given subject over the invisible air-waves then why shouldn't it be possible for CELESTIAL Beings to broadcast their messages to us? No brain specialist has dared to deny that in the brain of each individual there is some kind of mysterious receiving set. Every hour of every day Human Beings are saying "I was inspired to do this", or "I was tempted to do that". Thoughts, be they good or evil, must originate somewhere, from some "cause", and be transmitted to the human brain. The body is only the instrument which puts the dominating thought for "Good" or for "Evil" into effect.

7

One fundamental fact which all people, who believe in the existence of God, must never forget is this: — if we are on this earth for a period of trial; if we have been given our Free Will, it is to enable us to decide whether we want to go to God or want to go to the Devil. Therefore, if the Devil did not have the opportunity to influence the minds of men there would be no test.

If Almighty God sent his prophets and His son Jesus Christ, to show us clearly what is Good and what is Evil, then why wouldn't the Devil send his false Christs and his false prophets to try and prove to us that Evil is Good and that Good is Evil?

The simplest way to understand what is going on in the world to-day is to study the events of History as the moves being made in a continuing game of International Chess ... The leaders of the Illuminati have divided the people of the world into two main camps. They used Kings and Queens; Bishops and Knights; and the masses of the world's population, as pieces in their games. The ruthless policy of the leaders is to consider all other human beings as EXPENDABLE, providing the sacrifice of a Major piece, or a million Pawns, places them a move nearer their ultimate totalitarian goal. The despotism of Satan.

Professor Ritter is reported to have said the present phase of this game started in the Counting House of Amschel Mayer Bauer alias Rothschild, located at Frankfort-on-the-Main in Germany, when thirteen Gold and Silversmiths[9] decided they must remove all the Crowned Heads of Europe; destroy all existing governments; and eliminate all organized religions, before they could secure absolute control of the wealth, natural resources, and man-power of the entire world, and establish a Satanic Despotism. Dialectical and historical materialism was to be used to further these plans.

Strange though it may seem, history will prove that leaders of both the Semitic and Anti-Semitic groups have on occasion joined forces to fight against a common enemy such as the British Empire or the Christian religion. And while the masses fought, the Illuminati, who constitute the Secret Power behind the World Revolutionary Movements, jockeyed for the best position from which they would derive the greatest future benefit.

The leaders of both Communism and Nazism have crossed, and double crossed each other, but it is doubtful if many of the leaders realized, before it was too late, that even they were only tools controlled by the Agentur of the Illuminati who use all that is evil to further their ends. When the Secret Powers heading either group, even suspect one of their "tools" know too much, they ordered him Liquidated. Evidence will be produced to prove that the leaders of these two groups of totalitarian-minded men have instigated many individual assassinations, and caused many revolutions and wars, in which tens of millions of Human Beings have been killed, while millions have been wounded and rendered homeless. It is difficult to discover a military leader who can justify the decision to drop atomic bombs on Hiroshima or Nagasaki where, in the twinkling of an eye, approximately 100,000 people were killed, and twice

8

the number seriously injured. The Japanese Military forces had already been defeated. Surrender was only a matter of hours or days away when this diabolical act was perpetrated. The only logical conclusion is that The Secret Powers, who, it will be proved, influence and control the policies of most national Governments, decided that this most modern of all lethal weapons had to be demonstrated to remind Stalin what would happen if he became too obnoxious. This is the only excuse which provides even the resemblance of justification for such an outrage against humanity.

But the atomic bomb, and the hydrogen bomb, are no longer the world's most lethal weapons. Nerve gas, now being stockpiled by both Communist and Non-Communist nations, is capable of wiping out all living creatures in a country, a city, or a town. The extent of destruction of all human life in a nation can be adjusted to the military and economic requirements of those who decide to use Nerve Gas to reach their goal. Nerve Gas is said to be highly concentrated fluorine in its gaseous form. It is the most penetrating and deadly gas ever discovered by man. It is colorless, odorless, tasteless and economical to produce. One single drop, even when heavily diluted with water or oil will, if it comes in contact with a living body, cause paralysis of the breathing apparatus, and death. In a few minutes it will penetrate even through rubber clothing such as is worn by firemen when on duty. Nerve Gas will not seriously damage inanimate objects.

Within a few days after the Nerve Gas had been applied it would be safe for the invading force to enter the contaminated areas again. They would be areas of the Dead, but all buildings and machinery would be intact. The only known antidote to Nerve Gas is the drug Atropine. To be effective it must be injected into the veins of the victims immediately, and repeatedly, after they have been contaminated. This means of defense is not practical for densely populated areas. Both Communist and Anti-Communist governments have Nerve Gas. The knowledge that both sides have this Gas in quantity may cause both sides to hesitate to use it. But it is a well-known fact that desperate, and ruthless, men will resort to any extremes to gain their objectives. And, as will be proved, they have never hesitated to sacrifice millions upon millions of human beings — men, women and children, if by doing so they advance themselves only one step nearer to their ultimate goal.

We may well ask the question "How is the struggle now going on upon this earth going to end?" It is doubtful if there is a single living being who hasn't asked this question. It is a question young married couples anxiously ask each other when they debate if they should allow their connubial bliss to bring more children into this hate-dominated world. The most complete answer is to be found in the Gospel of Saint Matthew, Chapter XXIV, verses 15 to 34 — At that time Jesus said to His disciples : "When you shall see the abomination of desolation, which was spoken of by Daniel the Prophet, standing in the Holy Place (he that readeth let him understand), then they that are in Judea, let them flee to the mountains; and he that is on the house top let him not come down to take anything out of his house; and he that is in the field let him not go back to get his coat. And woe to them that are with child, and give suck in those days. But pray that your flight be not in winter or on the Sabbath; for there shall be great tribulation such as hath not been from the beginning of the world until now, neither shall be; and unless those days shall be shortened NO FLESH SHOULD BE SAVED; but for the sake of the elect, those days shall be shortened."

Christ then proceeded to deal with the problem of the false leaders and the anti-Christs who he foretold would use propaganda to befuddle men's thinking. He said : "Then if any man shall say to you Lo, here is Christ or There do not believe him; for there shall arise false Christs and false prophets who shall show great signs and wonders in so much as to deceive (if possible) even the elect. Behold I have told it to you beforehand. If therefore they shall say to you Behold, he is in the desert go ye not out. Behold he is in the closet believe it not. For as lightning cometh out of the East and appeareth even unto the West, so shall also the coming of the Son of Man be. Wheresoever the body shall be, there shall the eagles be gathered together. And immediately after the tribulations of those days, the sun shall be darkened, and the moon shall not give her light, and the stars shall be moved; and the powers of heavens shall be shaken. [10] And then shall appear the sign of the Son of Man in heaven, and then shall the tribes of the earth mourn; and they shall see the Son of Man coming in the clouds of heaven, with much power and majesty; and He shall send His angels with a trumpet, and a great sound and they shall gather together His elect from the four winds, from the farthest part of the heavens to the utmost bounds of them. And from the fig tree learn this parable; when the branch thereof is now tender, and the leaves come forth, you know that summer is nigh. So you also, when you shall see all these things, know ye that it is nigh even at the doors. Amen I say to you that this generation shall not pass till all these things shall be done."

The branch is indeed now tender, many leaves have budded out, we need only one more war in which both sides use atomic and hydrogen bombs, and nerve gas, and we shall have inflicted upon ourselves the abominations of desolation which shall reduce the human race to such chaotic conditions that Divine intervention will be our only salvation. Today it is common practice for people, especially those who act willfully or unwillfully, as the agents of the Evil Powers, to blame God for the sorry mess in which we find ourselves. The intelligent person will admit that God cannot be blamed. He gave us our Free Will. He gave us the Commandments as our guide. He gave us Christ as a teacher and living example. If we obstinately refuse to accept the teachings and example of Christ; if we also refuse to obey the Commandments of God, how can we reasonably blame any agency other than ourselves for allowing the Forces of Evil to gain supremacy in this World of Ours? Edmund Burke once wrote: "All that is necessary for the triumph of Evil, is that good men do nothing." He wrote a great truth.

The study of comparative religions, in relation to the conditions we are experiencing in the world to-day, brings the unbiased student to the conclusion that those human beings who worship God, and believe in another life after the death of our mortal bodies, enjoy a religion of Love and Hope. Atheism is a religion of Hate and blackest Despair. And yet, never before in the history of the world, has such a determined effort been put forth to introduce secularism into our lives as since 1846, when C.J. Holyoake, C. Bradlaugh, and others asserted their opinion "THAT HUMAN INTEREST SHOULD BE LIMITED TO CONCERNS OF THE PRESENT LIFE." These advocates of secularism were the predecessors of the most recent flock of false Christs and false Prophets — Karl Marx, Karl Ritter, Lenin, Stalin, Hitler and Mussolini. These men did deceive millions upon millions of people by working great signs and wonders. They deceived many professing Christians who should have known better.

NOTES:

1   The terms Nazi & Nazism are used to indicate and identify the extremist members of the "Right Wing" parties who gave allegiance and loyalty to the totalitarian minded Aryan War Lords who plotted to use Fascism to further their secret plans and ambitions in exactly the same way as the "International Group" consisting of bankers, monopolists and certain politicians have used Communism and all other groups "Left" of center to further their secret plane and Totalitarian ambitions.

2   The terms "True Communist" and "True Nazi" are used to identify the leaders and agents of the two totalitarian ideologies who have been initiated into the Satanic ritual of Illuminism in Grand Orient Freemasonry or the Pagan Aryan Rites used by German Nazi Military Grand Orient Lodges.

3   The reader must realize the difference between Nazism and Fascism because, contrary to what anti-Fascist propaganda has led so many people to believe, the Fascist Movement, as started in Italy in 1919, was intended to be a Christian Crusade to combat the Atheistic ideology of Karl Marx and to support "Nationalism" as against "Internationalism" as planned by the leaders of both German Nazi War Lords and the International Bankers, Industrialists and politicians.

4   The Aryan Nazi War Lords must not be confused with the more moderate Junkers who were young Germans who took military training to protect what they considered "Germany's National" Political and economic rights as threatened by International minded groups.

5   One of Britain's greatest Intelligence Officers is Godfather to my daughter Eileen. I have known him intimately since October 1914. I served with him, on occasions, in both World Wars. He and I both investigated this angle of Nazism independently but when we checked our evidence we found we were very close to complete agreement.

6   The term 'International Money-Barons' is used to define the International Group of men who control International Banking, Industries, and Trade and Commerce. They are the men who have used Communism to destroy

constituted authority, and existing political and religious institutions, in order that they may ultimately usurp undisputed control of the World's resources for themselves.

7   This is an illustration of how the Anti-Communist extremists also use the "Joint Stock Company Principle" and use others to serve their purpose while the actual directors and Instigators remain hidden and unknown to the general public.

8   When Hitler acted contrary to the fundamental principles laid down by Karl Ritter the German Generals who belonged to the Hard Core of the Nazi Leaders tried to have him assassinated, regardless of the fact that they had originally set him up as the Instrument of their Will.

9   ALL Goldsmiths were not Jewish. Only SOME turned to the practice of usury. One of the richest Goldsmiths is that of the London City Company dating from 1130.

10 The Greek word for Heavens is "Ouranor" from which the Planet Uranus and metal Uranium are named. This predicts the "A" and "H" bombs.

Chapter Two

The English Revolution 1640-1660

The Forces of Evil realize that in order to win undisputed control of the material assets of the world, and establish an Atheistic Materialistic Totalitarian Dictatorship, it is necessary to destroy all forms of constitutional government and organized religion. In order to do this the Forces of Evil decided they must divide the peoples of the world against each other on various issues. Dating back into antiquity the Aryan and Semitic races were driven into enmity against each other to serve the secret ambitions of their atheistic-materialistic leaders. Had the people of the Aryan and Semitic races remained steadfast to their belief in God, and faithful to His commandments, the Forces of Evil could never have accomplished their evil purpose.

The term Aryan actually denotes the lingual groups otherwise known as Indo-European or Indo- Germanic. It comprises two groups; The Western or European, and the Eastern or Armenian. The Aryan languages show a common origin by their vocabulary, system, and inflections. Actually the word Aryan means "An honorable Lord of the Soil". Thus it is that most leaders of the Aryan group in Europe were Landed Barons who maintained strong armed forces to protect their properties. From amongst these Barons came the Aryan War Lords. They in turn organized Nazism, and used Fascism, and all anti-semitic groups right of center to serve their purpose, and further their secret plans for world domination.

The Chief Divisions of the Aryan groups are the Teutonic, the Romanic, and the Slavic races, who settled in Western Europe. The Turks, the Magyars, the Basques, and the Finns are non- Aryan races. The common ancestors of the Aryan groups dwelt among the Pamirs at a period of remote antiquity.

On the other hand the Semitic groups are actually divided into two sections. One includes the Assyrian, the Aramaean, the Hebrew and Phoenician groups. The other section includes the Arabic and Ethiopian groups. The Arabic is the most copious group, and the Aramaean the poorest. The Hebrews occupy an intermediary position. [1]

Today the term Jew is used very loosely to define people who have at one time or another embraced the Jewish Faith. Many of these are not actually Semitic in racial origin. A great number of people who accepted the Jewish Faith are descendants of the Herodians who were Idumeans of Turkish-Mongol blood. They are actually Edomites.[2] The important fact to remember is that among the Jewish leaders, in exactly the same way as among the Aryan leaders, there always has been a small, hard core of men who have been, and still are, Illuminists or Atheists. They may have given lip-service to the Jewish or Christian religions to suit their own purpose, but they never believed in the existence of God. They are Internationalists now. They give allegiance to no particular nation although they have used, on occasion, nationalism to further their causes. Their only concern is to gain greater economic and political power. The ultimate objective of the leaders of both groups is identical. They are determined to win, for themselves, undisputed control of the wealth, natural resources, and man- power of the entire world. They intend to turn the world into THEIR conception of a Totalitarian - Godless Dictatorship.

The Non-Semitic and Turk-Finnish races infiltrated into Europe from Asia about the first century after the advent of Christ. They took the land route north of the Caspian Sea. These peoples are referred to in history as Khazars. They were a pagan people. They settled in Eastern Europe and established the powerful Khazar Kingdom. They expanded their domains by military conquests until, by the end of the 8th Century, they occupied the greater portion of Eastern Europe west of the Ural Mountains, and North of the Black Sea. The Khazars ultimately accepted Judaism as their religion in preference to Christianity or Mohammedanism. Synagogues, and schools for teaching Judaism, were built throughout their Kingdom. At the peak of their power the Khazars were collecting tribute from twenty-five conquered peoples.

The Great Khazar Kingdom flourished for almost five hundred years. Then, towards the end of the 10th century, the Khazars were defeated in battle by the Varangians (Russians) who swept down upon them from the North. The conquest of the Khazars was completed by the end of the 13th Century. The revolutionary movement inspired by the Khazar-Jews went on within the Russian Empire from the 13th Century until the Red October Revolution of 1917. The conquest of the Khazars in the 13th century explains how so many people, now commonly referred to as Jews, remained within the Russian Empire.

There is one other important fact which sheds light on the subject of Aryanism and Semitism. The Finns, and other groups generally classified as Varangians (Russians), were of non-Aryan origin and the German people generally speaking have treated them as enemies.

One act of Christ has a great deal of importance in the study of the World Revolutionary Movement. Christ was considered by many, a radical who based his reform movement on the worship of Almighty God, obedience to constituted authority, and love of one's neighbors. The story of the Life of Christ shows that he loved ALL people except one particular group. He hated the money-lenders with an intensity that seems strange in a man of so mild a character. Jesus repeatedly admonished the money-lenders for their practice of usury. He publicly denounced them as worshippers of Mammon. He said they were of the Synagogue of Satan. (Rev. 2:9). He emphatically expressed His extreme hatred of the money-lenders when he took a whip and drove them out of the Temple. He admonished them in these words: "This Temple was built as the house of God ... But you have turned it into a den of thieves." By performing this act of vengeance on the money-lenders Christ signed his own death warrant.

It was the Illuminati, and the false priests and elders in their day, who hatched the plot by which Christ would be executed by the Roman soldiers. It was they who supplied the thirty pieces of silver used to bribe Judas. It was they who used their propagandists to misinform, and mislead the Mob. It was the agents of the Illuminati who led the Mob when they accepted Barabbas and screamed that Christ be crucified. IT WAS THE ILLUMINATI WHO ARRANGED MATTERS SO THAT THE ROMAN SOLDIERS ACTED AS THEIR EXECUTIONERS. Then, after the foul deed had been done, and they had had their revenge, the conspirators stepped into the background and let their guilt rest on the masses of the Jews and their children. History proves they had a fiendish reason for putting the guilt for the death of Christ on the Jewish people. History proves that they intended to use the hate engendered amongst the Jewish people as the result of persecution, to serve their vile purposes, and further their secret totalitarian ambitions. Christ knew all these things. He made his knowledge known in the most dramatic manner possible. As he hung dying on the Cross he prayed to His Heavenly Father and He said: "Father forgive them for they know not what they do". Surely he was praying for the Mob? He was asking forgiveness for the men who had been USED by the Illuminati to be the INSTRUMENT of their revenge. History proves the International Money-Lenders have been using the Mob to further their secret ambitions ever since. In the Lenin Institute in Moscow the professors who lecture to aspiring revolutionary leaders from all over the world invariably refer to the Masses as 'The Mob'. The Illuminati direct all evil forces.

Study of the World Revolutionary Movement (W.R.M.), from the time of Christ to the present day, proves that it is unjust to blame the whole Jewish Race for the crimes committed against humanity by a small group of false priests and money-lenders. These men always have been, and still are, *The Secret Power* behind Internationalism. They use Communism today as their manual of action to further their secret pans for ultimate world domination.

Study of history will prove that it is equally unjust to blame the whole German and Italian people for the crimes against humanity committed by the small group of Aryan War Lords who organized Nazism, in the hope that they could defeat International Communism and Political Zionism and give them world domination by military conquest. History proves clearly that the leaders of the two opposing groups have divided the masses of the people regardless of race, color, or creed, into two opposing camps and then used them all as pawns in the game of International Chess. They play to decide which group will ultimately defeat the other and establish, once and for all, undisputed control over the world, its wealth, its natural resources, its man-power, and its religion. It must be remembered that as the purpose of the Devil is to win men's souls away from God, Satan uses both "Red" Communism and "Black" Nazism to influence the minds of men so that they will embrace EITHER Atheistic ideology. Those who accept EITHER Atheistic ideology sell their souls to the Devil.

Historical events prove the continuity of the evil purpose of the Illuminati.

Many theologians agree that this perfect continuity of their Long Range Plans is positive evidence that they are, as Christ named them, "Of the Synagogue of Satan". Theologians base their opinion on the theory that nothing human could have such a continuing record of evil down through the ages of time. The continuity of evil is the exact opposite of the Apostolic succession of the Roman Catholic Church. In this, as in many other things, we are forcibly reminded of the actual power of the super-natural forces to influence our individual lives, national policy, and international affairs. Arguments of this kind regarding evil minded Jews are equally applicable to evil minded Aryans, and evil minded men of all races, color and creeds.

History proves that Seneca (4 B.C. to 65 A.D.) died because he, like Christ, tried to expose the corrupt practices and evil influence of the money-lenders who had infiltrated into the Roman Empire. Seneca was a famous Roman philosopher. He was chosen tutor to Nero who became Emperor of Rome. For a long time Seneca was Nero's best friend, and most trusted advisor. Nero married Popaea who brought him under the evil influence of the money-lenders. Nero became one of the most infamous rulers the world has ever known. His licentious conduct, and depraved habits, developed in him a character so base that he lived only to persecute and destroy everything that was good. His acts of revenge took the form of atrocities usually committed in public upon the victims of his wrath. Seneca lost his influence over Nero but he never stopped publicly denouncing the money-lenders for their evil influence and corrupt practices. Finally the money-lenders demanded that Nero take action against Seneca who was very popular with the people. So as not to arouse the wrath of the people against himself, and the money-lenders. Nero ordered Seneca to end his own life.

This is the first recorded case in which the money-lenders made a person commit suicide because he had become troublesome to them, but it was by no means the last. History records dozens of similar suicides, and murders which were made to appear as accidents or suicides.

One of the most notorious in recent years was that of James V. Forrestal. In 1945 Forrestal had been convinced that the American Bankers were closely affiliated with the International Bankers who controlled the Banks of England, France and other countries. He was also convinced, according to his diaries, that the International Money-Barons were the Illuminati and directly responsible for the outbreak of World Wars One and Two. He tried to convince President Roosevelt, and other Top Level Government officials, of the truth. Either he failed, and committed suicide in a fit of depression, or he was murdered to shut his mouth forever. Murder, made to appear like suicide, has been accepted policy in the top levels of international intrigue for many centuries. [3]

Justinian I, (Flavius Anicius Justianiamus 483-565 A.D.) wrote his famous book of law "Corpus Juris Civilis". He tried to put an end to the illegal methods of traffic and trade indulged in by certain Jewish merchants. By engaging in illegal trade, and wholesale smuggling, the Jewish merchants, who

4

were only agents of the Illuminati, obtained unfair advantage over their Gentile competitors. They put them out of business. The book of law, written by Justinian, was accepted as the text book of law right down to the 10th Century. Even to-day it is considered the most important of all documents of jurisprudence. But the money-lenders were able to offset the good Justinian tried to do. [4] Funk & Wagnall's Jewish Encyclopedia has this to say about the Jews in those days — "They enjoyed full religious liberty ... Minor offices were open to them. The trade in slaves constituted the main source of livelihood for the Roman Jews, and decrees against this traffic were issued in 335, 336, 339, 384 A.D., etc."

There is the story in black and white. But history reveals that the Jewish merchants, and money-lenders, did not confine their illegal activities to the slave trade. It is recorded that they engaged in every form of illegal traffic including the drug trade, prostitution, wholesale smuggling of liquors, perfumes, jewels, and other dutiable goods. In order to protect their illegal trade and traffic they bribed and corrupted officials; by use of drugs and liquors, and women, they destroyed the morals of the people. History records that Justinian, although Emperor of the Roman Empire, wasn't strong enough to put a stop to their activities. [5]

Edward Gibbon (1737-1794) deals with the corrupting influence of the Jewish merchants and money-lenders. He credits them with contributing greatly to "The Decline and Fall of the Roman Empire". He wrote the book with that title. Gibbon gives considerable space to the part Popaea, Nero's wife, played in bringing about the conditions which started the people of Rome reeling drunkenly towards their own destruction. With the fall of the Roman Empire, Jewish predominance was established. The nations of Europe entered into what historians name "The Dark Ages".

The Encyclopedia Britannica has this to say on the subject. "There was an inevitable tendency for them (The Jewish merchants and money-lenders) to specialize in commerce for which their acumen, and ubiquity, gave them special qualifications. In the Dark Ages the commerce of Western Europe was largely in their hands, in particular, the Slave Trade."

Jewish control of trade and commerce, both legal and illegal, grew tighter and tighter. It spread far and wide, until every European country's economy was more or less in their hands. Evidence in the form of Polish and Hungarian coins bearing Jewish inscriptions gives some indication of the power they exerted in financial matters during those days. The fact that the Jews made a special effort, to issue and control currency, supports the opinion that the money- lenders had adopted the slogan "Let us issue and control the money of a nation and we care not who make its laws", long before Amschel Mayer Bauer [6] (1743-1812) used the slogan to explain to his co-conspirators the reason the Jewish money-lenders had obtained control of the Bank of England in 1694.

The barons, who were the leaders of Aryanism, determined they would

5

break the Jewish control of trade, commerce and money in Europe. It was with this purpose in mind that in 1095 they obtained the support of certain Christian rulers to start The Crusades or Holy Wars. [7] Between 1095 and 1271 eight Crusades were organized. Officially, the Crusades were military expeditions undertaken to ensure the safety of Pilgrims who wished to visit the Holy Sepulcher and set up Christian Rule in Palestine. In actual fact they were wars fomented for the purpose of dividing the population of Europe into two camps. One camp pro-Jewish and the other Anti-Jewish. In more recent years, the Secret Powers divided the white race into Semitic and Anti- Semitic groups. Some of the Crusades were successful, some were not. The net result was that, in 1271, Palestine still remained in the hands of the Infidels, although the countries of Christendom had spent MILLIONS IN MONEY and treasure to finance the Crusades and sacrificed MILLIONS OF HUMAN LIVES fighting those Holy Wars. Strange to relate, the Jewish money-lenders grew richer and stronger than ever.

There is one phase of the Crusades which must not be overlooked when the "Causes" are being studied in relation to the "Effects" they produced in later years. In 1215 the Roman Catholic Hierarchy held the Fourth Lateran Council. The main topic under consideration was Jewish aggression in all the countries of Europe. During this period of history the Rulers of the Church, and the Rulers of the State, worked in unity. The rulers of the Church, after due deliberation, expressed themselves in favor of continuing the Crusades. They also drew up, and passed Decrees, designed to put an end to usury and the Jewish money-lenders practice of using unethical methods in traffic and trade to obtain unfair advantage over Gentile competitors, and to curb corrupt and immoral practices. To achieve this purpose the dignitaries attending the Fourth Lateran Council decreed that in the future the Jews be restricted to living in their own quarters. Jews were absolutely prohibited from hiring Christians as their employees. This decree was passed because Jewish money-lenders and merchants operated on the Joint Stock Company principle. They employed Christians to act as their front men while they hid in the background directing operations. This was convenient because, when anything went wrong, the Christian front men got the blame, and the punishment, while they got off scot-free. In addition, by the Decrees, Jews were absolutely prohibited from employing Christian females in their homes and establishments. This decree was passed because evidence was produced to prove that young females were systematically seduced, and then turned into prostitutes; their masters used them to obtain control over influential officials. Other decrees made it unlawful for Jews to engage in many commercial activities. But even the power of the Church, supported by most Christian officials of the State, could not make the Money-Barons amenable to the law. All the decrees accomplished was to intensify the hatred the Illuminati had for the Church of Christ, and they started a continuing campaign to separate the Church from the State. To achieve this purpose they introduced the idea of secularism amongst the laity.

In 1253 the French government ordered the Jews expelled because they

6

refused to obey the law. Most of the Jews who were expelled went over to England. By 1255 the Jewish money- lenders had obtained absolute control of many Church dignitaries and most of the Nobility. [8] That the money-lenders, the Rabbis, and Elders belonged to the Illuminati was proved by evidence given during the investigation ordered by King Henry III into the ritual slaying of St. Hugh of Lincoln in 1255. Eighteen Jews were proved to have been the culprits. They were tried, found guilty, and executed. In 1272 King Henry died. Edward I became King of England. He determined the Jewish leaders must give up the practice of usury. In 1275 he had Parliament pass the Statutes of Jewry. They were designed to curb the power Jewish usurers were exerting over their debtors, both Christians, and fellow Jews. The Statutes of Jewry were probably the first legislation in which The Commons in Parliament had an active part. They cannot be classified as Anti-Semitic because they actually protected the interests of honest and law-abiding Jews. [9]

But, as had happened so often before, the Jewish money-lenders thought that the power they could exert over both the Church and the State, would permit them to defy the king's decree in the same way as they had set at naught those passed by the Lateran Council. They made a grave mistake. In 1290 King Edward issued another decree. ALL Jews were expelled from England. This was the start of what historians call *The Great Eviction.*

After Edward I started the ball rolling, all the Crowned Heads of Europe followed his example.

In 1306 France expelled the Jews. In 1348 Saxony followed suit. In 1360 Hungary; in 1370 Belgium; in 1380 Slovakia; in 1420 Austria; in 1444 the Netherlands; in 1492 Spain.

The expulsion of the Jews from Spain has special signification. It throws light on the Spanish Inquisition. Most people have the idea the Inquisition was instituted by Roman Catholics to persecute Protestants who had broken away from the Church. As a matter of fact the Inquisition, as introduced by Pope Innocent III, was a means of unmasking heretics, and infidels, who were masquerading as Christians for the purpose of destroying the Christian Religion from within. [10] It didn't make the slightest difference to the Inquisitors whether the accused was Jew or Gentile, black or white. The terrible ceremony of the "Auto-da-Fé" or "Act of Faith" was specially designed to be used in connection with the execution of all convicted heretics, and infidels, when Torquemada (1420-1498) was Grand Inquisitor. [11]

It is these hidden incidents which reveal so much truth. It was in Spain, during the 14th Century, that the Jewish money-lenders first succeeded in having the loans they made the State secure by the right to collect the taxes levied upon the people. They used such cruelty, when demanding their Pound of Flesh, that it only required the inflammatory oratory of the priest Fernando Martenez to produce mass action which ended in one of the bloodiest massacres recorded in history. Here again is a perfect example of how thousands of innocent Jews were victimized, for the sins and crimes committed

7

against humanity by just a few. [12]

In 1495 Lithuania expelled the Jews, in 1498 Portugal; in 1540 Italy; and in 1551 Bavaria. It is important to remember that during the general evictions certain wealthy and influential Jews managed to obtain sanctuary in Bordeaux, Avignon, certain Papal States, Marseille, Northern Alsace, and part of northern Italy. But, as stated in the Encyclopedia Britannica, "The masses of the Jewish people were thus to be found once more, in the East and in the Polish and Turkish Empires. The few communities suffered to remain in Western Europe were meantime subjected at last to all the restrictions which earlier Ages had usually allowed to remain as an ideal; so that, in a sense, the Jewish Dark Ages may be said to begin with the Renaissance. This admission would indicate there is some justification for the claim made by certain historians that not until the Western European nations wrested economic control from the Jewish money- lenders did the rebirth of western civilization occur.

Following the Great Eviction the Jews again resumed living in Ghettos or Kahals. Thus, isolated from the masses of the population, the Jews were under the direction and control of the Rabbis and Elders, many of whom were influenced by the Illuminati and the wealthy Jewish money-lenders who remained in their various sanctuaries. In the Ghettos, agents of the Illuminati inspired a spirit of hatred and revenge in the hearts of the Jewish people against those who had evicted them. The Rabbis reminded them that, as the chosen people of God, the day would come when they would have their revenge and inherit the earth.

It should be mentioned that most Jews who settled in Eastern Europe, were restricted to living within the "Pale of Settlement" located on the western borders of Russia and extending from the shores of the Baltic Sea in the north, to the shores of the Black Sea in the South. Most of them were Khazar Jews. [13] The Khazar Jews were noted for their Yiddish culture, their rapacious practices in financial matters, and their lack of ethics in commercial transactions. They should not be confused with the Biblical Hebrews who are mild mannered and, generally speaking, pastoral people.

Within the Ghettos, in an atmosphere of hatred, the desire for revenge was developed by the agents of the Illuminati. They organized these negative conditions, into the World Revolutionary Movement, based on Terrorism. From its very inception the international- minded Money-Barons, and THEIR High Priests, designed, financed, and controlled the World Revolutionary Movement. They used it as the instrument by which they would obtain their revenge on the Christian churches, and the Crowned Heads, of Europe.

History proves HOW the Money-Barons developed the revolutionary movement into International Communism as we know it to-day. They organized individual acts of terrorism into a disciplined revolutionary movement. They then planned systematic infiltration of the Jews back into the countries from which they had been expelled. Because their re-entry was illegal the only method by which infiltration could be accomplished was to establish Jewish Undergrounds. Because the Jews who infiltrated into the Undergrounds of the European cities could not obtain lawful employment they were supplied with funds with which to develop the Black Market system. They indulged in every kind of illegal traffic and trade. Working on the principle of the Joint Stock Co., the identity of the Money-Barons, who owned and controlled this vast underground system always remained secret. [14]

Count de Poncins; Mrs. Nesta Webster; Sir Walter Scott; and many other authors and historians have suspected that the Illuminati and a group of Internationalists were The Secret Power behind the World Revolutionary Movement, but it was not until recently that sufficient evidence was pieced together to prove that what they suspected was an actual fact. As the events of history are unrolled in their chronological sequence it will be seen how the Illuminati used the Semitic groups and the Aryan groups, to serve their purpose and involved millions upon millions of people in revolutions and wars to further their own secret and selfish ambitions. William Foss and Cecil Gerahty who wrote The Spanish Arena said: "The question of who are the leading figures behind the attempt of the JOINT STOCK COMPANY domination of the world, and how they obtain their ends, is beyond the scope of this book. But it is one of the important Libres a faire yet to be written. IT WILL HAVE TO BE WRITTEN BY A MAN OF THE HIGHEST COURAGE WHO WILL COUNT HIS LIFE AS NOTHING COMPARED WITH ENLIGHTENING THE WORLD AS TO WHAT THE SATANIC SELF-APPOINTED PRIESTHOOD WOULD ORDAIN."

How successful the plan, to infiltrate back into the countries from which they had been expelled, turned out to be can best be judged by the following records. The Jews were back in England in 1600; back in Hungary in 1500. They were expelled again in 1582; they were back in Slovakia in 1562 but were expelled again in 1744; they were back in Lithuania in 1700. But, regardless of how many times they were expelled, there always remained the Jewish underground from which the revolutionary activities of the *Secret Powers* were conducted.

Because King Edward I of England had been the first to expel the Jews, the Jewish Money-Barons in France, Holland, and Germany decided it would be poetic justice if they tried out their planned revolutionary technique in England first. They used their underground agents, or Cells, to cause trouble between the king and his government; employers and labor; ruling class and workers; Church and State. The plotters injected controversial issues into politics and religion, to divide the people into two opposing camps. [15] First they divided the people in England into Catholics and Protestants, and then they divided the Protestants into Conformists and Non-Conformists.

When King Charles I was brought into disagreement with his Parliament a Jewish Money-Baron in Holland, named Manasseh Ben Israel, had his agents contact Oliver Cromwell. They offered him large sums of money if he would carry out their plan to overthrow the British Throne. Manasseh Ben Israel and other German and French moneylenders financed Cromwell. Fernandez

Carvajal of Portugal, often referred to in history as The Great Jew, became Cromwell's Chief Military Contractor. He re-organized the Round Heads into a model army. He provided them with the best arms and equipment money could buy. Once the conspiracy was under way, hundreds of trained revolutionaries were smuggled into England and were absorbed into the Jewish Underground. The same thing goes on in America today.

The head of the Jewish underground in England at that time was a Jew named De Souze. The Great Jew, Fernandez Carvajal, had used his influence to have De Souze appointed Portuguese Ambassador. It was in his house, protected by diplomatic immunity that the leaders of the Jewish revolutionary underground remained hidden and worked out their plots and intrigue. [16]

Once the revolution had been decided upon, the Jewish plotters introduced Calvinism into England to split Church and State, and divide the people. Contrary to general belief, Calvinism is of Jewish origin. It was deliberately conceived to split the adherents of the Christian religions, and divide the people. Calvin's real name was Cohen! When he went from Geneva to France to start preaching his doctrine he became known as Cauin. Then in England it became Calvin. History proves that there is hardly a revolutionary plot that wasn't hatched in Switzerland; there is hardly a Jewish revolutionary leader who hasn't changed his name.

At the B'nai B'rith celebrations held in Paris, France, in 1936 Cohen, Cauvin, or Calvin, whatever his name may have been, was enthusiastically acclaimed to have been of Jewish descent. [17]

In addition to the religious controversy, the revolutionary leaders organized armed mobs to aggravate every situation injected into politics and labor by their masters. Isaac Disraeli, 1766-1848, a Jew, and father of Benjamin Disraeli who afterwards became Lord Beaconsfield, deals with this angle of the British Revolution in detail in his two-volume story *The Life of Charles II*. He remarks that he obtained considerable information from the records of Melchior de Salem, a Jew, who was French Envoy to the British Government at that time. Disraeli draws attention to the great similarity, or pattern, of the revolutionary activities which preceded both the British and the French revolutions. In other words the handiwork of the secret and real directors of the World Revolutionary Movement (W.R.M.) could clearly be seen in both, — a fact which we will proceed to prove.

The evidence which ABSOLUTELY convicts Oliver Cromwell of participating in the Jewish Revolutionary Plot was obtained by Lord Alfred Douglas, who edited a weekly review Plain English published by the North British Publishing Co. In an article which appeared in the issue of Sept. 3rd 1921 he explained how his friend, Mr. L.D. Van Valckert of Amsterdam, Holland, had come into possession of a missing volume of records of the Synagogue of Muljeim. This volume had been lost during the Napoleonic wars. The volume contains records of letters written to, and answered by the Directors of the Synagogue.

They are written in German. One entry, dated June 16th, 1647 reads: From O.C. (i.e. Olivier Cromwell) to Ebenezer Pratt.

"In return for financial support will advocate admission of Jews to England. This however impossible while Charles living. Charles cannot be executed without trial, adequate grounds for which do not at present exist. Therefore advise that Charles be assassinated, but will have nothing to do with arrangements for procuring an assassin, though willing to help in his escape."

In reply to this dispatch the records show E. Pratt wrote a letter dated July 12th, 1647 addressed to Oliver Cromwell.

"Will grant financial aid as soon as Charles removed, and Jews admitted. Assassination is too dangerous. Charles should be given an opportunity to escape. [18] His recapture will then make trial and execution possible. The support will be liberal, but useless to discuss terms until trial commences."

On November 12th that same year Charles was given the opportunity to escape. He was of course recaptured. Hollis and Ludlow, authorities on this chapter of history, are both on record as considering the flight as the stratagem of Cromwell. After Charles had been recaptured events moved apace. Cromwell had the British Parliament purged of most members he knew were loyal to the king. Notwithstanding this drastic action, when the House sat all night on December 5th, 1648, the majority agreed "That the concessions offered by the king were satisfactory to a settlement."

Any such settlement would have disqualified Cromwell from receiving the Blood-Money promised him by the International Money-Barons through their agent E. Pratt, so Cromwell struck again. He ordered Colonel Pryde to purge Parliament of those members who had voted in favor of a settlement with the King. What then happened is referred to, in school history books, as Pryde's Purge. [19] When the purge was finished fifty members remained. They are recorded as The Rump Parliament. They usurped absolute power. On January 9th, 1649, "A HIGH COURT OF JUSTICE" was proclaimed for the purpose of putting the king of England on trial. Two thirds of the members of the Court were "Levellers" from Cromwell's Army. The conspirators couldn't find an English lawyer who would draw up a criminal charge against King Charles. Carvajal, instructed an alien Jew, Isaac Dorislaus, Manasseh Ben Israel's Agent in England, to draw up the indictment upon which King Charles was tried. Charles was found guilty of the charges leveled against him by the International Jewish money-lenders, not by the people of England. On January 30th, 1649, he was publicly beheaded in front of the Banqueting House at Whitehall London. The Jewish money-lenders, directed by the High Priests of the Synagogue of Satan, had had their revenge because Edward I had expelled the Jews from England. Oliver Cromwell received his Blood-Money just as Judas had done.

History proves that the International Jewish money-lenders had a purpose other than revenge for getting rid of Charles. They removed him to obtain control of England's economy and government. They planned to involve many

European countries in war with England. Great sums of money are needed to fight wars. By loaning the Crowned Heads of Europe the money required to fight wars they fomented, the Internationalists were enabled to rapidly increase the National Debts of all European Nations.

The chronological sequence of events from the execution of King Charles in 1649 to the institution of the Bank of England in 1694, shows how the National Debt was increased. The International Bankers used intrigue and cunning to throw Christians at each other's throats.

1649   Cromwell financed by Jews, waged war in Ireland. Captures Drogheda and Wexford. British Protestants blamed for persecution of Irish Catholics.

1650   Montrose in rebellion against Cromwell. Captured and executed.

1651   Charles II invades England. Defeated and flees back to France.

1652   England involved in war with Dutch.

1653   Cromwell proclaims himself Lord Protector of England.

1654   England involved in more wars.

1656   Trouble started in American Colonies.

1657   Death of Cromwell — Son Richard named Protector.

1659   Richard, disgusted with intrigue, resigns.

1660   General Monk occupies London Charles II proclaimed King.

1661   Truth revealed regarding intrigue entered into by Cromwell and his cohorts Ireton, and Bradshaw, causes serious public reaction. Bodies are exhumed and hung from gallows on Tyburn Hill, London.

1662   Religious strife is engendered to divide members of the Protestant denominations. Non- Conformists to the established Church of England are persecuted.

1664   England is again involved in war with Holland.

1665   A great depression settles over England. Unemployment and shortages of food undermine the health of the people and the Great Plague breaks out. [20]

1666   England involved in war with France and Holland.

1667   Cabal agents start new religious and political strife. [21]

1674   England and Holland make Peace. The men directing international intrigue change their characters. They become matchmakers. They elevate plain Mr. William Stradholder to the rank of Captain-General of the Dutch Forces. He became William Prince of Orange. It was arranged that he meet Mary, the eldest daughter of the Duke of York.

The Duke was only one place removed from becoming King of England.

1677   Princess Mary of England married William Prince of Orange. To place William Prince of Orange upon the Throne of England it was necessary to get rid of both Charles II, and the Duke of York, who was slated to become James II.

1683   The Rye House Plot was hatched. The intention was to assassinate both King Charles II and the Duke of York. It failed.

1685   King Charles II died. The Duke of York became King James II of England. Immediately a campaign of L'Infamie was started against James II. The Duke of Monmouth was persuaded, or bribed, into leading an insurrection to overthrow the king. On June 30th, the Battle of Sedgemoor was fought. Monmouth was defeated and captured. He was executed July 15th. In August Judge Jeffreys opened, what historians have named, "The Bloody Assizes". Over three hundred persons concerned in the Monmouth Rebellion were sentenced to death under circumstances of atrocious cruelty. Nearly one thousand others were condemned to be sold as slaves. This was a typical example of how the Secret Powers, working behind the scenes, create conditions for which other people are blamed. Others are aroused to take active opposition against those they blame. They in turn are liquidated. King James still had to be disposed of before William of Orange could be placed on the throne to carry out their mandate. Every person in England was bewitched and bewildered. They were not allowed to know the truth. They blamed everyone, and everything except the "Secret Powers" who were pulling the strings. Then the conspirators made their next move.

1688   They ordered William Prince of Orange to land in England at Torbay. This he did on November 5th. King James abdicated. He fled to France. He had become unpopular by reason of the campaign of L'Infamie, intrigue and his own foolishness and culpability.

1689   William of Orange and Mary, were proclaimed King and Queen of England. King James did not intend to give up the Throne without a fight. He was a Catholic, so the Secret Powers set up William of Orange as the Champion of the Protestant Faith. On February 15th, 1689, King James landed in Ireland. The Battle of The Boyne was fought by men of definite, and opposing, religious convictions. The Battle has been celebrated by Orangemen on the 12th of July ever since. There is probably not one Orangeman in ten thousand who knows that all the wars and rebellions fought from 1640 to 1689 were fomented by the International money-lenders for the purpose of putting themselves in position to control British politics and economy. Their first objective was to obtain permission to institute a Bank of England and consolidate and secure the debts Britain owed them for

13

loans made to her to fight the wars they instigated. History shows how they completed their plans.

In the final analysis, none of the countries and people involved in the wars and revolutions obtained any lasting benefits. No permanent or satisfactory solution was reached regarding the political, economic, and religious issues involved. THE ONLY PEOPLE TO BENEFIT WERE THE SMALL GROUP OF MONEY-LENDERS WHO FINANCED THE WARS AND REVOLUTIONS, AND THEIR FRIENDS AND AGENTS, WHO SUPPLIED THE ARMIES, THE SHIPS, AND THE MUNITIONS.

It is important to remember that no sooner was the Dutch General sitting upon the throne of England than he persuaded the British Treasury to borrow £1,250,000 from the Jewish bankers who had put him there. The school book history informs our children that the negotiations were conducted by Sir John Houblen and Mr. William Patterson on behalf of the British Government with money-lenders WHOSE IDENTITY REMAINED SECRET.

Search of historical documents reveals that in order to maintain complete secrecy the negotiations regarding the terms of the loan were carried on in a church. In the days of Christ the money-lenders used the Temple. In the days of William of Orange they desecrated a church.

The international money-lenders agreed to accommodate the British Treasury to the extent of £1,250,000 providing they could dictate their own terms and conditions. This was agreed to. The terms were in part:

1. That the names of those who made the loan remain secret; and that they be granted a Charter to establish a Bank of England.[22]
2. That the directors of the Bank of England be granted the legal right to establish the Gold Standard for currency by which —
3. They could make loans to the value of £10 for every £1 value of gold they had on deposit in their vaults.
4. That they be permitted to consolidate the national debt; and secure payment of amounts due as principal and interest by direct taxation of the people.

Thus, for the sum of £1,250,000, King William of Orange sold the people of England into economic bondage. The Jewish money-lenders gained their ambitions. They had usurped the power to issue and control the currency of the nation. And, having secured that power, they cared not who made the laws.

Just what the acceptance of the Gold Standard meant is best illustrated by citing a simple transaction. — The directors of the Bank of England could loan £1,000 for every £100 worth of gold they had on deposit as security. They collected interest on the full £1,000 loan. At 5 per cent this amounted to £50 a year. Therefore at the end of the first year the bankers collected back 50 per cent of the amount they had originally put up to secure the loan. If a private individual wished to obtain a loan, the bankers made him put up security, in the form of property, stocks, or bonds, much in excess of the value of the loan he required. If he failed to meet payments of principal and interest, foreclosure proceedings were taken against his property, and the moneylenders obtained many times the value of the loan.

The international bankers never intended that England be allowed to pay off the national indebtedness. The plan was to create international conditions which would plunge ALL nations concerned deeper and deeper into their debt. [23]

As far as England is concerned, in only four years, 1694 to 1698, the national debt was increased from one to sixteen million pounds sterling. This debt accumulated because of wars. It is interesting to note that John Churchill, 1650-1722, became the leading military figure during this period of English history. Because of his military genius, and his services to Britain, he was created the first Duke of Marlborough. [24]

The Secret Power behind the World Revolutionary Movement pulled the necessary strings and brought about The Wars of the Spanish Succession. In 1701 the Duke of Marlborough was made Commander-in-chief of the armed forces of Holland. No less an authority than the Jewish Encyclopedia records the fact that FOR HIS MANY SERVICES THE DUKE OF MARLBOROUGH RECEIVED NOT LESS THAN £6,000 A YEAR FROM THE DUTCH JEWISH BANKER, SOLOMON MEDINA.

The events leading up to the French Revolution show how between 1698 and 1815 the National Debt of Britain was increased to £885,000,000. By 1945 the British National Debt had reached the astronomical figure of £22,503,532,372, and for the years 1945-46 the carrying charges alone amounted to £445,446,241. As an Irish economist remarked "Only a Jewish controlled organization would insist on the odd pound."

NOTES:
1 See Pears Cyclopedia Pages 514 and 647.
2 See Jewish Encyclopedia Vol. 5, p. 41: 1925. It states "Edom is in Modern Jewry". Also Professor Lothrop Stoddard the eminent Ethnologist states: "The Jews' own records admit that 82 per cent of those who subscribe to the Political Zionist movement are Ashkenazim, so-called Jews, but not Semitic. There are many different opinions on these racial matters.
3 The Forrestal Diaries Viking press, New York, 1951.
4 Some readers claim Justianiamus had no such purpose. I claim knowledge of wrong spurs men to create corrective legislation and laws.
5 The same evil influences are responsible for the same evil conditions which exist in all big cities to-day.
6 Bauer is the Jewish Goldsmith who established "The House of Rothschild", in Frankfort-on-the-Main. He and his (confreres) plotted the French Revolution of 1789.

7 Because hate and revenge are the Stock-in-Trade of the forces of evil they will use any pretext to foment wars and revolutions even to using the name of God, whom they hate.

8 The book "Aaron of Lincoln". Shapiro-Valentine & Co. gives interesting information regarding this period of history. Valentine's Jewish Encyclopedia has this to say. "Their numbers and prosperity increased. Aaron of Lincoln (whose house still stands to this day) became the richest man in England. His financial transactions covering the whole country and concerning many of the leading Nobles and Churchmen... On his death his properties passed to the Grown, and a special branch of the Exchequer had to be created to deal with the estates.

9 The Statutes of Jewry were printed in detail as appendix 1 in The Nameless War by Captain A.H.M. Ramsay.

10 Because the Jews were being evicted from all European countries Chemor, Rabbi of Arles in Provence, sought advice from the Sanhedrin then located in Constantinople. His appeal was dated Jan. 13th 1489. The reply arrived back November 1459. It was signed V.S.S. - V.F.F. Prince of the Jews. It advised the Rabbis to use the tactics of "The Trojan Horse" Christian and make their sons Priests, Laymen, lawyers, and doctors, etc. so they could destroy the Christian structure from within.

11 The Encyclopedia Britannica on page 67, Vol. 13, 1947 has this to say: "The 14th Century was the Golden Age of the Jews in Spain. In 1391, the preaching of a Priest of Seville, Fernando Martenez, led to the first general massacre of the Jews who were envied for their prosperity and hated because they were the king's tax collectors.

12 This is dealt with more fully in the chapters on Spain.

13 H.G. Wells defines the differences very clearly in his Outline of History, pages 493-494.

14 It does even today. Illegal entry into the United States and into Palestine has reached unprecedented numbers since the end of World War Two. Evidence will be produced to prove the Underground is invariably associated with the Anti-Social characters that constitute the Underworld.

15 Sombirt's work — "The Jews and Modern Capitalism", and the "Jewish Encyclopedia", bear out the above statement.

16 This policy has been common practice ever since. The Soviet Embassies in every country have been turned into the Headquarters of intrigue and espionage as further evidence will prove.

17 This fact was commented upon in the Catholic Gazette in February of that year.

18 Charles was in custody at this time.

19 It is important to note that school history books make no mention of the two opposing groups of men who have been the "Secret Power" behind International Affairs who made history. This policy seems to have been by tacit agreement. —Author.

20 The outbreak of the Great Fire of London, known as "The Great Cleaner" ended the plague.

21 The word Cabal is closely related to Cabala a mysterious Hebrew theosophy dating back into antiquity but which became very active during the 10th and succeeding centuries. Cabala was announced as "a special revelation" which enabled Rabbis to explain to the Jewish people the hidden meanings of the sacred writings. Pear's Cyclopedia 57th edition, page 529 says "Cabalism was later carried to great excess". Cabal list leaders pretending to read signs, and evidence, in letters and forms, and numbers, contained in the Scriptures. The French named this mysterious rite Cabale. The French used the term Cabale to designate any group of political or private intriguers. The English coined the name Cabal because the chief personages concerned with Cabalistic intrigue in England were Clifford Ashley, Buckingham, Arlington, and Lauderdale, in that order. The first letter of their names spells Cabal! Cabalists were the instigators of various forms of political and religious unrest during the unhappy reign of Charles II.

22 The identity of the men who control the Bank of England still remains a secret. The Macmillan Committee appointed in 1929 to throw light on the subject failed completely. Mr. Montague Norman, the official Head of the Bank of England was most evasive and non-committal in any answer he made to the committee. For further particulars read — Facts about the Bank of England by A.N. Field, p. 4.

23 If such a policy is carried to its logical conclusion it is only a matter of time before the international money- lenders control the wealth, natural resources, and man-power of the entire world. History shows how rapidly they have progressed toward their goal since 1694.

24 The duke is the direct ancestor of Sir Winston Churchill, the Prime Minister of England today... i.e. 1954 — Churchill is self-acknowledged as having been the foremost Zionist of this era. He is the man most responsible for influencing the United Nations to create the State of Israel.

Chapter Three

The Men Who Caused The French Revolution, 1789

In the previous chapter evidence was given to prove how a small group of foreign money- lenders, operating through their English agents, remained anonymous while they secured control of that nation's economy for the modest sum of £1,250,000. Evidence will now be produced to identify some of these International Jewish money-lenders and prove they, or their successors, plotted and planned, and helped finance, the Great French Revolution of 1789, exactly the same way as they had plotted and planned and financed the English Revolution of 1640-1649. In succeeding chapters evidence will be produced to prove that the descendants of these same International Jewish Financiers have been The Secret Power behind every war and revolution from 1789 onwards.

The Jewish Encyclopedia says *Edom is in modern Jewry*. This is a very important admission, because the word *Edom means Red*. History reveals that a Jewish Goldsmith, Amschel Moses Bauer, tired of his wandering in Eastern Europe, decided in 1750 to settle down in Frankfort-on- the-Main in Germany. He opened a shop, or Counting House, in the Jundenstrasse district. Over the door of his shop he placed as his sign of business A RED SHIELD. It is of the greatest importance to remember that the Jews in Eastern Europe, who belonged to the revolutionary movement based on terrorism, had also adopted the *Red Flag* as their emblem because it represented Blood.

Amschel Moses Bauer had a son born in 1743 and he named him Amschel Mayer Bauer. The father died in 1754 when his son was only eleven years of age. The boy had shown great ability, and extraordinary intelligence, and his father had taught him everything possible about the rudimentary principles of the money-lending business. It had been the father's intention to have his son trained as a Rabbi but death intervened.

A few years after his father's death Amschel Mayer Bauer was employed by the Oppenheimer Bank as a clerk. He soon proved his natural ability for the banking business and was rewarded with a junior partnership. Later he returned to Frankfort where he secured control and ownership of the business which had been established by his father in 1750. The Red Shield was still proudly displayed over the door. Knowing the secret significance of the Red Shield Amschel Mayer Bauer decided to adopt it as the new family name. Red Shield in German is Roth Schild and thus The *House of Rothschild* came into being.

Amschel Mayer Bauer lived until 1812. He had five sons. All of them were specially-trained to become Captains of High Finance. Nathan, one of the sons, showed exceptional ability and, at the age of twenty-one, went to England with the definite purpose of securing control of the Bank of England. The purpose was to use this control to work in conjunction with his father and other brothers to set up, and consolidate, an International Banking Monopoly in Europe. The combined wealth of the International Banking Pool could then be used to further the secret ambitions his father had made known to all his sons. To prove his ability, Nathan Rothschild turned £20,000, with which he had been entrusted, into £60,000 in three years.

In studying the World Revolutionary Movement it is important to remember that the *Red Flag* was the symbol of the French Revolution and every revolution since. More significant still is the fact that when Lenin, financed by International Bankers, overthrew the Russian Government and established the first Totalitarian Dictatorship in 1917, the design of the flag was a Red Flag, with a Hammer and Sickle, and *THE STAR OF JUDEA* imposed.

In 1773, when Mayer Rothschild was only thirty years of age, he invited twelve other wealthy and influential men to meet him in Frankfort. His purpose was to convince them that if they agreed to pool their resources they could then finance and control the World Revolutionary Movement and use it as their Manual of Action to win ultimate control of the wealth, natural resources, and man-power of the entire world.

Rothschild revealed how the English Revolution had been organized. He pointed out the mistakes and errors that had been made. The revolutionary period had been too long. The elimination of reactionaries had not been accomplished with sufficient speed and ruthlessness. The planned reign of terror, by which the subjugation of the masses was to be accomplished speedily, had not been put into effective operation. Even after all these mistakes had been made the initial purpose of the revolution had been achieved. The bankers who instigated the revolution had established control of the national economy and consolidated the national debt. By means of intrigue carried out on an international scale they had increased the national debt steadily by loaning the money to fight the wars and rebellions they had fomented since 1694.

Basing his arguments on logic and sound reasoning, Mayer Rothschild pointed out that the financial results obtained as the result of the English Revolution would be as nothing when compared to the financial rewards to be obtained by a French Revolution provided those present agreed to unity of purpose and put into effect his carefully thought out and revised revolutionary plan. The project would be backed by all the power that could be purchased with their pooled resources. This agreement reached, Mayer Rothschild unfolded his revolutionary plan. By clever manipulation of their combined wealth it would be possible to create such adverse economic conditions that the masses would be reduced to a state bordering on starvation by unemployment. By use of cleverly conceived propaganda it would be easy to place the blame for the adverse economic conditions on the King, His Court, the Nobles, the Church, Industrialists, and the employers of labor. Their paid propagandists would arouse feelings of hatred and revenge against the ruling classes by exposing all real and alleged cases of extravagance, licentious conduct, injustice, oppression, and persecution. They, would also invent infamies to bring into disrepute others who might, if left alone, interfere with their overall plans. [1]

After the general introduction to build up an enthusiastic reception for the plot he was about to unfold, Rothschild turned to a manuscript and proceeded to read a carefully prepared plan of action. The following is what I have been assured is a condensed version of the plot by which the conspirators hoped to obtain ultimate undisputed control of the wealth, natural resources, and man-power of the entire world.

1. The speaker started to unfold the plot by saying that because the majority of men were inclined to evil rather than to good the best results in governing them could be obtained by using violence and terrorism and not by academic discussions. The speaker reasoned that in the beginning human society had been subject to brutal and blind force which was afterwards changed to LAW. He argued that LAW was FORCE only in disguise. He reasoned it was logical to conclude that "By the laws of nature right lies in force".

2. He next asserted that political freedom is an idea and not a fact. He stated that in order to usurp political power all that was necessary was to preach 'Liberalism' so that the electorate, for the sake of an idea, would yield some of their power and prerogatives which the plotters could then gather together into their own hands.

3. The speaker asserted that the Power of Gold had usurped the power of liberal rulers even then, i.e. 1773. He reminded his audience that there had been a time when FAITH had ruled but stated that once FREEDOM had been substituted for FAITH the people did not know how to use it in moderation. He argued that because of this fact it was logical to assume that they could use the idea of FREEDOM to bring about "CLASS WARS". He pointed out that it was immaterial to the success of HIS plan whether the established governments were destroyed by internal or external foes because the victor had of necessity to seek the aid of 'Capital' which "Is entirely in our hands." [2]

4. He argued that the use of any and all means to reach their final goal was justified on the grounds that the ruler who governed by the moral code was not a skilled politician because he left himself vulnerable and in an unstable position on his throne. He said "Those who wish to rule must have recourse to cunning and to make-believe because great national qualities like frankness and honesty, are vices in politics"[3]

5. He asserted "Our right lies in force. The word RIGHT is an abstract thought and proves nothing. I find a new RIGHT ... to attack by the RIGHT of the strong, and to scatter to the winds all existing forces of order and regulation, to reconstruct all existing institutions, and to become the sovereign Lord of all those who left to us the RIGHTS to their powers by

laying them down voluntarily in their 'Liberalism'."

6. He then admonished his listeners with these words *"The power of our resources must remain invisible until the very moment when it has gained such strength that no cunning or force can undermine it."* He warned them that any deviation from the Line of the strategical plan he was making known to them would risk bringing to naught "THE LABORS OF CENTURIES".

7. He next advocated the use of '**Mob Psychology**' to obtain control of the masses. He reasoned that the might of the Mob is blind, senseless, and unreasoning and ever at the mercy of suggestion from any side. He stated *"Only a despotic ruler can rule the Mob efficiently because without absolute despotism there can be no existence for civilization which was carried out NOT by the masses, but by their guide, whosoever that person might be."* He warned *"The moment the Mob seizes FREEDOM in its hands it quickly turns to anarchy."*

8. He next advocated that the use of **alcoholic liquors, drugs, moral corruption, and all forms of vice**, be used systematically by their "Agenturs" [4] to corrupt the morals of the youth of the nations. He recommended that the special 'agenturs' should be trained as tutors, lackeys, governesses, clerks and by our women in the places of dissipation frequented by the Goyim.[5] He added *"In the number of these last I count also the so-called society ladies who become voluntary followers of the others in corruption and luxury. We must not stop at bribery, deceit, and treachery when they should serve towards the attainment of our end."*

9. Turning to **politics** he claimed they had the RIGHT to seize property by any means, and without hesitation, if by doing so they secured submission, and sovereignty. He pronounced *"Our STATE marching along the path of peaceful conquest has the RIGHT to replace the horrors of wars by less noticeable and more satisfactory sentences of death necessary to maintain the 'terror' which tends to produce blind submission."*

10. Dealing with the use of slogans he said *"In ancient times we were the first to put the words 'Liberty', 'Equality' and 'Fraternity' into the mouths of the masses ... words repeated to this day by stupid poll parrots; words which the would-be wise men of the Goyim could make nothing of in their abstractness, and did not note the contradiction of their meaning and inter-relation."* He claimed the words brought under their directions and control 'legions' *"Who bore our banners with enthusiasm."* He reasoned that there is no place in nature for 'Equality', 'Liberty' or 'Fraternity'. He said *"On the ruins of the natural and genealogical aristocracy of the Goyim we have set up the aristocracy of MONEY. The qualification for this aristocracy is WEALTH which is dependent upon us."*

11. He next expounded his theories regarding **war**. In 1773 he set down a principle which the governments of Britain and the United States publicly announced as their joint policy in 1939. He said it should be the policy of those present to foment wars but to direct the peace conferences so that neither of the combatants obtained territorial gains. He said the wars

21

should be directed so that the nations engaged on both sides would be placed further in their debt, and in the power of 'Our' Agenturs.

12. He next dealt with **administration.** He told those present that they must use their wealth to have candidates chosen for public office who would be *"servile and obedient to our commands, so they may readily be used as Pawns in our game by the learned and genius men we will appoint to operate behind the scenes of government as official advisers."* He added *"The men we appoint as 'Advisers' will have been bred, reared, and trained from childhood in accordance with our ideas to rule the affairs of the whole world."*

13. He dealt with **propaganda,** and explained how their combined wealth could control all outlets of public information while they remained in the shade and clear of blame regardless of what the repercussions might be due to the publication of libels, slanders, or untruths. The speaker said *"Thanks to the Press we have got gold in our hands notwithstanding the fact that we had to gather it out of the oceans of blood and tears... But it has paid us even though we have sacrificed many of our own people. Each victim on our side is worth a thousand Goyim."*

14. He next explained the necessity of having their '**Agentur**' always come out into the open, and appear on the scene, when conditions had reached their lowest ebb, and the masses had been subjugated by means of want and terror. He pointed out that when it was time to restore order they should do it in such a way that the victims would believe they had been the prey of criminals and irresponsibles. He said *"By executing the criminals and lunatics after they have carried out our preconceived 'reign of terror', we can make ourselves appear as the saviors of the oppressed, and the champions of the workers."* The speaker then added *"We are interested in just the opposite ... in the diminution, the killing out of the Goyim."*

15. He next explained how **industrial depressions and financial panics** could be brought about and used to serve their purpose saying *"Enforced unemployment and hunger, imposed on the masses because of the power we have to create shortages of food, will create the right of Capital to rule more surely than it was given to the real aristocracy, and by the legal authority of Kings."* He claimed that by having their agentur control the 'Mob', the 'Mob' could then be used to wipe out all who dared to stand in their way.

16. The infiltration into continental Freemasonry was next discussed extensively. The speaker stated that their purpose would be to take advantage of the facilities and secrecy Freemasonry had to offer. He pointed out that they could organize their own Grand Orient Lodges within Blue Freemasonry in order to carry on their subversive activities and hide the true nature of their work under the cloak of philanthropy. He stated that all members initiated into their Grand Orient Lodges should be used for proselytizing purposes and for spreading their atheistic- materialistic ideology amongst the Goyim. He ended this phase of the discussion with the words. *"When the hour strikes for our sovereign Lord of all the World*

to be crowned these same hands will sweep away everything that might stand in his way."

17. He next expounded the value of systematic deceptions, pointing out that their agentur should be trained in the use of high sounding phrases, and the use of popular slogans. They should make the masses the most lavish of promises. He observed *"The opposite of what has been promised can always be done afterwards ... that is of no consequence."* He reasoned that by using such words as Freedom and Liberty, the Goyim could be stirred up to such a pitch of patriotic fervor that they could be made to fight even against the laws of God, and Nature. He added *"And for this reason after we obtain control the very NAME OF GOD will be erased from the 'Lexicon of life'."*[6]

18. He then detailed the plans for **revolutionary war**; the art of street fighting; and outlined the pattern for the 'Reign of Terror' which he insisted must accompany every revolutionary effort *"Because it is the most economical way to bring the population to speedy subjection."*

19. **Diplomacy** was next discussed. After all wars secret diplomacy must be insisted upon *"in order that our agentur, masquerading as 'political', 'Financial', and 'Economic' advisers, can carry out our mandates without fear of exposing who are 'The Secret Power' behind national and international affairs."* The speaker then told those present that by secret diplomacy they must obtain such control *"that the nations cannot come to even an inconsiderable private agreement without our secret agents having a hand in it."*

20. **Ultimate World Government the goal**. To reach this goal the speaker told them *"It will be necessary to establish huge monopolies, reservoirs of such colossal riches, that even the largest fortunes of the Goyim will depend on us to such an extent that they will go to the bottom together with the credit of their governments ON THE DAY AFTER THE GREAT POLITICAL SMASH."* The speaker then added *"You gentlemen here present who are economists just strike an estimate of the significance of this combination."*

21. **Economic war.** Plans to rob the Goyim of their landed properties and industries were then discussed. A combination of high taxes, and unfair competition was advocated to bring about the economic ruin of the Goyim as far as their national financial interests and investments were concerned. In the international field he felt they could be encouraged to price themselves out of the markets. This could be achieved by the careful control of raw materials, organized agitation amongst the workers for shorter hours and higher pay, and by subsidizing competitors. The speaker warned his co-conspirators that they must arrange matters, and control conditions, so that *"the increased wages obtained by the workers will not benefit them in any way."*

22. **Armaments**. It was suggested that the building up of armaments for the purpose of making the Goyim destroy each other should be launched on such a colossal scale that in the final analysis *"there will only be the*

23

masses of the proletariat left in the world, with a few millionaires devoted to our cause ... and police, and soldiers sufficient to protect our interests."

23. **The New Order**. The members of the One World Government would be appointed by the Dictator. He would pick men from amongst the scientists, the economists, the financiers, the industrialists, and from the millionaires because *"in substance everything will be settled by the question of figures."*

24. **Importance of youth**. The importance of capturing the interest of youth was emphasized with the admonition that *"Our agenturs should infiltrate into all classes, and levels of society and government, for the purpose of fooling, bemusing, and corrupting the younger members of society by teaching them theories and principles we know to be false."*

25. National and International Laws should not be changed but should be used as they are, to destroy the civilization of the Goyim *"merely by twisting them into a contradiction of the interpretation which first masks the law and afterwards hides it altogether. Our ultimate aim is to substitute ARBITRATION for LAW."*

The speaker then told his listeners *"You may think the Goyim will rise upon us with arms, but in the WEST we have against this possibility an organization of such appalling terror that the very stoutest hearts quail ... the 'Underground'... The Metropolitans ... The subterranean corridors ... these will be established in the capitals and cities of all countries before that danger threatens."*

The use of the word 'WEST' has great significance. It makes it plain that Rothschild was addressing men who had joined the World Revolutionary Movement which was started in the Pale of Settlement in the 'EAST'. It must be remembered that before Amschel Moses Bauer settled down in Frankfort, Germany, he had followed his trade as a gold and silversmith, travelling extensively in the 'East' of Europe, where he had undoubtedly met the men his son Amschel Mayer addressed after he developed from a money-lender into a banker and established THE HOUSE OF ROTHSCHILD in the Jundenstrasse where the above meeting is said to have taken place in 1773.

As far as can be ascertained the original plan of the conspiracy ended at the point where it terminated above. I am satisfied that the documents which fell into the hands of Professor S. Nilus in 1901, and which he published under the title 'The Jewish Peril' in 1905 in Russia, were an enlargement of the original plot. There appears to be no change in the first section but various additions disclose how the conspirators had used Darwinism, Marxism, and even Nietzcheism. More important still, the documents discovered in 1901 disclose how Zionism was to be used. It must be remembered that Zionism was only organized in 1897.

This matter is referred to later, when the intrigue leading up to the abdication of King Edward VIII is explained. The translation Mr. Victor Marsden made of The Jewish Peril was published by The Britons Publishing

Society, London, England, under the title The Protocols of The Learned Elders of Zion in 1921. This book is also discussed. It appears logical to say that the discovery of the later document confirms the existence of the earlier one. Little, if anything is changed, but considerable material is added probably due to the rapid development of the international conspiracy. The only point upon which there seems to be grounds for disagreement is in regard to the titles chosen by Prof. Nilus and Mr. Marsden for their books. Mr. Marsden definitely states the contents of his book are the Protocols of the meetings of the Learned Elders of Zion whereas it would appear it was a plot presented to moneylenders, Goldsmiths, Industrialists, Economists, and others, by Amschel Mayer Rothschild who had graduated from money-lender to banker.

Once the spirit of revolt against constituted authority had been aroused within the hearts and minds of the masses, the actual revolutionary effort would be carried out under the impetus of a preconceived Reign of Terror. The Reign of Terror would be conceived by the leaders of the Jewish Illuminati. They in turn would have their agents infiltrate into the newly organized French Freemasonry and establish therein Lodges of Grand Orient Masonry to be used as the revolutionary underground and as their instrument for proselytizing the doctrine of atheistic dialectical and historical materialism. Rothschild ended his discourse by pointing out that if proper precautions were taken their connection with the revolutionary movement need never be known.

The question may well be asked "How can it be proved these secret meetings were held?" — and "If they were held how is it possible to prove what matters were discussed at such meetings?" The answer is simple. The devilish plot was made known by "An Act of God".

In 1785 a courier was galloping madly on horseback from Frankfort to Paris carrying detailed information regarding the World Revolutionary Movement in general, and instructions for the planned French Revolution in particular. The instructions originated with the Jewish Illuminati in Germany and were addressed to Grand Master of the Grand Orient Masons in France. The Grand Orient Lodges had been established as the revolutionary underground by the Duc D'Orleans after he, as Grand Master of French Masonry, had been initiated into the Jewish Illuminati in Frankfort by Mirabeau. The courier was struck by lightning while passing through Ratisbon, and killed. The documents he carried fell into the hands of the police who turned them over to the Bavarian Government. A record of historical events told in chronological order connects the House of Rothschild with the Jewish Illuminati in Frankfort and the Illuminati within French Free Masonry known as the Grand Orient Lodges as will be shown.

It has been recorded how the Jewish Rabbis claimed the power to interpret the secret and hidden meanings of the writings of Holy Scripture by special revelation obtained through Cabala. Claiming to have such powers was of little avail unless they had an organization, or instrument, in their hands to put the inspiration they claimed to have received into effect. The money-lenders, certain High Priests, Directors, and Elders decided to organize a very secret society to serve their evil purpose — they named it "The Illuminati". The word *Illuminati* is derived from the word Lucifer, which means *Bearer of the Light*, or *Being of extraordinary brilliance*. Therefore the *Illuminati* was Organized to carry out the inspirations given to the High Priests by Lucifer during the performance of their Cabalistic Rites. Thus Christ is proved justified when he named them of the Synagogue of Satan. The Supreme Council of the Jewish Illuminati numbered thirteen. They were, and still remain, the executive body of *The Council of Thirty Three*. The heads of the Jewish Illuminati claim to possess superlative knowledge in everything pertaining to religious doctrine, religious rites, and religious ceremonies. They were the men who conceived the Atheistic-materialistic ideology which in 1848 was published as "The Communist Manifesto" by Karl Marx. Marx was the nephew of a Jewish Rabbi but he disassociated himself officially from the Jewish High Priesthood when designated to perform his important duties, putting into practice once again the Joint Stock Co. principle of operation.

The reason the Supreme Council numbered thirteen was to remind the members that their one and only duty was to destroy the religion founded by Christ and his twelve Apostles. [7] To ensure secrecy and avoid the possibility of Judas-like betrayal, every man initiated into the Illuminati was required to take an oath of Unlimited Obedience to the head of the Council of Thirty Three and to recognize no mortal as above him. In an organization, such as the Illuminati, this meant that every member acknowledged the head of the Council of Thirty Three as his God upon this earth. This fact explains how high level Communists, even today, swear an oath that they do not give allegiance to Russia. They don't. They give allegiance only to the head of the directors of the World Revolutionary Movement.

The Supreme Council decided they would use the Ingoldstadt Lodge to organize a campaign by which the agents or Cells of the Illuminati would infiltrate into Continental Freemasonry and, under the cloak of social enjoyment and public philanthropy, organize their revolutionary underground. Those who infiltrated into Continental Freemasonry were ordered to establish Lodges of the Grand Orient and use them for proselytism so they could quickly contact non- Jews of wealth, position, and influence connected with both Church and State. Then, by using the age-old methods of bribery, corruption and graft, they could make them become willing, or unwilling, disciples of Illuminism. They could make them preach the inversion of the Ten Commandments of God. They could make them advocate atheistic-materialism.

Once this policy had been decided upon, agents of the Supreme Council contacted the Marquis of Mirabeau as the most likely person in France to serve their ends. He belonged to the nobility. He had great influence in court circles, he was an intimate friend of the Duc D'Orleans whom they had decided they would use as Front Man to lead the French Revolution. But more important still, the Marquis of Mirabeau was devoid of morals and his licentious excesses had led him heavily into debt.

It was a simple matter for the money-lenders to have their agents contact Mirabeau, the famous French orator. Under the guise of friends and admirers they offered to help him out of his financial difficulties. What they actually did was lead him down the "Primrose Path" into the very depths of vice and debauchery until he was so deeply in their debt that he was forced to do their bidding. At a meeting to consolidate his debts, Mirabeau was introduced to Moses Mendelssohn, one of the big Jewish financiers who took him in hand. Mendelssohn in due time introduced Mirabeau to a woman, famous for her personal beauty and charm but without moral scruples.

This stunning Jewess was married to a man named Herz, but, to a man like Mirabeau, the fact that she was married only made her more desirable. It wasn't long before she was spending more time with Mirabeau than she was spending with her husband. Heavily in debt to Mendelssohn, tightly ensnared by Mrs. Herz, Mirabeau was completely helpless ... He had swallowed their bait hook, line, and sinker. But, like good fishermen, they played him gently for a time. If they exerted too great a pressure the leader might break and their fish might get away. Their next move was to have him initiated into Illuminism. He was sworn to secrecy and unlimited obedience under pain of death. The next move was to lead him into compromising situations which mysteriously became public. This method of destroying a man's character became known as the practice of L'Infamie. Because of scandals and organized detraction, Mirabeau was ostracized by many of his social equals. His resentment produced a desire for revenge and thus he embraced the revolutionary Cause.

Mirabeau's task was to induce the Duc D'Orleans to lead the Revolutionary Movement in France. It was implied that once the King had been forced to abdicate he would become the Democratic Ruler of France. The real plotters of the French Revolution were careful not to let either Mirabeau or the Duc D'Orleans know they intended to murder the King and Queen, and thousands of the nobility. They made Mirabeau and the Duc D'Orleans believe that the purpose of the revolution was to free politics and religion from superstition and despotism. Another factor which made the men who were The Secret Power behind the revolutionary movement decides that the Duc D'Orleans should be their Front man was the fact that he was Grand Master of French Freemasonry.

Adam Weishaupt was given the task of adapting the ritual and rites of Illuminism for use of initiation into the Grand Orient Masonry. He also lived in Frankfort, Germany. Mirabeau introduced the Duc D'Orleans and his friend Talleyrand to Weishaupt who initiated them into the secrets of Grand Orient Masonry. By the end of 1773 Phillipe, Duc D'Orleans had introduced the Grand Orient Ritual into French Freemasonry. By 1788 there were more than two thousand lodges in France affiliated with Grand Orient Masonry and the number of individual adepts exceeded one hundred thousand. Thus the Jewish Illuminati under Moses Mendelssohn was introduced into Continental Freemasonry by Weishaupt under the guise of Lodges of the Grand Orient. The Jewish Illuminati next organized secret revolutionary committees within the lodges. Thus the revolutionary underground directors were established throughout France.

Once Mirabeau had succeeded in having the Duc D'Orleans amalgamate the *Blue or National freemasonry* in France with the Grand Orient rites, he led his friend down the same "Primrose Path" which had led to his own social ostracism. In exactly four years, the Duc D'Orleans was so heavily in debt that he was PERSUADED to engage in every form of illegal traffic and trade to recuperate his losses. But in some mysterious manner his ventures always seemed to go wrong and he lost more and more money.

By 1780 he owed 800,000 livres. Once again the money-lenders came forward and offered him advice in regard to his business transactions and financial aid. They very nicely maneuvered him into the position of signing over to them as security for their loans, his palace, his estates, his house, and the Palais Royal. The Duc D'Orleans signed an agreement under which his Jewish financiers were authorized to manage his properties and estates so as to ensure him sufficient income to meet his financial obligations and leave him a steady and adequate income.

The Duc D'Orleans had never been too bright in regard to financial matters. To him the agreement he signed with his Jewish Bankers appeared to be a sound financial deal. They had offered to manage his business affairs and turn them from a dismal failure into a great financial success. What more could he want? It is doubtful if the Duc D'Orleans even suspected that there was a nigger hidden deep in the wood-pile. It is doubtful if he even suspected he had sold himself body and soul to the Agents of the Devil... But he had done so. He was completely in their hands. [8]

The Secret Powers directing the French Revolution appointed Choderlos de Laclos to manage the Palais Royal and the Duc D'Orleans' estates. De Laclos is thought to have been a Jew of Spanish origin. When he was appointed manager of the Palais Royal he was acclaimed as the author of *Les Liaisons Dangereuses* and other pornographic works. He publicly defended his extreme immorality on the grounds that he studied the politics of love in all its varied aspects because of his love of politics.

It matters little who Choderlos de Laclos was, it is what he did that is of importance. He turned the Palais Royal into the greatest and most notorious house of ill-fame the world has ever known. In the Palais Royal he established every kind of lewd entertainment, licentious conduct, shameless shows, obscene picture galleries, pornographic libraries, and staged public exhibitions of the most bestial forms of sexual depravity. Special opportunities were provided for men and women who wished to indulge in every form of debauchery. The Palais Royal became the center in which details of the campaign for the systematic destruction of the French religious faith and public morals were conceived and carried out. This was done on the Cabalistic theory that *the best revolutionary is a youth devoid of morals.*

Associated with de Laclos was a Jew from Palermo named Cagliostro, alias

Joseph Balsamo. He turned one of the Duc's properties into a printing house from which he issued revolutionary pamphlets. Balsamo organized a staff of revolutionary propagandists. In addition to literature they organized concerts, and plays, and debates calculated to appeal to the very lowest instincts of human nature and further the revolutionary cause. Balsamo also organized the Spy-rings which enabled the men who were The Secret Power behind the revolutionary movement to put into operation their plan of *L'Infamie* to be used for systematic character assassination.

Men and women, who were enticed into the Web spun by de Laclos and Balsamo, could be blackmailed into doing their bidding. Thus it was the Duc D'Orleans' estates were turned into the Centre of Revolutionary Politics while, under the guise of Lecture Halls, Theatres, Art Galleries, and Athletic Clubs, the gambling rooms, brothels, and wine and drug shops did a roaring trade. In this revolutionary underworld potential leaders were first ensnared. Their consciences were at first deadened by evil associations and then killed by indulgence in evil practices. The estates of the Duc D'Orleans were turned into factories in which the Secret Power behind the World Revolutionary Movement manufactured the Pieces they intended to use in their game of International Chess. Scudder, who wrote *"Prince of the Blood"* says of the Palais Royal: "It gave the police more to do than all other parts of the city". But as far as the public was concerned, this infamous place was owned by the Duc D'Orleans, the cousin of the king. Only a mere handful of men and women knew that the money-lenders controlled it and used it to create a revolutionary organization which was to be the instrument of their revenge and their manual of action to further their secret aims and ambitions.

After the secret documents found on the body of the Courier had been read by the police, the documents were passed on to the Bavarian Government. The Bavarian Government ordered the police to raid the headquarters of the Illuminati. Further evidence was obtained which exposed the wide-spread ramifications of the World Revolutionary Movement. The Governments of France, England, Poland, Germany, Austria and Russia were informed of the International Nature of the revolutionary plot, but as has happened repeatedly since, the governments concerned took no serious action to stop the diabolical conspiracy. Why? The only answer to this question is this: The power of the men behind the world revolutionary movement is greater than the power of any elected government. This fact will be proved time and time again as the story unfolds.

The malevolent men who plot and plan the W.R.M. have another advantage over decent people. The average person, who believes in God and finds pleasure and enjoyment in the beautiful things with which God has blessed us, just cannot bring himself, or herself, to believe a diabolical plan of hatred and revenge could be conceived by human beings. Although all Christians believe most sincerely that the Grace of God enters their own souls as the result of attending their religious services, receiving the Sacraments, and saying their prayers, they cannot make themselves believe that through the ceremonies and

Rites of the Illuminati, be it the Semitic Cabala or the Aryan Pagan Grand Orient type, the Devil does inoculate his evil influence and powers into the hearts and souls of the men and women who accept, as their religion, Satanism or atheism, and put the theories of their High Priests into practice.

A few illustrations will be given to show how individuals and governments have remained just as stupid and naive in regard to warnings given them concerning the evil mechanism of the real leaders of the World Revolutionary Movement.

After various governments failed to act on the information made known by the Bavarian police in 1785, the sister of Marie Antoinette wrote her personal letters warning her of the revolutionary plot; the connection of the International Bankers; the part Freemasonry was destined to play, and her own danger. Marie Antoinette (1755 - 1793) was the daughter of the Emperor Francis I of Austria. She married Louis XVI of France. She just couldn't bring herself to believe the terrible things her own sister told her were being plotted by the Illuminati. To the repeated warnings sent by her sister, Marie Antoinette wrote long letters in reply. In regard to her sister's claim that evidence had been obtained that the Illuminati operating under the guise of Philanthropic Freemasonry planned to destroy both the Church and State in France, Marie Antoinette replied: "I believe that as far as France is concerned, you worry too much about Freemasonry. Here it is far from having the significance it may have elsewhere in Europe."

How wrong she proved to be is a matter of history. Because she refused consistently to heed her sister's repeated warnings she and her husband died under the guillotine.

Between 1917 and 1919 the British Government was given full particulars regarding the international bankers who were at that time The Secret Power behind the W.R.M. The information was submitted officially by British Intelligence Officers, American Intelligence Officers and confirmed by Mr. Oudendyke and Sir M. Findlay. Mr. Oudendyke was the representative of the Netherlands Government in St. Petersburg (now Leningrad) at the time. He looked after Britain's interests after The Mob had wrecked the British Embassy, and killed Commander E.N. Cromie. This aspect of the W.R.M. is dealt with in detail in subsequent chapters on Russia.

The majority of students of history believe Marie Antoinette was a woman who entered fully into the spirit and gaiety of the French Court. It is generally accepted as a fact that she engaged in many affairs d'amour with her husband's close friends, and indulged in reckless extravagances. That is the picture Balsamo and his propagandists painted of her. The fact that they made their L'Infamie stick enabled them to have the mob demand her life. But their version of the conduct of Marie Antoinette is a pack of lies, as historians have proved. The fortitude with which she bore the sufferings inflicted upon her by her enemies, the dignity with which she met her fate and the resignation and courage with which she offered up her life on the scaffold, cannot be reconciled with the characteristics of a wanton woman.

In order to defame Marie Antoinette, Weishaupt and Mendelssohn thought up the idea of the *Diamond Necklace*. At the time, the financial resources of France were at their lowest ebb and the government of France was begging the International Money-Barons to grant them further credit. A secret agent of the arch-conspirators ordered a fabulous diamond necklace to be made by the Court Jewelers. The order for this necklace, the estimated value of which was a quarter of a million livres, was placed in the name of the Queen. When the Court Jewelers brought the Diamond Necklace to the Queen for her acceptance she refused to have anything to do with it. She disclaimed all knowledge of the transaction. But the news of the fabulous necklace leaked out as the plotters intended it should. Balsamo put his propaganda machine into operation. Marie Antoinette was deluged with criticism; her character was smeared; her reputation dragged in the mire by a whispering campaign of character assassination. And, as usual, nobody could ever put a finger on the person or persons who started the slanders. After this build-up, Balsamo uncorked his own special master-piece. His printing presses turned out thousands upon thousands of pamphlets which claimed a secret lover of the Queen's had sent the necklace as a mark of appreciation for her favors.

But those who operated *L'Infamie* thought up even more diabolical slanders to circulate regarding the Queen. They wrote a letter to Cardinal Prince de Rohan to which they forged the signature of the Queen. In the letter he was asked to meet her at the Palais Royal about midnight to discuss the matter of the diamond necklace. A prostitute from the Palais Royal was engaged to disguise herself as the Queen, and involve the Cardinal. The incident was played up in newspapers and pamphlets and the foulest innuendoes were circulated involving two of the highest personages of both Church and State.

History records that after the diamond necklace had served its foul purpose it was taken over to England and taken apart. A Jew named Eliason is said to have retained the majority of the valuable diamonds used in its original composition.

Another piece of evidence which connects the English Jewish moneylenders with the plot to bring about the French Revolution was unearthed by Lady Queensborough, author of "Occult Theocrasy". While doing some research work she read a copy of "L'Anti-Semitisme" written by a Jew named Bernard Lazare and published in 1849. With the leads obtained from this book Lady Queensborough claims Benjamin Goldsmid, his brother Abraham, and their partner Moses Mecatta, and his nephew Sir Moses Montifiore, were Jewish financiers in England who were definitely affiliated with their continental Jewish brethren in the plot to bring about the revolution in France. Further evidence was found to tie Daniel Itsig of Berlin and his son-in- law David Friedlander, and Herz Gergbeer of Alsace in with the Rothschilds and the plot. Thus are revealed the men who at that time constituted the *Secret Power* behind the World Revolutionary Movement.

Knowledge of the methods these men used to maneuver the French Government into financial difficulty is of importance, because it set the pattern they followed in America, Russia, Spain and other countries afterwards.

Sir Walter Scott in Vol. two of *The Life of Napoleon*, gives a clear story of the initial moves. He then sums up the situation with these words — "These financiers used the Government (French) as bankrupt prodigals are treated by usurious money-lenders who, feeding the extravagance with one hand, with the other wring out of their ruined fortunes the most unreasonable recompenses for their advances. By a long succession of these ruinous loans, and various rights granted to guarantee them, the whole finances of France were brought to a total confusion". [9]

After the Government of France was forced into the position of seeking huge loans because of debts incurred in fighting wars to further the secret ambitions of the International Conspirators, they very kindly offered to supply the money providing they could write the terms of the agreement. On the surface their terms were most lenient. But again they had placed a nigger in the wood-pile in the person of one M. Necker. He was to be appointed to the French King's Council as his Chief Minister of Financial Affairs. The Jewish financiers pointed out that this financial wizard would pull France out of her monetary troubles in less than no time at all. What he actually did during the next four years was to involve the French Government so badly with the Jewish financiers that the National Debt increased to £170,000,000.

Captain A.H.M. Ramsay sums up the situation aptly in *The Nameless War*. He says: "Revolution is a blow struck at a paralytic. ... When the debt-grip has been firmly established, control of every form of publicity and political activity soon follows, together with a full grip on industrialists, [both management and labor]. The stage is then set for the revolutionary blow. The grip of the right hand of finance establishes the paralysis; while the revolutionary left hand that holds the dagger and deals the fatal blow. Moral corruption facilitates the whole process."

While Balsamo's propaganda sheets damned the higher officials of both Church and State, special agents of the Illuminati organized the men who were to be used as leaders in the Reign of Terror planned to accompany the revolutionary effort. Among these leaders were Robespierre, Danton, and Marat. To conceal their real purpose, the men who were to release the prisoners and lunatics to create the necessary atmosphere for instituting the preconceived Reign of Terror, met in the Jacobean Convent. Within the walls of the sacred edifice the details of the bloody plan were worked out. The lists of reactionaries marked down for liquidation were compiled. It was explained that while the criminals and lunatics ran wild terrorizing the population by committing mass murders and publicly performing rapes, the organized underground workers, under direction of Manuel, Procurer of the Commune, would round up all the important political figures, heads of the clergy, and military officers known to be loyal to the King. [10] The men who were to emerge from the Jewish organized underground were formed into Jacobin

Clubs. Under leaders, who were well versed in the duties required of them to direct the "Reign of Terror", they conducted the mass atrocities so they would serve the purpose of their hidden masters, and move them further towards their ultimate goal.

NOTES:

1 These were the original theories on which Class War was ultimately organized.

2 This statement in the original documents convince all but the biased that the speaker was not a Rabbi or Elder of the Jews nor was he addressing Elders and Rabbis because it was the Goldsmiths, the money-lenders and their affiliates in commerce and industry who in 1773 had the wealth of the world in their hands as they have it still in their hands in the 20th Century.

3 The Red Fog explains how this theory has been put into effect in America since 1900.

4 The word "agentur" means the complete organized body of agents ... spies, counter-spies, blackmailers, saboteurs, underworld characters, and everything and everybody outside the LAW which enables the international conspirators to further their secret plans and ambitions.

5 The word "Goyim" means all others than their own group. The unimportant people.

6 The "Lexicon of Life" he referred to, was Almighty God's plan of creation.

7 There were also thirteen tribes of Israel which could have some bearing on the matter of numbers.

8 The same Evil Geniuses used their agents to involve William Pitt in debt and forced him to resign as Prime Minister of England because during the early part of his ministry he obstinately refused to allow England to become involved in wars they planned to further their own secret plans and ambitions. Pitt had learned a great deal regarding the part the International Money-Barons played in International Affairs when Chancellor of the Exchequer — 1785.

9 Because of his alleged anti-semitic utterances Sir Walter Scott's important works consisting of a total of nine volumes dealing with many phases of the French Revolution have been given the silent treatment by those who control the publishing houses as well as the biggest portion of the press. They are almost unattainable except in Museum Libraries and are never listed with his other works.

10 Sir Walter Scott — "Life of Napoleon", Vol. 2, P. 30 says "The demand of the Communauté de Paris, now the Sanhedrin of the Jacobin, was of course, for blood."

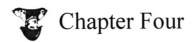 # Chapter Four

The Downfall of Napoleon

The international bankers planned the French Revolution so they could become *The Secret Power* behind the governments of Europe and further their Long Range Plans.

With the outbreak of the revolution the Jacobins took over control. They were men who had been hand-picked by the Illuminati and Grand Orient Masonry. They used the Duc D'Orleans to serve their purpose right up to the time he was required to vote for the death of his cousin the King. The Duc believed he would be made the constitutional monarch, but the Jacobins had other instructions. Once he had voted for the death of the King, and assumed the blame, he left the real plotters free from suspicion. Then those who comprised The Secret Power behind the revolution ordered him liquidated also. They switched the full force of their propaganda, and L'Infamie, against him. In an unbelievably short time, he was on his way to the guillotine. While riding over the cobble stones on the death-cart he heard himself reviled, and execrated, by all classes of the people.

Once Mirabeau realized what a terrible instrument of vengeance he had helped to bring into being, he repented. Wild and dissolute as he had been, he just couldn't stomach witnessing the terrible and shocking atrocities which the Jacobins were systematically perpetrating on all those who were *fingered* for outrage and death by their secret masters. Mirabeau was actually opposed to any violence being done to the King. His personal plan had been to reduce Louis XVI to a Limited Monarch, and then have himself appointed his chief advisor. When he realized that his Masters were determined to kill the King he tried to arrange for Louis to escape from Paris so he could place himself under the protection of his loyal Generals who still commanded his army. When his plans were betrayed to the Jacobins, Mirabeau was ordered liquidated also. In his case a public execution could not be arranged because his enemies did not consider they had time to frame charges against him and make them stick, so he was poisoned. His death was made to look like suicide. A book was written about *The Diamond Necklace* already referred to. In it is the significant remark "Louis was not ignorant of the fact that Mirabeau had been poisoned".

Danton and Robespierre were the two devil's incarnates who stepped up the Reign of Terror designed by the Illuminati to give them revenge upon their enemies, and to remove personages they considered obstacles in their path. Yet, when they had served their purpose, their two chief executioners were arrested and charged with their many infamies and then executed. [1]

Lafayette was a Mason. He was a good man. He joined the revolutionary forces because he honestly believed revolutionary action was necessary to bring about much needed reforms speedily. But Lafayette never thought for a moment he was leading the people of France from their old oppression into a new subjection. When he tried to save the King he was packed off to fight a war in Austria. Since the French Revolution of 1789, up to the revolutions going on to- day, the Secret Power behind them have used many Duc D'Orleans, Mirabeaus and Lafayettes. Although the men have borne different names they have all been used as tools and played similar parts. They have been used to foment the revolutions and, after having served their purpose, they have been liquidated by the very men they served. Their deaths are always so arranged that they die under a blanket of guilt which should rightfully have covered the shoulders of the men who still remain *The Secret Power* behind the scenes in International Intrigue.

Sir Walter Scott understood a great deal about how The Secret Power behind the French Revolution worked. Any person who reads his Life of Napoleon will sense that the author thought he detected the Jewish origin of the plots. [2]

Sir Walter points out that the real key figures in the revolution were mostly *foreigners*. He observed that they used typically Jewish terms such as Directors and Elders, in their work. He points out that a man named Manuel was in some mysterious manner appointed *Procurer of the Commune*. Sir Walter states that this one man was responsible for the arrest and detention, in prisons all over France, of the victims of the pre-arranged massacres which took place in September 1792. During the massacres 8,000 victims were murdered in the prisons of Paris alone. Sir Walter also noted that the Communauté de Paris (the Paris County Council) became the SANHEDRIN of the Jacobins who cried for blood and more blood. Scott relates that until they had served their purpose Robespierre, Danton, and Marat shared the high places in the SYNAGOGUE of the Jacobins. (My emphasis) It was Manuel who sparked the attack against King Louis and Marie Antoinette which finally led them to the guillotine. Manuel was well supported by a man named David who, as a leading member of the Committee of Public security, tried Manuel's many victims. David's voice always called for blood and death.

Sir Walter records that David used to preface his "bloody work of the day with the professional phrase Let us grind enough of the Red." It was David who introduced The Cult of the Supreme Being. The heathen ritual was Cabalistic mummery which was substituted for every external sign of rational devotion. Scott also mentions that Choderlos de Laclos, thought to have been of Spanish origin, was manager of the Palais Royal which played such a devilish part in the preparations for the outbreak of the Revolution. Another matter of importance is this; after Robespierre had been ordered liquidated two men named Reubel and Gohir were appointed Directors of The Council of Elders. With three others they became the actual government of France for a time. The five men referred to were known as *The Directoires*. It is a very remarkable fact that Sir Walter Scott's *Life of Napoleon* (in nine volumes) which reveals so much of the real truth is practically unknown.

35

Mention must be made of G. Renier's *Life of Robespierre*. He writes as if some of the secrets were known to him. He says: "From April 27th to July 28th, 1794 (when Robespierre was defeated), the reign of terror was at its height. It was never a dictatorship of a single man, least of all Robespierre. Some 20 men shared in the power". Then again — "On July 28th Robespierre made a long speech before the Convention ... a Philippic against ultra-terrorists ... during which he uttered vague and general accusations". Robespierre is quoted to have said "I dare not name them at this moment and in this place. I cannot bring myself entirely to tear asunder the veil that covers this profound mystery of iniquity. But I can affirm most positively that among the authors of this plot are the agents of that system of corruption and extravagance, the most powerful of all the means invented by the Foreigners for the undoing of the Republic: I mean the impure apostles of Atheism; and the immorality that is its base". Mr. Renier added: "Had he (Robespierre) not spoken these words he might still have triumphed".

Robespierre had said too much. He was deliberately shot in the jaw to silence him effectively until he could be dragged to the guillotine the following day. Thus another Mason, who knew too much, was disposed of. As the events which led up to the Russian and Spanish revolutions are reviewed, it will be shown that the Hidden Revolutionary Section of the Illuminati within the Grand Orient Lodges of Continental Freemasonry was the instrument of the men who constituted The Secret Power behind the World Revolutionary Movement. Thousands of individuals are publicly blamed, and many organizations brought into disrepute, simply because it was within the power of the secret leaders of the W.R.M. to saddle them with the blame for their crimes and thus conceal their own identity. There are not many people living to-day who know that Robespierre, Marat and Danton, were only the instruments used by the thirteen directors of the Illuminati who plotted and directed the Great French Revolution. It was the men behind the scene who preconceived the pattern of The Reign of Terror as the means of gratifying their desire for revenge. Only during a Reign of Terror could they remove human obstacles from their path.

Having run out of victims, the men who directed the French Revolution decided to engage in international intrigue again. For the purpose of increasing their economic and political power Anselm Mayer Rothschild trained his son Nathan Mayer for the special purpose of opening up a House of Rothschild in London, England. His intention was to consolidate, more strongly than ever, the connections between the men who controlled the Bank of England and those who controlled the Banks of France, Germany and Holland. Nathan undertook this important task at the age of 21. He tripled his fortune. The Bankers then decided to use Napoleon as the Instrument of their will. They organized the Napoleonic Wars to topple several more of the Crowned Heads of Europe.

After Napoleon swept over Europe he pronounced himself Emperor in 1804. He appointed his brother Joseph, King of Naples. Louis, King of

Holland; Jerome, King of Westphalia. At the same time Nathan Rothschild arranged matters so that his four brothers became the kings of finance in Europe. They were the Secret Power behind the newly established thrones. The international money-lenders set up headquarters in Switzerland. It was agreed between them that, in their interests, and for their security, Switzerland should be kept neutral in all disputes. In their Swiss headquarters at Geneva they organized the different combines and cartels on an international scale. They arranged things so that no matter who fought who, or who won and who lost, the members of the International Money-Lenders Pool made more and more money. This group of men soon obtained control of the munition plants, the ship-building industry, the mining industry, chemical plants, drug supply depots, steel mills, etc. The only fly in the ointment was the fact that Napoleon grew more and more egotistical until he finally had the temerity to denounce them publicly. Thus he also decided his own fate. It was not the weather, nor the cold, that turned his victorious invasion of Russia into one of the most tragic military defeats the world has ever known. The failure of munitions and supplies to reach his armies was due to the sabotaging of his lines of communications.

The secret strategy used to defeat Napoleon, and force his abdication, has been accepted as essential for all revolutionary efforts since that date. It is very simple. The leaders of the revolutionary movement arrange to place their agents secretly in key positions in the departments of supply, communication, transport and intelligence, of the armed forces they plan to overthrow. By sabotaging supplies, intercepting orders, issuing contradictory messages, tying up or misrouting transports, and by counter intelligence work, revolutionary leaders have discovered they can create utter chaos in the most efficient military organization on land, at sea, or in the air. Ten Cells secretly placed in key positions are worth ten thousand men in the field. The methods used to bring Napoleon to ruin in the early part of the nineteenth century were used to bring about the defeat of the Russian Armies in the war against Japan in 1904, and again to cause mutiny in the Russian Armies, in 1917, and mutiny in the German Army and Navy in 1918.

Communist infiltration into key positions was the real reason the German Generals asked for, and were granted, an Armistice in November 1918. The same methods were used to destroy the effectiveness of the Spanish Army, Navy and Air Force in 1936. Exactly the same tactics were used to bring about the defeat of Hitler after his victorious advances into Russia in World War Two. Thus history repeats itself, because the same powers use the same methods over and over again. But most important of all, it was the descendants of the men who brought about Napoleon's downfall who brought about the defeat of China's National Forces in 1945 and onwards. Mysterious orders were given which caused millions upon millions of dollars' worth of arms and ammunition to be dumped into the Indian Ocean when they should have gone to Chiang-Kai-Shek. The true story of the manner in which British and American politicians betrayed our anti-Communist Chinese and Korean allies will prove that it was the agents of the International Bankers, maneuvering to let Communism obtain control of Asia, who deceived and ill-advised our top-level statesmen. Communism is to-day what it always has been since 1773, — the instrument of destruction and the manual of action used by the international arch- conspirators to further their own secret plans by which, in the final analysis, they intend to obtain control of the wealth, natural resources, and manpower of the entire world.

History records how Napoleon was forced to abdicate in Paris in 1814, then he was sent into exile on St. Elba, he escaped and tried to make a come-back, but he was playing against men who use loaded dice. Nathan Rothschild, and his international clique, had backed Germany to defeat Napoleon. They had planned to make money regardless of the outcome of the struggle. When the Battle of Waterloo was about to be fought Nathan Rothschild was in Paris. He had obtained, as his place of residence, a palace which overlooked that occupied by Louis XVIII. He could, when he wished, look right into the window of the palace occupied by the aspirant to the throne of France. He had arranged also to have agents on the field of battle dispatch to him by carrier pigeon information regarding the fighting. Nathan Rothschild also arranged to have false information sent to England by carrier pigeons regarding the results of the battle. Once he was sure Wellington had been victorious he had his agents inform the British public that Wellington had been defeated and that Napoleon was on the rampage again. The fact that carrier-pigeons played such an important role in this conspiracy gave birth to the expression A little bird told me. (If a person in England asks another "Where did you get that information?" the person questioned will most likely say "Oh! A little bird told me", and let it go at that).

Nathan Rothschild's little birds told lies of such magnitude, regarding the battle of Waterloo, that the people of Britain went into a panic. The bottom dropped out of the stock market. English pounds could be bought, for a Song or a shilling. Values of everything fell to an all-time low. Nathan chartered a small vessel for the sum of £2,000 to take him from France to England. Upon arrival he, and his financial associates, bought up all the stocks, bonds, shares, other properties, and securities they could get their hands on. When the truth regarding Wellington's victory became known, values returned to normal. The International money- lenders made astronomical fortunes.

Why they were not assassinated by some of the people they ruined is beyond comprehension. As a token of their joy and gratitude for the marvelous feat of arms performed by Wellington and Blücher, the Rothschilds LOANED England £18,000,000 and Prussia £5,000,000 of this ill- gotten gain, TO REPAIR THE DAMAGES OF WAR. When Nathan Rothschild died in 1836, he had secured control of the Bank of England and the National Debt which, after his big financial killing in 1815, reached £885,000,000.

It is most unlikely that one Freemason in a thousand knows the TRUE story of how the heads of the Grand Orient Illuminati infiltrated their agents into Continental Freemasonry. Because the facts related are the truth, the Grand Masters of English Freemasons have warned their Brother Masons that they must have no truck with Grand Orient Masons or affiliate with them in any way. The fact that The Revolutionary Illuminati established itself within Continental Freemasonry, caused Pope Pius IX to publicly denounce Communism, and prohibit Catholics from becoming Masons. To convince any reader, who may still have doubts, regarding the part Freemasonry played in the French Revolution, part of a debate, which took place on the subject in the French Chamber of Deputies in 1904, will be quoted. The Marquis of Rosanbe, after some searching questions related to proving French Freemasonry was the author of the French Revolution said: "We are then in complete agreement on the point that Freemasonry was the only author of the revolution, and the applause which I receive from the Left, and to which I am little accustomed, proves gentlemen, that you acknowledge with me that it was Masonry which made the French Revolution?"

To this statement M. Jumel, a well-known Grand Orient Mason, replied: "We do more than acknowledge it ... we proclaim it". [4]

In 1923 at a big banquet attended by many men prominent in International Affairs, some of whom were connected with the League of Nations organization, the President of the Grand Orient gave this toast. — "To the French Republic, daughter of French Freemasonry. To the universal republic of to-morrow, daughter of universal Masonry."[5]

To prove that The Grand Orient Freemasons have controlled French politics from 1923 onwards a brief review of historical events will be given. The most important victory the International Bankers gained, after their agents had acted as advisors to the political leaders who devised and finally ratified the infamous Treaty of Versailles, was to have M. Herriot elected to power in France in 1924. Every political policy dictated by the heads of Grand Orient Freemasonry in 1923 was put into effect by the Herriot Government within a year.

1. In January 1923 the G.O.L. (Grand Orient Lodges) decreed the suppression of the embassy to the Vatican. The French Parliament carried out this order October 24th, 1924.

2. In 1923 the G.O.L. demanded the triumph of the idea of Laicity (this is the primary principle essential to the establishment of the Grand Orient's ideology of an Atheistic State) Herriot made his public ministerial declaration in favor of this policy June 17th, 1924.

3. On January 31st, 1923 the G.O.L. demanded a full and complete amnesty for condemned persons and traitors. Several prominent Communist leaders were to benefit, amongst them Marty who afterwards became notorious as the organizer of the International Brigades which fought on the Communist side in Spain 1936-39. The Chamber of Deputies voted for a general Amnesty July 15th, 1924 and thus turned loose on an unsuspecting society a number of International Gangsters whose master was the Supreme Council of Grand Orient Masonry, the Illuminati.

4. In October 1922 the G.O.L. had started a campaign to popularize the idea that diplomatic relations be opened with the SOVIET Government as

established in Moscow. This movement didn't get very far until after the election of M. Herriot to power. This Friendship with Russia campaign was started in France when the Bulletine Official de la Grand Loge de France published an article on the subject in the October issue of 1922 on page 286. Political relations were established with the Communist Revolutionary Leaders by Herriot on October 28th, 1924. [6] The same forces of evil are advocating the recognition of Red China today.

One of the leaders of the Grand Orient at this time was Leon Blum. He was being primed to become a political instrument ready to do the bidding of his leaders. High-ranking members of the Military Lodges in Spain who defected (after they found out they were being used as tools by leaders of the W.R.M.), disclosed that every Grand Orient Mason was required to take an oath of UNLIMITED OBEDIENCE to the head of the Council of Thirty Three and to recognize no human as above him. An oath of this kind taken by an avowed atheist literally means that he recognized the State as above everything else, and the head of the State as his God. A great deal of detail about Grand Orient intrigue in France and Spain, from 1923 to 1939 is told in *The Spanish Arena* written by William Foss and Cecil Gerahty and published by *The Right Book Club*, London, England, in 1939. To establish continuity of the International Banker's plot, it is sufficient to touch on just a few highlights.

Leon Blum was born in Paris in 1872 of Jewish parents. He was noted for the part he played in the Dreyfus affair. He was elected French Premier June 1936. He retained office until June 1937. He was re-elected in March, and remained until April 1937. His supporters managed to get him back into politics as Vice-Premier June 1937 to January 1938. Mendes-France is being used the same way today.

During the whole of this time Leon Blum's task was to mold French governmental policy so that it would aid the plans of the leaders of the W.R.M. in regard to Spain. In order to throw suspicion away from themselves the arch-conspirators made it appear that it was Franco, and his military associates, who were the planners and plotters of the events which led up to the Civil War in Spain. It is now proved that Stalin, and his revolutionary experts the Comintern, were the conspirators who carried out the plans of The Secret Power behind the W.R.M. They planned to duplicate what they had achieved in both the French Revolution in 1789, and the Russian Revolution in 1917. As early as 1929 M. Gustave pointed out in his paper "La Victoire" the truth regarding Leon Blum and his associates. He had the courage to declare: "The Collectivist Party of Leon Blum, the second branch of Freemasonry ... is not only anti- religious, but a party of class-war, and of social revolution".

Leon Blum put into effect the plans of the leaders of the W.R.M. to supply Spanish Loyalists with arms, munitions, and finances. He was instrumental in keeping the Pyrenees open but he followed a one-sided policy of non-intervention... It only applied to the Nationalists of Franco's forces.

Evidence is produced, in the chapters dealing with the revolution in Spain, to prove that the French and Spanish Grand Orient Lodges were the line of communications between the directors of the W.R.M. and their agents in Moscow, Madrid and Vienna. [7]

Should the reader think too much importance is being placed on the influence Grand Orient Masonry has on International Affairs A.G. Michel, author of La Dictature de la Franc- Maçonnerie sur la France, gives evidence to prove that the Grand Orient of France decreed in 1924, to make The League of Nations "An international tool for Freemasonry". Trotsky wrote in his book Stalin: "To-day there is a Tower of Babel at the service of Stalin, and one of its principal centers is Geneva, that hot-bed of intrigue."

The importance of what Trotsky says lies in the fact that the accusations he made regarding the evil influence of Grand Orient Masons within the League of Nations applies equally to the bad influence they have in the United Nations today. The student who studies to-day's happenings in the United Nations will see their handiwork especially in regard to strange policies which just don't make sense to the average man-in-the-street. But these strange policies become extremely clear if we study them to see how they will further the long range plan of the W.R.M. To do this we only have to remember one or two important facts : First, that the Illuminati consider it necessary to destroy all existing forms of constitutional government, regardless of whether they be monarchy or republic; Second, that they intend to introduce a World Dictatorship just as soon as they consider they are securely in position to usurp absolute control. M.J. Marques- Rivière [8] had this to say "The center of the International Freemasons is at Geneva. The offices of the International Masonic Association are at Geneva. This is the meeting place of delegates of nearly all the forms of Masonry throughout the world. The interpretation of the League and the I.M.A. is easy, apparent and confessed."

One can well understand the exclamation in 1924 by Brother Barcia, Past Grand Master of the Spanish Grand Orient, at the Convent of the Grand Orient when he returned from Geneva: "I have assisted at the work of the commissions. I have heard Paul-Boncour, Jeuhaux, Loucheur, de Jouvenal. All the French had the same spirit. Beside me were representatives of American Freemasons, and they asked each other: 'Are we in a secular assembly or a Masonic Order? ... Brother Joseph Avenal is the Secretary-General of the League'."

It is well to remember that the International Illuminati chose Geneva as their headquarters nearly a century before the above event was recorded. They had, in accordance with their policy, kept Switzerland a neutral nation in all international disputes because they had to have one place where they could meet and instruct their agents who were doing their bidding and carrying out their secret policies. The United States Government refused to join the League of Nations. Certain interests promoted the Isolationist Policy. The Secret Powers were determined to exploit those who honestly support the idea of a One World form of Super- government to assure peace and prosperity. They determined to wreck the League of Nations and substitute The United Nations.

World War Two gave them this opportunity. In 1946 the remnants of the League of Nations were picked up and used in the quilted pattern of the United Nations which included the U.S.S.Rs and the U.S.A. as the two most powerful members. The fact that the United Nations gave Israel to the Political Zionists, which they had been after for half a century, and on the advice of these same men, turned over China, Northern Korea, Manchuria, Mongolia, the Dutch East Indies, and parts of Indo-China, to Communist leaders, proves how successfully the Secret Powers laid, and carried out, their plans. It must be remembered that Lenin predicted that the forces of Communism would, in all probability, sweep over the western world from the East. People, who study the MERCATOR'S PROJECTION of the world, fail to understand how the nations of the Far East could sweep over the nations of the Western world like a tidal wave. To those who study Global War, Lenin's statements are as clear as crystal. What is even more important — When Lenin had outlived his usefulness he died, or was removed. Few people can understand how it was that Stalin, by a few ruthless, murderous moves, removed all those who, by reason of their activities in the Russian Revolution, were considered better qualified for leadership in the U.S.S.Rs, and usurped power for himself.

Those who study the W.R.M. from the evidence presented in this book will understand why Stalin was chosen to follow Lenin. The old Joint Stock Company principle was being put into effect again. American and British Intelligence Officers had exposed the part the International Bankers had played in the Russian Revolution, to their Governments. In April 1919 the British Government had issued a *White Paper* on this subject. It was quickly suppressed, but a certain amount of damage had been done. The International Bankers had been accused of financing International Jewry to put their plans for an International Dictatorship into effect. The International Bankers had to find some means of countering these impressions and ideas. The true picture of their utter ruthlessness is seen when it is pointed out that Stalin, a Gentile, was chosen by the International money-lenders, and that, acting on their instructions, he put Trotsky out of the way and proceeded to liquidate hundreds of thousands of Russian Jews in the purges which put him in power, following Lenin's death. This should prove to sincere, but misguided people, everywhere, that the International Bankers, and their carefully selected agents and friends, don't consider the MASSES of the people of any race, color, or creed, as other than expendable pawns in the game. It is true that many Jews became Communists and followers of Karl Marx. They worked and fought to bring into being Karl Marx's published theories for an International of Soviet Socialist Republics. But they, like many Gentiles, were deceived. By the time Stalin was firmly seated in Moscow as the head agent of the International Bankers, it was difficult to find any members of the First and Second Internationals alive. The manner in which the Arch-conspirators used Grand Orient Masons, and then had them liquidated as soon as they had served their purpose, is just another illustration of the ruthlessness of those whose only god is Satan.

Further evidence will be produced to prove that the International Bankers are not interested in anything else other than obtaining for their own small and very select group, ultimate undisputed control of the wealth, natural resources, and man-power of the entire world.[9] The only honest thought in any of their minds is that they obviously believe that they are so superior in mental ability to the rest of mankind that they are better able, than any other group of individuals, to manage the World's affairs. They are convinced that they can work out a plan of world government that is better than God's plan. For this reason they are determined to ultimately obliterate from the minds of all human beings all knowledge of God and of His Commandments and substitute their own New Order based on the theory that the State is Supreme in all things and the Head of the State is, therefore, God Almighty upon this earth. The attempted deification of Stalin is proof of this statement. Once people become convinced of this great truth they will realize that men of all races, colors, and creeds have been used, and are still being used, as "Pawns in the Game".

NOTES:

1   It is of interest to note. Protocols of Zion Number 15 reads "We execute Masons in such wise that none save the brotherhood can ever have a suspicion of it" — and again "In this way we shall proceed with those GOY masons who get to know too much". E. Scudder, in his "Life of Mirabeau" says — "He (Mirabeau) died at a moment when the revolution might still have been checked".

2   My investigations prove that the men who have constituted *The Secret Powers* behind the scenes of International Intrigue and directed the W.R.M. and the Nazi plan for World Conquest, have not all been of Semitic origin or members of the Jewish religion. I feel certain they were all of the Illuminati, regardless of racial origin. Money- Barons, Industrial Monopolists, Grasping Politicians, never hesitated to blame Jews and Gentiles alike, for the crimes they committed against humanity.

3   The volumes are never mentioned or reprinted with his other works. They are almost unobtainable. As the story of *The Secret Power* unfolds the reader will realize the importance of this significant fact which illustrates how the channels of publicity are controlled.

4   This was quoted in the Convent du Grand Orient 1923, p. 402, The Illuminati control masonry.

5   Henry Delassus' passage quoted in *La Conjuration Anti-Chrétienne* Vol. I, p. 146; re-quoted in "The Spanish Arena," p. 143.

6   A.G. Michel in *La Dictature de la Franc-Maçonnerie la France* requoted in the Spanish Arena, p. 143.

7   All political events which have occurred in France from the outbreak of world War Two to the recent refusal by Mendes-France to agree to the E.D.C. must be studied, with due regard to the Long Range [Plan] of the

Illuminati whose agents, the grand Orient Freemasons, are members of all levels of the French government, and all political parties. At the last check more than one hundred members of the French Parliament were Grand Orient Masons.

8   J. Marques-Rivière is the author of *Comment la Franc-Maçonnerie fait une Révolution.*

9   The reason the International Bankers backed Political Zionism from 1914 to date is explained in another chapter dealing with events which led to World War Two. It is sufficient to say here that the International Bankers were interested in securing control of the Five Trillion Dollars' worth of minerals and oil which had been discovered in Palestine by Cunningham-Craig, consulting Geologist to the British Government and others, prior to 1918. These geological reports were kept secret. In 1939 Cunningham-Craig was recalled from Canada to make another survey in the Middle East. He died under mysterious circumstances immediately after he had completed his task. To-day, i.e. 1954, arrangements are being made quietly by the big money people to exploit these resources.

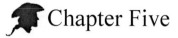 # Chapter Five
American Revolution

In order to understand how men who obtained control of the Bank of England, and the British National Debt, also obtained control of the trade and commerce, and the monetary system of Britain's American colonies, it will be sufficient if we pick up the threads of the story at the time Benjamin Franklin (1706-1790) went over to England to represent the interests of the men who had been associated with him in building up the prosperity of the American Colonies.

Robert L. Owen, former chairman, Committee on Banking and Currency, United States Senate, explains the matter on page 98 of Senate Document No. 23. He states that when associates of the Rothschild's asked Franklin how he accounted for the prosperous conditions prevailing in the colonies, he replied: "That is simple — In the Colonies we issue our own money. It is called Colonial Script — we issue it in proper proportion to the demands of trade and industry."

Robert L. Owen remarked that not very long after the Rothschilds heard of this they realized the opportunity to exploit the situation with considerable profit to themselves. The obvious thing to do was to have a law passed prohibiting the Colonial officials from issuing their own money and make it compulsory for them to obtain the money they required through the medium of the Banks. Amschel Mayer Rothschild was still in Germany but he was supplying the British Government with Mercenary Troops at £8 per man. Such was his influence that in 1764 he succeeded, through the Directors of the Bank of England, in having laws passed in accordance with his dictates.

The authorities in the Colonies had to discard their Script money. They had to mortgage the Colonial assets and securities to the Bank of England in order to borrow the money they needed to carry on business. Referring to those facts Benjamin Franklin stated. "In one year the conditions were so reversed that the era of prosperity ended, and a depression set in, to such an extent that the streets of the Colonies were filled with unemployed." Franklin stated: "The Bank of England refused to give more than 50 per cent of the face value of the Script when turned over as required by law. The circulating medium of exchange was thus reduced by half". [1]

Mr. Franklin disclosed the primary cause of the Revolution when he said: "The Colonies would gladly have borne the little tax on tea and other matters had it not been that England took away from the Colonies their money, which created unemployment and dissatisfaction."

Dissatisfaction became general, but very few Colonials realized that the taxation, and other economic sanctions being imposed on them, was the results of the activities of a small group of International Gangsters, who had succeeded in obtaining control of the British Treasury, after they had obtained control of the Bank of England. It has already been shown how they jumped Britain's National Debt from £1,250,000 in 1694 to £16,000,000 in 1698, and increased it progressively to £885,000,000 by 1815, and £22,503,532,372 by 1945.

On April 19th 1775, the first armed clashes between British and Colonials took place at Lexington and Concord. On May 10th the Second Continental Congress met at Philadelphia and George Washington was placed at the head of the Naval and Military Force. He took command at Cambridge. On July 4th, 1776 Congress adopted the Declaration of Independence.

For the next seven years the International money-lenders urged and financed the Colonial War. The Rothschilds made plenty of money supplying the British with German Hessian soldiers with which to fight the Colonists. The average Brit had no quarrel with his American cousins. [2] He secretly sympathized with them.

On October 19th, 1781 the British Commander, General Cornwallis, surrendered his whole army, including what was left of the Hessians. On September 3rd, 1783 the Independence of the United States was recognized by the Peace Treaty of Paris. The only real losers were the British people. Their National Debt had been increased tremendously and the International money-lenders (who were in reality the Secret Power behind the World Revolutionary Movement) had succeeded in the first stage of the long range plans towards the dissolution of the British Empire. [3]

The agents of the international bankers worked industriously to prevent unity. By keeping the various states in America separated it was much easier to exploit them. To prove the continuity of the foreign money-lenders meddling in the affairs of every nation it is sufficient to record that the Founding Fathers of the United States meeting at Philadelphia in 1787 talked over the importance of bringing in some form of legislation which would protect them against the exploitation of the International Bankers.

The agents of the international bankers organized active lobbying. They used intimidation. But despite all their efforts paragraph 5, of Section 8, of the First article of the new American Constitution read: "CONGRESS SHALL HAVE THE POWER TO COIN MONEY AND REGULATE THE VALUE THEREOF".

The vast majority of the United States' citizens consider the Constitution an honored, and almost sacred, document. All laws passed since then are SUPPOSED to conform with the provisions of the Constitution. The fact that subsequent legislation dealing with finance and currency, have been in violation of the provisions laid down in Article 1, Section 8, paragraph 5, proves how powerful the bankers have been in the political field.

The history of how the international money-lenders obtained economic control of the United States in order to further their long range plans is decidedly interesting.

Using the good old reliable Joint Stock Company principle, the Directors of the Bank of England appointed one of their hirelings named Alexander Hamilton, to represent their interests in the United States. In 1780 this man, a supposed patriot, proposed the establishment of a Federal Bank. It was to be owned by PRIVATE INTERESTS as an alternative to those who insisted the issue and control of money should remain in the hands of the government elected by the people. Alexander Hamilton suggested that his proposed Federal Bank be capitalized for $12,000,000. The Bank of England would provide $10,000,000; the remaining $2,000,000 would be allocated to wealthy people in America. In 1783 Alexander Hamilton, and his business partner Robert Morris, organized the Bank of America. As Financial Superintendent of the Continental Congress, Morris was able to reduce the United States Treasury to a state of indigence by the end of seven years of war. This is another illustration of how the Secret Power use wars to further their plan for the W.R.M. To make absolutely sure the United States' Financial cupboard was bare, Hamilton transferred the last $250,000 from the Treasury Department, and invested it in the Bank's Capital Stock. The directors of the Bank of America were agents of the Bank of England. The Illuminati controlled both. The fact that they sold their souls to Satan in order to gain the world is the truth they wish to conceal.

The Fathers of American Independence realized that if the Directors of the Bank of England obtained monopolistic control of America's money system they would recover any money they had lost by the simple process of mortgage and foreclosure. The net result of this struggle for economic control of the nation was that Congress refused to grant the Bank of America a charter.

Benjamin Franklin died in 1790 and the agents of the International Jewish money-lenders immediately made another bid to obtain control of America's finances. They succeeded in having Alexander Hamilton appointed Secretary of the Treasury. Hamilton had the Government charter the bank his principals had been clamoring for. It was then a simple matter to usurp the rights to issue currency based on public and private debts. The most forceful arguments the bankers' agents had used to defeat their opposition was that money issued by Congress, on the credit of the Nation, would be valueless in dealing abroad; while money obtained on loan from the bankers, at interest, would be welcomed as legal security in all kinds of transactions. Thus the public fell prey to the exploitation of the men who professed to be their friends. Alexander Hamilton, and Morris, were never more than hirelings of the international money-lenders.

The new Bank was capitalized for $35,000,000. Of this amount $28,000,000 was subscribed by European bankers, which the Rothschilds controlled. It is suspected that the international bankers decided that Hamilton knew too much and couldn't be trusted any longer. He was inveigled into a duel with an expert named Aaron Burr, who acted as his executioner.

47

While American citizens were used as *Front* men by the international bankers, policy was determined in Europe. The Rothschild interests gave orders that the American bankers were to extend almost unlimited credit for good security and put plenty of money into circulation. The propaganda media played up on the highest notes of optimism. Prosperity was assured. The Americans were destined to become the greatest people on Earth. Everybody was urged to invest in the future of his great nation.

When everyone of any worth had mortgaged himself to the hilt, orders were given to tighten up credits, recall outstanding loans, and reduce the amount of money in circulation. An artificial depression was created. Citizens could not meet their financial obligations and the Money Barons obtained millions of dollars' worth of property, and securities, at a fraction of their normal value. Admittedly everything was done by due process of law, but Al Capone and his gangsters, were gentlemen in comparison with the international bankers.

Many great Americans have commented on this phase of the history of the United States, but their expressed opinions don't seem to have prevented their successors from falling into the same traps and pit-falls. John Adams (1735-1826) wrote to Thomas Jefferson in 1787. He said: "All the perplexities, confusion and distress arise not from the defects of the Constitution, not from want of honor and virtue so much as, from downright ignorance of the nature of coin, credit and circulation."

Thomas Jefferson said: "I believe that banking institutions are more dangerous to our liberties than standing armies. Already they have raised up a money aristocracy that has set governments at defiance. The issuing power should be taken from the banks and restored to the people to whom it properly belongs".

Andrew Jackson said: "If Congress has a right, under the Constitution to issue paper money, it was given them to use by themselves, not to be delegated to individuals or corporations."

These outspoken comments warned the International Bankers to expect serious opposition when their Charter for the Bank of the United States ran out in 1811. To prepare for this eventuality Amschel Mayer Rothschild, had obtained absolute control of the Bank of England in order to strengthen his control of the World's economy. His son Nathan had been specially trained to undertake this tremendous task as previously mentioned. Nathan proved to have exceptional talent and ability for financial affairs. He trained himself only to think in terms of profits, just as the professional politician thinks only in terms of votes. In 1798, at the early age of twenty-one, he went over from Germany to secure control of the Bank of England. He was entrusted with the modest sum of £20,000. To demonstrate his financial wizardry he speculated, and in a comparatively short time [3 years], he increased his capital to £60,000. By 1811, when the matter of the renewal of the Charter for the Bank of America was due for a hearing, Nathan Rothschild was in control of the International Bankers. He issued his ultimatum. "Either the application for renewal of the charter is granted or the United States will find itself involved in a most disastrous war."

President Andrew Jackson didn't believe the International Bankers would foment a war. He decided to call their bluff. He told them bluntly: "You are a den of thieves — vipers. I intend to rout you out, and by the Eternal God I will rout you out." But President Jackson had underestimated the power of the Rothschilds. Nathan Rothschild issued orders. "Teach these impudent Americans a lesson. Bring them back to Colonial status."

The British Government [of that British Empire which the money power wanted to dissolve], always subservient to the Bank of England, launched the war of 1812. This war was calculated to impoverish the United States to such an extent the legislators would have to plead for peace, and seek financial aid. Nathan Rothschild stipulated that no financial aid would be forthcoming except in return for the renewal of the charter for the Bank of America.

Nathan Rothschild's plan worked to perfection. It mattered not to him, how many men were killed and wounded; how many women were widowed; how many children were made orphans; how many people were rendered destitute. He and his co-conspirators rejoiced in the fact that they had achieved their objective and in so doing they had created more and more dissatisfaction amongst the masses of the people who blamed the blundering policies of their own governments, while the *Secret Power* behind the scenes remained unsuspected by all except a very few people.

In 1816 The United States Congress granted the renewal of the Charter for the Bank of the United States as requested. There are many authorities who state quite frankly that the Members of Congress were bribed, or threatened, into voting for the legislation which put the American people back into financial bondage. [4]

The men who plot and plan to secure economic and political control of the world don't hesitate to prostitute *Love* to achieve their ends, any more than they hesitate to order murder committed to rid them of men who stand in their way. In 1857 the marriage of Lenora, daughter of Lionel Rothschild, to her cousin Alfonso of Paris (they believe in keeping things within the family) brought many international personages to London, England, where the ceremony was performed. Benjamin Disraeli, the noted English Statesman, who was made Prime Minister in 1868 and again in 1874, was invited to be present.

Disraeli is reported to have said during his speech on that memorable occasion — "Under this roof are the heads of the family of Rothschild, a name famous in every capital of Europe, and every division of the globe. If you like we shall divide the United States into two parts, one for you James, and one for you Lionel. Napoleon will do exactly — and all that I advise him to do; and to Bismarck will be suggested such an intoxicating program as to make him our abject slave."

History records that Judah P. Benjamin, a Rothschild relative, was appointed as their professional strategist in America. The American Civil War, which split the Union in two, became an accomplished fact.

Napoleon III was persuaded by the Bankers to extend his French Empire into Mexico. The British Government was persuaded that the Northern States could be made into a colony again. The Civil War in the United States was an economic war brought about by the International Bankers. By applying economic pressure it was a simple matter to aggravate the economic difficulties the Northern States encountered after the slaves had been given their freedom. Abraham Lincoln admitted "No nation can long endure half free and half slaves."[5]

The international bankers loaned unlimited credit to all forces engaged by the South fighting the forces of the North. They loaned Napoleon III, 201,500,000 francs for his Mexican campaign. When the Confederacy needed assistance in 1863 the Powers-that-be offered Napoleon Texas and Louisiana in exchange for French intervention against the Northern States.

The Tzar of Russia heard of these preposterous offers and he informed the Governments of England and France that should they actively intervene, and give military aid to the South, Russia would consider such action as a declaration of war against the Imperial Russian Empire. To strengthen his ultimatum Russian warships were sent to New York and San Francisco and placed at Lincoln's disposal. [6]

When the Northern authorities found themselves in financial difficulties the International Bankers didn't refuse to loan the money. They simply stipulated that the rate of interest to the Northern States would be 28 per cent. After all, they were in business as money-lenders. An important aspect of the American Civil War is that it would in all probability have reached a conclusion in a few months had not the international money-lenders made fresh loans. These loans were usury. They were based on terms and rates of interest which were calculated to give international bankers control of the economy of the whole country. When they considered it time they ended the war.

Lincoln tried to break the financial bonds with which his Northern States were bound. To him Article 1, Section 8, paragraph 5 of the Constitution was sufficient authority. He disregarded the bankers' overtures. He caused $450,000,000 of *honest* money to be printed. He placed the *Credit of the Nation* as security behind this money. The International Bankers retaliated by causing a Bill to be passed through Congress ruling that *Lincoln's Greenbacks* would not be accepted as payment of interest on government bonds nor import duties. The Bankers caused Lincoln's money to become almost valueless by refusing to accept the Greenbacks except at a heavy discount. Having beaten down the value of Greenback dollars to 30 cents they bought them all in. They then turned around and bought government bonds with them demanding dollar for dollar value. In this way they overcame a serious threat and made 70 cents on the dollar.

An article, inspired by the International Bankers, appeared in the London

Times. It concerned Abraham Lincoln's issue of Greenbacks. It said: "If this mischievous financial policy, which has its origin in North America, shall become indurated down to a fixture, then that Government will furnish its own money without cost. It will pay off debts and be without debt. It will have all the money necessary to carry on its commerce. It will become prosperous without precedent in the history of the world. The brains and wealth of all countries will go to North America. THAT COUNTRY MUST BE DESTROYED OR IT WILL DESTROY EVERY MONARCHY ON THE GLOBE."[7]

The Hazard Circular was supplied to all banking interests from overseas. It read "Slavery is likely to be abolished by war power. This, I and my European friends are in favor of, because slavery is but the owning of labor, and carries with it the care of the laborers, while the European plan, led on by England, is that capital shall control labor by controlling wages.

"The great debt, that Capitalists will see is made out of the war, must be used to control the value of money. To accomplish this government bonds must be used as a banking basis. We are now waiting for the Secretary of the Treasury of the United States to make that recommendation. It will not do to allow Greenbacks, as they are called, to circulate as money for any length of time as we cannot control that. But we can control the bonds, and through them, the banking issues."

The Bankers financed the election campaigns of enough Senators, and Congressmen, to assure them that the National Banking Act would become law. The National Banking Act did become law in 1863 despite the vigorous protests of President Lincoln. Thus the International Bankers won another round. The people of the world had been brought one step nearer to economic, political and religious bondage.

On the letter head of Rothschilds' Brothers, Bankers, London, England, under date of June 25th, 1863, the following was written to Messrs. Ikelheimer, Morton and Vandergould, No. 3 Wall Street, New York, U.S.A.

Dear Sirs:

A Mr. John Sherman has written us from a town in Ohio, U.S.A., as to profits that may be made in the National Banking business, under a recent act of your Congress; a copy of this Act accompanies this letter. Apparently this Act has been drawn up on the plan formulated by the British Bankers Association, and by that Association recommended to our American friends, as one that, if enacted into law, would prove highly profitable to the banking fraternity throughout the world.

Mr. Sherman declares that there has never been such an opportunity for capitalists to accumulate money as that presented by this act. It gives the National Bank almost complete control of the National finance. The few who understand the system he says will either be so interested in its profits, or so dependent on its favors, that there will be no opposition from that class, while on the other hand, the great body of the people, mentally incapable of comprehending the tremendous advantages that capital derives from the system, will bear its burden without complaint, and perhaps without even suspecting that the system is inimical to their interests...

Your respectful servants,

ROTHSCHILD BROTHERS

In reply to the above letter Messrs. Ikelheimer, Morton and Vandergould replied:

Dear Sirs:

We beg to acknowledge receipt of your letter of June 25th, in which you refer to a communication received from Honorable John Sherman, of Ohio, with reference to the advantages, and profits, of an American investment under the provisions of the National Banking Act.

Mr. Sherman possesses, in a marked degree, the distinguishing characteristics of a successful financier. His temperament is such that whatever his feelings may be they never cause him to lose sight of the main chance. He is young, shrewd and ambitious. He has fixed his eyes upon the Presidency of the United States and already is a member of Congress (he has financial ambitions too). He rightfully thinks he has everything to gain by being friendly with men, and institutions, having large financial resources, and which at times are not too particular in their methods, either of obtaining government aid, or protecting themselves against unfriendly legislation.

As to the organization of the National Bank here, and the nature and profits of such investments, we beg leave to refer to our printed circulars enclosed herein, viz:

Any number of persons not less than five may organize a National Banking Corporation.

Except in cities having 6,000 inhabitants or less, a National Bank cannot have less than $1,000,000 capital.

They are private corporations organized for private gain, and select their own officers and employees.

They are not subject to control of State Laws, except as Congress may from time to time provide.

They may receive deposits and loan the same for their own benefit. They can buy and sell bonds and discount paper and do general banking business.

To start a National Bank on the scale of $1,000,000 will require purchase of that amount (par value) of U.S. Government Bonds. U.S. Bonds can now be purchased at 50 per cent discount, so that a bank of $1,000,000 capital can be started at this time for only $500,000. These bonds must be deposited with the United States Treasury at Washington as security for the National Bank currency that will be furnished by the government to the bank.

The United States Government will pay 6 per cent interest on all bonds in gold, the interest being paid semi-annually. It will be seen that at the present price of bonds the interest paid by the government itself is 12 per cent in gold on all money invested.

The United States Government on having the bonds aforesaid deposited with the Treasurer, on the strength of such security will furnish National currency to the bank depositing the bonds, at an annual interest of only one per cent per annum.

The currency is printed by the U.S. Government in a form so like Greenbacks that the people do not detect the difference. Although the currency is but a promise of the bank to pay.

The demand for money is so great that this money can be readily loaned to the people across the counter of the Bank at a discount at the rate of 10 per cent at thirty or sixty days' time, making it about 12 per cent interest on the currency.

The interest on the bonds, plus the interest on the currency which the bond secures, plus the incidentals of the business, ought to make the gross earnings of the bank amount to from 28 per cent to 33 and one-third per cent.

National Banks are privileged to increase and contract their currency at will, and of course, can grant or withhold loans, as they may see fit. As the banks have a National organization and can easily act together in withholding loans or extending them, it follows that they can by united action in refusing to make loans cause stringency in the money market, and in a single week or even a single day cause a decline in all products of the country.

National Banks pay no taxes on their bonds, nor on their capital, nor on their deposits.

Requesting that you will regard this as strictly confidential.

Most respectfully yours,

IKELHEIMIER, MORTON and VANDERGOULD

Following the exchange of the above letters the American Bankers put into practice once again the manipulations mentioned. They reaped another rich harvest by foreclosures on property and securities left with them as security for loans, which their clients could not repay because the Bankers, acting in unity, withdrew currency, and restricted credits, to a degree that made it impossible for the vast majority of borrowers to meet their financial obligations.

Abraham Lincoln felt that after this sad, and costly, experience the

American people might be ready to listen to sense so, once again, he launched a public attack upon the bankers.

In an address he said: "I see in the near future a crisis approaching that unnerves me, and causes me to tremble for the safety of my Country; corporations have been enthroned, an era of corruption in high places will follow, and the money power of the country will endeavor to prolong its reign by working upon the prejudices of the people, until the wealth is aggregated in a few hands and the Republic is destroyed."

Shortly after making this momentous speech Abraham Lincoln was re-elected President but before he could have legislation enacted which would have curbed the avaricious practices of the bankers he was assassinated by John Wilkes Booth while attending a theatrical performance, on the night of April 14th, 1865. Very few Americans know why President Lincoln was assassinated. The true answer was found when investigators located a coded message amongst Booth's effects. The key to that coded message was in possession of Judah P. Benjamin who was Rothschild's agent in America. While the coded message had no direct bearing on the murder, it definitely established the contact Booth had with the International Bankers. Once again they remained hidden behind the scenes while the Jew, Booth, was blamed for the death of a great man. Had Abraham Lincoln lived he would most certainly have clipped the wings, and trimmed the sails, of the international moneylenders.

Before Lincoln was murdered, Salmon P. Chase, who was Secretary of the U.S. Treasury 1861-1864, stated publicly: "My agency in promoting the passage of the National Banking Act was the greatest financial mistake of my life. It has built up a monopoly which affects every interest in the country. It should be repealed, but before that can be accomplished the people will be arrayed on one side and the banks on the other, in a contest such as we have never seen before in this country."[8]

In 1866 there was $1,906,687,770 in currency in circulation in the United States. This represented $50.46 per capita. At the end of 1876 there was only about $605,250,000 in circulation representing a per capita amount of $14.60. The currency of the nation had been reduced by bank withdrawals to the extent of over $1,300,000,000. The importance of these figures will be better understood by the average man when he learns that the net result of the bankers' policy was a total of 56,446 business failures representing a loss of $2,245,105,000 in cash investments. The larger proportion of the losses was incurred by mortgage foreclosures. In other words, by withdrawing currency and restricting credits the bankers had enriched themselves by well over $2,000,000,000 in a little over ten years. There is plenty of evidence to prove that the American Bankers and the European Bankers, have been affiliated ever since, and that the subsequent depressions were created by similar financial manipulations, as will be explained in other chapters.

NOTES:

1 Direct quotations from Senate Document No. 23 supports the above statements.

2 The Earl of Chatham and his son William Pitt (1769-1806) both denounced the policy of the international Money-Barons in regard to the Colonies prior to 1783. Young William Pitt was chosen by King George III to be Prime Minister because he convinced the King the money-lenders were involving European countries in wars to serve their own selfish purposes.

3 Just stop and think for a moment how far they have advanced that part of their plans since then. Jefferson and John Adams (Roosevelt's kinsman) both became ardent Illuminists. This explains Roosevelt's policy.

4 The fact that Franklin, Adams, and Jefferson all became members of the Illuminati and the fact that the Great Seal of America is actually the insignia of the Illuminati proves the power of the Synagogue of Satan.

5 It is just as impossible for half a World which employs paid labor and enjoys a high Standard of living to compete forever with the other half which employs slave labor under a Dictatorship.

6 This act of interference caused the International Bankers to decide to overthrow the Russian Government.

7 This is a typical example of the Illutninati's double-talk. Monarchy really meant money lender.

8 For more detailed information on this angle of the world Revolutionary Movement read *Lightning Over The Treasury Building* by John R. Elsom and *The Federal Reserve Conspiracy* by Eustace Mullins.

 Chapter Six

Monetary Manipulation

When the Rothschilds obtained control of the Bank of England, following Nathan's spectacular financial "killing" in 1815, he and his associates insisted that Gold be made the only base for the issuance of paper money. In 1870 the European Bankers experienced a little annoyance in their control system due to the fact that in America a considerable amount of silver coin was used. The European Bankers decided that silver must be demonetized in the United States. At that time England had much gold and very little silver: America had much silver and very little gold. [1] The bankers on both sides of the Atlantic knew that while this difference continued they could not obtain absolute control of the economy of the nation and absolute control is essential for the success of big scale manipulation.

The European International Bankers sent Ernest Seyd over to America and placed at his disposal in American banks $500,000 with which to bribe key members of the American legislature. In 1873, at the instigation of the bankers, their agents introduced a "Bill", innocently named "A Bill to reform Coinage and Mint Laws". It was cleverly drafted. Many pages of writing concealed the real purpose behind the Bill. The Bill was sponsored by none other than Senator John Sherman, whose letter to the House of Rothschild has already been referred to. Sherman was supported by Congressman Samuel Hooper. After Senator Sherman gave a very plausible, but misleading, report regarding the purpose of the Bill, it was passed without a dissenting vote. Three years passed before the full import of the Bill began to be realized. It was a camouflaged Bill to demonetize silver. President Grant signed the Bill without reading the contents after he had been assured it was just a routine matter necessary to make some desirable reforms in the coinage and monetary laws. According to the Congressional Record none but the members of the Committee which introduced the Bill understood its meaning.

The International Bankers considered the passage of the Bill so essential to their plans, to obtain absolute control of the monetary system of the United States, that Ernest Seyd was instructed to represent himself as an expert on coining of money. After organizing the formation of a committee favorable to his master's objectives, he sat in with the committee, in a professional advisory, capacity, and helped draft the Bill in accordance with the Rothschilds' instructions.

Congressman Samuel Hooper introduced the Bill in the House on April 9th, 1872. He is recorded as saying: "Mr. Ernest Seyd, of London, a distinguished writer, has given great attention to the subject of mints and coinage. After examining the first draft of the Bill, he furnished many valuable suggestions which have been incorporated in the Bill." Mr. John R. Elsom in his book *Lightning over the Treasury* Building on page 49 declares: *According to his*

(Seyd's) own statement, made to his friend Mr. Frederick A. Lukenback, of Denver, Colorado, who has, under oath, given us the story, he (Seyd) said "I saw the Committee of the House and Senate and paid the money, and stayed in America until I knew the measure was safe".

In 1878 a further withdrawal of currency, and restricting of credits, caused 10,478 business and banking failures in the United States. In 1879 the issuance of more coin at the insistence of Congress halted the artificially created recession and reduced business failures to 6,658. But in 1882 the "Secret Power" behind International affairs issued orders that there was to be no more pussy-footing. They reminded their banking associates in the States that sentiment has no place in business. These admonishments produced results as spectacular as they were drastic. Between 1882 and 1887 the per capita money in circulation in the United States was reduced to $6.67. This action increased the total business failures from 1878 to 1892, to 148,703, while proportionate foreclosures were made on farms and private dwellings. Only the bankers and their agents, who made the loans and took foreclosure proceedings, benefited.

It would appear that the International bankers were deliberately creating conditions of poverty, and despair, in the United States in order to produce conditions which would enable their instrument the Word Revolutionary Party to recruit revolutionary forces. This accusation is supported by a letter issued to all American Bankers, by the American Bankers Association. It has been proved that this association was intimately affiliated with Rothschild's European Monopoly, if not actually controlled by the House of Rothschild, at that time. The letter reads:

March 11, 1893

Dear Sir:

The interests of the National Banks require immediate financial legislation by Congress. Silver certificates, and Treasury notes, must be retired, and national bank notes, upon a gold basis, made the only money. This will require the authorization of new bonds in the amount of $500,000,000 to $1,000,000,000 as the basis of circulation. You will at once retire one-third of your circulation and will call one-half of your loans. Be careful to create money stringency among your patrons, especially among influential business men. The life of the National Banks, as fixed and safe investments, depends upon immediate action as there is an increasing sentiment in favor of government legal tender and silver coinage.

This command was obeyed immediately and the panic of 1893 was created. William Jennings Bryan tried to counteract the bankers' conspiracy, but once again the public believed the false accusations circulated in the Press by the bankers' propagandists. The man in the street blamed the government. The average citizen never even suspected the part the bankers had played in creating chaos in order to feather their own nests. William Jennings Bryan was unable to do anything constructive. His voice, like the voices of many other honest and loyal citizens, was a voice crying in the wilderness.

In 1899 J.P. Morgan, and Anthony Drexel, went to England to attend the International Bankers' Convention. When they returned, J.P. Morgan had been appointed head representative for the Rothschild's interests in the United States. He was probably chosen as Top-man because of the ingenuity he had shown when he made a fortune selling his government Union Army rifles which had already been condemned. [2]

As the result of the London Conference J.P. Morgan & Co. of New York, Drexel & Co. of Philadelphia, Grenfell & Co. of London, Morgan Harjes & Co. of Paris, M.M. Warburgs of Germany & Amsterdam and the House of Rothschild were all affiliated.

The Morgan-Drexel combination organized the Northern Securities Corporation in 1901 for the purpose of putting the Heinze-Morse group out of business. The Heinze-Morse controlled considerable banking, shipping, steel and other industries. They had to be put out of business so the Morgan-Drexel combination could control the forthcoming Federal election.

The Morgan-Drexel combination succeeded in putting in Theodore Roosevelt in 1901. This delayed the prosecution which had been started against them by the Justice Department because of the alleged illegal methods used to rid themselves of competition. Morgan-Drexel then affiliated with Kuhn-Loeb & Co. To test their combined strength it was decided to stage another financial "killing". They created "The Wall Street Panic of 1907". The public reaction to such methods of legalized gangsterism was sufficient to make the Government take action, but the evidence which follows clearly proves how the public was betrayed.

The Government appointed a *National Monetary Commission*. Senator Nelson Aldrich was appointed head of the commission. He was charged with the duty of making a thorough study of financial practices, and then formulating banking and currency reforms by submitting the necessary legislation to Congress. Aldrich, it was discovered afterwards, was financially interested with the powerful Rubber and Tobacco Trusts. He was just about the last man in the Senate who should have been entrusted with such a task. Immediately after his appointment Aldrich picked a small group of trusted lieutenants and they all departed for Europe. While in Europe they were given every facility to study the way the international bankers controlled the economy of European countries. After Aldrich had spent two years, and over $300,000 of the American tax-payers' money in Europe, lie returned to the U.S.A. All the public received for their money was to be told by Aldrich that he hadn't been able to arrive at any definite plan which would prevent recurring financial panics which had upset business, created unemployment, and destroyed many small fortunes in the U.S.A. since the Civil War. Aldrich was so close to the Rockefellers that J.D. Jr married his daughter Abby.

Prior to the tour of Europe Aldrich had been advised to consult Paul

Warburg. This Paul Moritz Warburg was a unique character. He had arrived in the U.S.A. as a German immigrant about 1902. It turned out afterwards that he was a member of the European Financial House of M.M. Warburg & Co. of Hamburg and Amsterdam. This company was as we have seen, with the House of Rothschild. Paul Warburg had studied International finance in Germany, France, Great Britain, Holland and other countries before entering America as an immigrant. The U.S. A. proved to be his land of golden opportunity because, in no time at all, he purchased a partnership in Kuhn-Loeb & Co. of New York. He was voted a salary of $500,000 a year. One of his new partners was Jacob Schiff who had previously purchased into the firm with Rothschild gold. This Jacob Schiff is the man evidence will prove financed the Terrorist Movement in Russia from 1883, onwards to 1917.

Schiff hadn't done too badly for himself, and his backers. He had managed to achieve undisputed control over the transportation, the communication systems, and the supply lines in the United States. As has been proved, control of these is absolutely essential for successful revolutionary effort in any country. [3]

On the night of November 22nd, 1910 a private railway coach was waiting at the Hoboken, New Jersey, Railway Station. Senator Aldrich arrived with A. Piatt Andrews, a professional economist and treasury official, who had been wined and dined in Europe. Shelton, Aldrich's private secretary, also turned up. He was followed by Frank Vanderlip, president of the National City Bank of New York; this Bank represented the Rockefeller Oil Interests and the Kuhn-Loeb railway interests. The directors of the National City Bank had been publicly charged with helping to foment a war between the U.S.A. and Spain in 1898. Regardless of the truth or otherwise, of the charges, the fact remains that the National City Bank owned and controlled Cuba's sugar industry when the war ended. Others who joined Aldrich were H.P. Davison, senior partner of J.P. Morgan & Co., Charles D. Norton, president of Morgan's First National Bank of New York. These last three had been accused in the American legislature of controlling the entire money and credit of the U.S.A. Last to arrive were Paul Warburg and Benjamin Strong. Warburg was so wealthy and powerful by this time that he is said to have inspired the famous comic strip ("Orphan Annie") in which Warbucks is featured as the most wealthy and influential man in the world; a man who can, when he so wishes, use superhuman or supernatural powers to protect himself and his interests. Benjamin Strong came into prominence during the preliminary manipulations of high finance which led to the Wall Street Panic of 1907. As one of J.P. Morgan's lieutenants he had earned a reputation for carrying out orders without question and with ruthless efficiency.

Aldrich's private coach was attached to the train. Newspaper reporters learned of this gathering of the men who controlled America's oil, finances, communications, transportations and heavy industries. They began to swarm down upon the private car like locusts ... But they couldn't get anyone to speak. Mr. Vanderlip finally brushed off the reporters' demands for information with the explanation "We are going away for a quiet week-end".

It took years to discover what happened that quiet week-end. A secret meeting was held on Jekyll Island, Georgia. This hide-away was owned by J.P. Morgan, and a small group of his financial affiliates. The business discussed at the meeting referred to was "Ways and means to ensure that proposed legislation to curb financial racketeering and monetary manipulation in the U.S.A. be sabotaged and legislation favorable to those attending the secret meeting be substituted." To achieve these two important objectives was no easy task. Mr. Paul Warburg was asked to suggest solutions. His advice was accepted.

Subsequent meetings were held by the same group to iron out details in New York. The conspirators named their group the *First Name Club* because, when meeting together, they always addressed each other by their first names to guard against strangers becoming interested should they hear the surnames of national and international financiers being spoken. To make a long story short, Aldrich, Warburg and Company, drew up the monetary legislation which Aldrich ultimately presented as the work of his special committee. He had it passed by Congress in 1913 under the title "The Federal Reserve Act of 1913". The vast majority of American citizens honestly believed that this act protected their interests, and placed the Federal Government in control of the nation's economy.

Nothing is further from the truth. The Federal Reserve System placed the affiliated bankers in America and Europe in position to bring about and control World War One. This statement will be proved. World War One was fought to enable the International Conspirators to bring about the Russian Revolution in 1917.

These facts illustrate how history does repeat itself and why. By means of similar plots, and intrigue, the International Bankers had brought about the English Revolution in 1640-1649; and the Great French Revolution of 1789. [4]

In 1914 the Federal Reserve System consisted of twelve banks which had bought $134,000,000 worth of Federal Reserve Stock. According to Congressional Record of May 29th, 1939; 8896, they had made a profit of $23,141,456,197. In 1940 the assets of the Federal Reserve were shown as five billion dollars. In 1946 they were declared to be forty five billion dollars. The bankers made forty billion dollars profit out of their transactions in World War Two.

The majority of citizens in the United States believe that the Federal Reserve System benefits the people of the Nation as a whole. They think the Federal Reserve System protects the depositors' money by making bank failures an impossibility. They think that profits made by the Federal Reserve Banks benefit the National Treasury. They are wrong on all suppositions.

What the majority of the people think is exactly what the Federal Reserve System was originally intended to accomplish, but the legislation drawn up on

Jekyll Island, Georgia in 1910, and passed by the American Congress in 1913, did not benefit the people or the government of the U.S.A. It benefited only the American Bankers, who were interlocked with the International Bankers of Europe.

The President of the United States nominates four of the men who are charged with the responsibility of operating the Federal Reserve System. They are paid $15,000 a year for their services. Congressional records will prove that the member banks shared illegally the profits made right from its inception. It wasn't until 1922 that the original Act was amended so the bankers could take the profits legally.

Regarding the delusion that the Federal Reserve System protects people who deposit their money for safe-keeping in American Banks against possible bank failures, statistics show that since the Federal Reserve System came into operation in 1913 over 14,000 banks have failed. Millions upon millions of the depositors' hard earned money were lost to the rightful owners. As money or wealth, generally speaking, is indestructible somebody got what the others lost. That is what we term "Smart Business" today.

NOTES:

1 It was to aggravate this situation that agents of the International Conspirators in America organized the gangs of stage-coach and train-robbers to intercept shipments of gold being sent from various mines to the U.S. Treasury during this period. This connection between international Bankers and the Underworld will be proved to exist even today.

2 Gustavus Myers deals with J.P. Morgan's and his father's connections with the House of Rothschild in much greater detail and all Americans who wish to stop history repeating itself should read how they were sold down the river in the middle of last century. It is explained in another Chapter how the International Bankers met in one section of London and planned policy while the revolutionary leaders met in another and worked out the details of intrigue which would put the wars and revolutions planned by the master-minds into effect.

3 Investigations in several countries already subjugated prove that the Financial Tycoons who owned and controlled the transportation systems on land and sea, and affiliated industries deliberately brought about conditions which led to general strikes immediately prior to the date set for a revolutionary effort to take place. It must be obvious that these international Tycoons cannot form dictatorships as they did in Russia until existing governments and institutions have been overthrown. This book proves how this purpose was achieved in Russia.

4 For full details of the Federal Reserve. Conspiracy read the book of that title written by Eustace Mullins and published by Common Sense, Union, New Jersey. 1954.

♟ Chapter Seven
Events Preceding the Russian Revolution

The invasion of Russia in 1812 by Napoleon shook the Russian people to the core. Tzar Alexander I set about the task of organizing a recovery program. In the hope that he could bring about a united effort throughout the Russian Empire, he relaxed many of the restrictions which had been imposed on the Jews when they were confined to the Pale of Settlement in 1772. Special concessions were made to the artisans and professional classes. A determined effort was made to establish Jews in agriculture. Under Alexander I they were given every encouragement to assimilate themselves into the Russian way of life.

Nicholas I succeeded Alexander I in 1825. He was less inclined to favor the Jews, because he viewed their rapid inroads into the Russian economy with alarm. His government viewed with great displeasure the determination of the Jews to maintain their separate culture, language, mode of dress, etc.

In order to try to assimilate the Jews into the Russian society Nicholas I, in 1804, made it compulsory for all Jewish children to attend Public School. Nicholas thought that if the young Jews could be convinced that they would be welcomed into Russian society it would go a long way to eliminate misunderstandings. His avowed purpose was to offset the one-sided story of religious persecution which was drilled into their minds from early infancy.

The net results of the Russian experiment didn't turn out as expected. Education for non-Jewish children was not compulsory. The Jews became the best educated segment in Russia. [1]

Alexander II followed Nicholas I to the throne of Russia in 1855. Benjamin Disraeli referred to Alexander II as "The most benevolent prince that ever ruled over Russia". Alexander devoted his life to improving the conditions of the peasants, poorer classes, and the Jews. In 1861 he emancipated 23,000,000 serfs. This unfortunate class had been FORCED to work on the land. They were LITERALLY slaves. They could be transferred from one owner to another in all sales, or leases, of landed estates.

Many Jews, who had taken advantage of the compulsory education, entered universities. They found themselves severely handicapped after graduation when seeking employment. To correct this injustice Alexander II ruled that all Jewish graduates be allowed to settle and hold government positions in Greater Russia. In 1879 Jewish apothecaries, nurses, mid-wives, dentists, distillers and skilled craftsmen were permitted to work and reside, anywhere in Russia.

But the Jewish revolutionary leaders were determined to continue their movement for Popular World Revolution. Their terrorist groups committed one outrage after another. They worked to enlist the support of disgruntled

Russian intellectuals and to plant the general idea of violent revolution in the minds of the industrial working population. In 1866 they made their first attempt on the life of Alexander II. They tried to murder him a second time in 1879. In some miraculous manner both attempts failed. It was then decided a very special effort had to be made to remove Alexander. His benevolent rule was completely upsetting their claim "That much needed reforms can only be brought about speedily by revolutionary action". The conspirators hatched their next plot against the life of Alexander II in the home of the Jewess Hesia Helfman. The Tzar was murdered in 1881.

While the Revolutionary Forces within Russia were trying to embarrass the government in every way possible, and committing all kinds of outrages, including assassination, the "Secret Powers" behind the W.R.M. from their headquarters in England, Switzerland and the United States were trying once again to involve Britain in war with Russia. In such a war neither Empire could make any appreciable gains. The final outcome of such a war would be to weaken both Empires materially and leave them easier prey for revolutionary action afterwards.

In the *Nineteenth Century*, October issue, 1881, Goldwyn Smith, professor of modern history at Oxford University wrote: "When I was last in England we were on the brink of war with Russia, which would have involved the whole Empire — the Jewish interests throughout Europe, with the Jewish Press of Vienna as its chief organ, was doing its utmost to push us in." [2]

The assassination of the Russians' "Little Father" in 1881 caused widespread resentment which was expressed by a spontaneous outbreak of violence against the Jewish population in many parts of Russia. The Russian Government passed "The May Laws". These were harsh laws passed because the Russian officials who sponsored them argued "That if the Jews could not be satisfied and reconciled by the benevolent policy of Alexander II then it was obvious that they would be satisfied with nothing less than the absolute domination of Russia." Once again the whole Jewish Race was being punished for the sins of a few self-appointed revolutionary leaders.

On May 23rd, 1882 a Jewish delegation, headed by Baron Ginzberg, [3] called on the new Tzar Alexander III and officially protested the May Laws. The Tzar promised a thorough investigation into the whole matter concerning the conflict between the Jewish and non-Jewish factions of the Empire's population. On September 3rd he issued this statement: "For some time the government has given its attention to the Jews, and their problems and their relations to the rest of the inhabitants of the Empire with a view to ascertaining the sad conditions of the Christian population brought about by the conduct of the Jews in business matters. During the last twenty years the Jews have not only possessed themselves of every trade and business in all its branches but also of a great part of the land by buying or farming it. With few exceptions they have, as a body, devoted their attention not to enriching, or benefiting the country, but to defrauding the Russian people by their wiles. Particularly have the poor inhabitants suffered, and this conduct has called forth protests from the people as manifested in acts of violence against the Jews. The government, while on one hand doing its best to put dawn these disturbances; and to deliver the Jews from oppression and slaughter; on the other hand thought it a matter of urgency, and justice, to adopt the stringent measures to put an end to oppression as practiced by the Jews on the other inhabitants, and to rid the country of their malpractices, which were, as is well known, the original cause of the anti-Jewish agitations."

The May Laws had been passed by the Government not only as an act of resentment because of the assassination of Tzar Alexander II, but also because Russian economists had been urgently warning the Government that the national economy was in danger of being ruined if measures were not taken to curb the illegal activities of the Jews. The economists pointed out that while the Jews only represented 4.2 per cent of the whole population they had been able to entrench themselves so well in the Russian economy that the nation was faced with economic disaster. How correct the economists proved to be is shown by the action taken after Baron Ginzberg's deputation failed to have the May Laws rescinded. The International Bankers imposed economic sanctions against the Russian Empire. They almost reduced the nation to bankruptcy. They exercised an embargo on Russian trade and commerce. In 1904, after they involved the Russian Empire in a disastrous war with Japan, the English Banking House of Rothschild repudiated its promise of financial aid and tried to render the Russian Empire bankrupt, while Kuhn-Loeb & Co. New York extended to Japan all the credit asked for.

Encyclopedia Britannica, page 76, Vol. 2 — 1947 says this of the May Laws: "The Russian May Laws were the most conspicuous legislative monument achieved by modern anti-semitism... Their immediate results were a ruinous commercial depression which was felt all over the empire and which profoundly affected the national credit. The Russian Minister was at his wits end for money. Negotiations for a large loan were entered into with the House of Rothschild and a preliminary contract was signed when the Finance Minister was informed that unless the persecutions of the Jews were stopped, the great banking house would be compelled to withdraw from the contract... In this way anti-semitism, which had already so profoundly influenced the domestic policies of Europe, set its mark on the International relations of the Powers, for it was the urgent need of the Russian Treasury, quite as much as the termination of Prince Bismarck's secret treaty of mutual neutrality, which brought about the Franco-Russian Alliance."

Many orthodox Jews were worried because of the ruthless terrorism being practiced by their compatriots. They knew that a similar policy was being carried out in France, Germany, Spain and Italy. The less radical Jews worried because they feared a continuation of such terrorism would result in such a wave of anti-semitism that it could quite possibly end with the extermination of the Jewish race. Their worst fears were confirmed by a German Jew, Theodore Herzl, who informed them of Karl Ritter's anti-semitic policy and warned them that it was rapidly being spread throughout Germany. He suggested the organization of a Jewish Back to Israel Movement on the part of orthodox Jews. This was the beginning of the Zionist movement. [4]

After Tzar Alexander III had issued his verdict blaming AVARICIOUS Jews as the cause of the Empire's unrest, and economic ruin, the leaders of the revolutionaries organized "The Social Revolutionary Party". An utterly ruthless man named Gershuni was appointed organizer of the Terrorist Groups. A tailor named Yevno Azev was appointed to organize the "Fighting Sections". The leaders of the Social Revolutionary Party also emphasized the importance of enlisting Gentiles in the movement. Gentiles, who passed the tests to which they were submitted, became full members. It was this decision that brought Alexander Ulyanov into the party. Before the revolutionary leaders would admit him into full membership he was ordered to take part in the plot to assassinate Tzar Alexander III. The attempt on the Tzar's life failed. Alexander Ulyanov was arrested. He was tried, and condemned to death. His execution caused his younger brother, Vlasimir, to dedicate himself to the revolutionary cause. Vlasimir rose in power until he became leader of the Bolshevik Party. He assumed the name of Lenin. He ultimately became the first Dictator of the U.S.S.Rs.

Between 1900 and 1906, in addition to causing serious labor trouble, and creating terrible misunderstanding between all levels of Russian society, the Revolutionary Party rubbed the sore of religious bigotry until it developed into a festering boil. This boil was brought to a head by the hot applications of wholesale murders and assassinations. The boil burst in the form of the revolution of 1905.

The officials assassinated by the Social Revolutionaries Terrorist Section were Bogolepov, Minister of Education in 1901. This assassination was perpetrated to register Jewish resentment against the educational clause in the previously referred to May Laws. This clause limited the number of Jews attending state-supported schools, and universities, to a number in ratio to the Jewish population as compared to the whole Russian population. This measure was passed because the State financed schools had become flooded with Jewish students. A group of young Jews who had "suffered" when boys, because of the educational clause in the May Laws of 1882, were given the task of murdering the Minister of Education. They had to prove their courage and ability to qualify them for duty with the Terrorist section of the Social Revolutionary Party.

Next year (1902) Sipyagin, Minister of the Interior, was assassinated to emphasize Jewish resentment against the May Law which had reversed the policy of Alexander II, and prohibited Jews from living outside the Pale of Settlement. Jews who had been evicted from their homes in Greater Russia as children under the May Law were chosen to carry out this "Execution". They made no mistake.

In 1903 Bogdanovich, Governor of Ufa was assassinated; in 1904 Vischelev von Plehve, the Russian Premier was killed; in 1905 the first full scale Russian

Revolution broke out. The Grand Duke Sergius, uncle of the Tzar, was assassinated on February 17th. In December, 1905, General Dubrassov suppressed the revolutionaries, but in 1906 he was assassinated by the Terrorist Section.

After the Tzar had blamed the Jews for the unsatisfactory state of affairs in Russia, Baron Ginzberg was instructed to work to bring about the destruction of the Russian Empire. It was agreed that to start the Russo-Japanese War the Rothschild interests in Europe would pretend to be friendly with Russia. They would finance the war on Russia's behalf while secretly the Rothschild's partners, Kuhn-Loeb & Co. of New York, would finance the Japanese government. The defeat of Russia was to be made certain by the Rothschilds withdrawing financial aid when it was most needed. Chaos and confusion was to be created within the Russian armed forces in the far East by sabotaging the lines of transport and communication crossing Siberia. This caused both the Russian Army and Navy to run short of supplies and reinforcements. [5]

Then again, a Russian Naval Officer bound from the Baltic to Port Arthur in the Far East, ordered his ships to fire on a British Trawler Fleet fishing on the Dogger Bank in the North Sea. No logical reason was ever forthcoming to explain this wanton act of cruelty and mass murder against a supposedly friendly power. Public reaction in England was such that war was narrowly averted. Because of this incident many British Naval Officers and British Merchant Officers volunteered their services to Japan.

The Japanese government was financed by international loans raised by Jacob Schiff (New York). Schiff was senior partner in Kuhn-Loeb & Co. He co-operated with Sir Ernest Cassels (England) and the Warburgs (Hamburg). Jacob Schiff justified his action of financing the Japanese in the war against Russia in a letter he wrote to Count Witte, the Tzar's emissary who attended the Peace negotiations held at Portsmouth, U.S.A. in 1905.

"Can it be expected that the influence of the American Jew upon public opinion will be exerted to the advantage of the country which systematically degraded his brethren-in-race?... If the Government, now being formed, should not succeed in assuring safety, and equal opportunity throughout the Empire, to the Jewish population, then indeed the time will have come for the Jews in Russia to quit their inhospitable fatherland. While the problem with which the civilized world will then be faced will be enormous, it will be solved, and you, who are not only a far- seeing statesman, but also a great economist, know best that the fate of Russia, and its doom, will then be sealed."

The hypocrisy of Jacob Schiff can be better appreciated when it is explained that from 1897 he had financed the Terrorists in Russia. In 1904 he helped finance the revolution which broke out in Russia in 1905. He also helped to organize on an international basis the financing of the Russian Revolution which broke out early in 1917, and gave him and his associates their first opportunity to put their Totalitarian Theories into effect. [6]

The Russo-Japanese War was fomented by the international bankers in order to create the conditions necessary for the success of a revolutionary effort to overthrow the power of the Tzars. The plans of the International Bankers were upset when the Jewish-led Mensheviks started a revolution independently in Russia in 1905. When the International Bankers withheld financial support the revolution failed right at the moment it appeared to have reached the pinnacle of success.

Because the Jewish-dominated Mensheviks acted on their own initiative the International Bankers decided that Lenin would conduct their revolutionary program in Russia from that date onwards.

Lenin was born in the city of Simbirsk, located on the banks of the river Volga. He was the son of a government official who had the title of "Actual State Counselor". This title was not inherited, but had been awarded to his father for outstanding service as a school supervisor. Lenin received a university education and was admitted to the practice of Law but he never set himself up in business. Jewish students had persuaded him that it was time to overthrow the power of the privileged classes and time that the masses ruled their own countries. It was while Lenin was toying with the idea that "Necessary reforms could only be brought about speedily by revolutionary action" that his brother was arrested by the police and executed.

Lenin was quickly recognized as an intellectual. He was associating with the leaders of the Revolutionary Party when in his early twenties. It has been previously stated that the wealthy direct influential international money-lenders had helped finance and direct the revolutionary activities within the Pale of Settlement. Lenin wanted to find out all he could about the people who directed the various national revolutionary groups which were united in the common cause of Popular Revolution. In 1895, at the age of twenty-five, he went to Switzerland and joined Plekhanov who had fled there from Russia to escape the fate of Lenin's older brother Alexander.

While in Switzerland, Lenin and Plekhanov, who were Gentiles, joined forces with Vera Zasulich, Leo Deutch, P. Axelrod, and Julius Tsederbaum, who were all Jews. They formed a Marxist Movement on a world wide scale which they named the "Group for the Emancipation of Labor". Tsederbaum was a young man like Lenin. He had earned a reputation in "The Pale of Settlement" as a ruthless terrorist, and accomplished agitator. He changed his name to Martov. He became leader of the Mensheviks. Lenin ruled the Bolsheviks in Russia.

The abortive revolutionary attempt by the Mensheviks in 1905 convinced Lenin that the only way to have a successful revolution was to organize an International Planning Committee which would first plan and then direct any agreed upon revolutionary effort. Lenin brought into being the Comintern, as the Central International Revolutionary Planning Committee. The International

Bankers picked him as their top-level agent in Russia. Lenin had made a serious study of the Great French Revolution. When he learned that the *Secret Power* which had brought about the French Revolution was still in active operation he threw in his lot with them. His plan was to let the members of the Comintern think they were the Brains, but to influence their thinking, so that they furthered the Long Range Plans of the International Bankers. If the day came when the revolutionary leaders couldn't be controlled then they could always be liquidated. Evidence will be given to show how this actually happened.

Having decided his own policy, Lenin returned to Russia with Martov to organize his Money Raising Campaign which consisted of blackmail, bank robbery, extortion, and other kinds of illegal practices. Lenin argued that it was only logical to take money from the people whose government they plotted to overthrow. He made it a principle of his party that all young people who aspired to membership should, like his older brother Alexander, be tested for physical courage and mental alertness. Lenin insisted that part of every young revolutionary's training should include robbing a bank, blowing up a police station, and liquidating a traitor or spy.

Lenin also insisted that the revolutionary leaders, in all other countries, should organize an underground system. In discussing, this matter, and writing about it, Lenin declared "everything legal and illegal which furthers the revolutionary movement is justified". He warned, however, that "the legal party should always be in control of the illegal". This practice is in force today, particularly in Canada and the United States. Communists who openly acknowledge their membership in the Labor Progressive Party take great care not to get involved in a criminal way with the illegal activities of the Communist party's underground organization. But the "Apparatus" secretly directs operations and benefits financially, as a result.

It is a fact that few of the early leaders of Communism were members of the proletariat. Most of them were well educated intellectuals. In 1895 they caused a series of strikes. Some of these were successfully turned into riots. Thus they brought about one of the fundamental principles of revolutionary technique "developing a minor disturbance until it became a riot, and brought the citizens into actual physical conflict with the police."

Lenin, Martov, and a number of other revolutionaries, were arrested and sentenced to prison. Lenin finished his prison term in 1897.

It is not generally known that in those days in Russia political offenders exiled to Siberia were not imprisoned if they had not been convicted of any other CRIMINAL offence. Therefore, Lenin took his beautiful young Jewish wife, and her Yiddish speaking mother, into exile with him. During his term of exile Lenin drew an allowance of seven rubles and forty copecks a month from the Russian Government. This was just about enough to pay for room and board. Lenin worked as a bookkeeper to earn extra money. It was while in exile that Lenin, Martov, and an accomplice named Potresov, decided upon their release to publish a newspaper for the purpose of combining the brains and energies of the entire revolutionary movement which at that time was broken up into many factions.

In February 1900 Lenin finished his exile. He was granted permission to return to Switzerland for a visit. He joined the other revolutionary leaders and the agents of the *Secret Powers*. They approved his idea; and Iskra (The Spark) was published. The editorial board consisted of the older revolutionary leaders — Plekhanov, Zasulich and Axelrod — with Lenin, Potresov and Martov representing the younger members. Lenin's wife was secretary of the board. Trotsky joined the editorial staff two years later. For a while the paper was actually printed in Munich, Germany. The editorial board met in London. [7] In 1903 it was moved back to Geneva. The copies were smuggled into Russia, and other countries, by way of the underground system organized by the Grand Orient Masons. Because the paper was named "Iskra", the revolutionaries who subscribed to the Party Line, as defined by the editorial board, became known as Iskrists.

The paper called for a Unification Congress to take place in Brussels in 1903 for the purpose of uniting various Marxist groups. The Russian Social Democrats, Rosa Luxemberg's Polish Social Democrats, the group for the Emancipation of Labor, and the Maximalist group, were represented. Early in August the Belgium police took action, and the delegates moved over to London en masse. This Congress is of historical importance because during this Congress the ideological split developed between the Iskrists. Lenin became leader of the Bolshevik (or majority group) while Martov became leader of the Mensheviks (or minority group).

When the Mensheviks pulled off the abortive revolution in Russia in 1905, Trotsky proved himself a leader of ability. It is difficult for the uninitiated to understand just what caused the effort to fold up, because the revolutionaries had control of St. Petersburg from January to December 1905. They formed the Petersburg Soviet, Lenin and many of his top-level revolutionary leaders stayed aloof. They let the Menshevik Party handle this revolution.

Lenin had been in Geneva consulting with the *Secret Powers* when the revolution broke out following the Bloody Sunday tragedy in St. Petersburg in January 1905. He didn't return to Russia until October. The Bloody Sunday tragedy was blamed on the intolerance of the Tzar, but many who investigated the happenings found ample evidence to convince them that the Bloody Sunday incident had been planned by the Terrorist Group for the purpose of arousing anger and hatred in the hearts of the non-Jewish workers against the Tzar. The incident enabled the leaders of the revolutionary movement to enlist the support of thousands of non-Jewish men and women who, until that sad day, had remained loyal to the Tzar, and spoken of him as "The Little Father". Bloody Sunday is of great historical importance.

In January, 1905, Russia was at war with Japan. Transportation on the railway across the Russian waste-lands from west to east had been broken down. Reinforcements and supplies had failed to get through to the eastern front due to sabotage. On January 2nd the Russian people were shocked with the news that Port Arthur had fallen to the Japanese. They had lost the war against what they had considered a very second class power.

The Imperial Government, in its attempt to gain the favor of the industrial population, had adopted the policy of encouraging the formation of legal trade unions. Known revolutionaries had to be barred from membership. One of the most active leaders in organizing the Legal Trade Unions was the Russian Orthodox Priest, Father Gapon. The liberal reforms, obtained by non-radical citizens, didn't please the leaders of the revolutionary party who claimed that "necessary reforms could only be brought about speedily by revolution". Father Gapon had won so much respect he was welcomed by the Tzar, and his ministers, any time he wished to discuss a weighty labor problem.

On January 2nd, when the bad war news swept the Empire, organized labor disturbances broke out in St. Petersburg's huge Putilov Works. A strike was called, but because of the general situation, Father Gapon said he would settle the matters in dispute by direct appeal to the Tzar. The idea appealed to the majority of the workers, but the "Radicals" opposed it. However, on Sunday afternoon January 22nd, 1905, thousands of workmen, accompanied by their wives and children, formed into a procession to accompany Father Gapon to the palace gates. According to the authentic reports the procession was entirely orderly. Petitioners carried hastily made banners expressing loyalty to the "Little Father". At the palace gates, without the slightest warning, the procession was thrown into utter confusion by a withering volley of rifle and machine gun fire. Hundreds of workers and their families were slaughtered. The square in front of the Palace was turned into a space of agonized chaos. January 22nd, 1905 has been known as "Bloody Sunday" ever since. Was Nicholas II responsible? It is a proven fact that he was not in the Palace, or in the city, at the time. It is known that an officer of the guard ordered the troops to fire. It is quite possible he was a "Cell" carrying out the terrorist policy of his superiors. This act was the "spark" that touched the "tinder" provided by the revolutionary leaders. The "blaze" of a full scale revolution followed.

Regardless of who was responsible, tens of thousands of previously loyal industrial workers joined the Socialist Revolutionary Party, and the movement spread to other cities. The Tzar tried to stem the tide of rebellion. Early in February he ordered an investigation into the St. Petersburg events, by the Shidlovsky Commission. In August he announced provision had been made for the establishment of a democratic representative legislature. This became the Duma. He offered amnesty to all political offenders. It was under this amnesty that Lenin, and his Bolshevik leaders, returned to Russia in October from Switzerland, and other countries abroad. But nothing the Tzar did could stem the tide of revolution.

On October 20th, 1905, the Menshevik-led all Russian Railway Union went on strike. On October 25th general strikes were effective in Moscow, Smolensk, Kursk, and other cities. On October 26th the Revolutionary

Petersburg Soviet was founded. It assumed the functions of a national government. The Soviet government was dominated by the Menshevik faction of the Russian Social-Democratic Labor Party although the Social Revolutionary Party had representation. The first President was Menshevik Zborovisk. He was quickly displaced by Georgi Nosar. He in turn was superseded by Lev Trotsky who became President on December 9th, 1905. On the 16th of December, a military force arrested Trotsky and 300 members of the Soviet government. There wasn't a single prominent Bolshevik amongst those arrested. This should prove that Lenin was acting for, and protected by, the Secret Powers which operate behind the government.

The revolution wasn't quite over. On December 20th a Jew named Parvus assumed control over a new Soviet Executive. He called a general strike in St. Petersburg and 90,000 workers responded. The next day 150,000 workers went on strike in Moscow. Open insurrection broke out in Chita, Kansk and Rostov. On December 30th the troops, and government officials, who had remained loyal to the Tzar, in some miraculous manner regained control. They put an end to the revolution. [8] Tzar Nicholas II kept his promise. The Duma was formed and an elected legislature established.

In 1907 the Fifth Congress of the Russian Social Democratic Labor Party was held in London. Lenin with 91 delegates represented the Bolshevik party; the Mensheviks led by Martov had 89 delegates; Rosa Luxemberg led her Polish Social democrats with 44 delegates; the Jewish Bund led by Rafael Abramovitch had 55; the Lettish Social Democrats, led by Comrade Herman (Danishevsky) made up the remainder. All told there were 312 delegates of which 116 were, or had been, workers.

This Congress had been called for the purpose of holding a postmortem on the abortive Russian Revolution of 1905. Lenin blamed the failure of the revolutionary effort on lack of co-operation between the Mensheviks and other group leaders. He told the 312 delegates that the Mensheviks had run the whole show and made a mess of things generally. He called for unity of policy and unity of action. He argued that revolutionary action should be planned well in advance, and the element of surprise used to full advantage.

Martov hit back at Lenin. He accused him of failing to give the Menshevik revolutionary effort the support he should have done. He accused him particularly of withholding financial assistance. Martov and the other Jewish groups led by Ross. Luxemberg and Abrahamovitch were annoyed that Lenin had been able to finance the attendance of the largest number of delegates. They accused him of financing his Bolshevik party by robbery, kidnappings, forgery and theft. They reprimanded him for refusing to contribute a fair proportion of his ill-gotten gains to the central unifying organization. One big laugh was created when one of the Mensheviks accused Lenin of marrying off one of his top officials to a rich widow in order to enrich his party treasury.

Lenin is alleged to have admitted he had done this for the good of the Cause. He maintained that the official he had married oft to the widow was a fine, strong, healthy specimen of humanity. He thought the widow would agree she had gotten full value for her money. It was at this Congress that Stalin, then a very minor character, became attached to Lenin. The Congress finally agreed to closer cooperation between the leaders of the various revolutionary groups and decided who should edit their revolutionary newspapers. They put great emphasis upon propaganda. At this Congress they laid the foundation for a re-organization of their propaganda machine with the understanding that all publications should adopt the same editorial policy "The Party Line".

In 1908 the Bolsheviks started publishing the "Proletarie". Lenin, Dubrovinsky, Zinoviev and Kamenev were the editors. The Mensheviks published "Golos Sotsial-Demokrata". Plekhanov, Axelrod, Martov, Dan and Martynov (Pikel) were the editors. All editors were Jewish except Lenin and Plekhanov. Trotsky started a semi-independent publication named "Vienna Pravda".

In 1909 Lenin won the unconditional support of two Jewish leaders, Zinoviev and Kamenev. They became known as "The Troika" and this friendship endured until Lenin's death in 1924.

After the Fifth Congress of the Russian Social Democrats Labor Party held in London in 1907, Lenin decided to find out how courageous and trustworthy his new disciple Stalin was. He also wished to convince the leaders of the other revolutionary groups that he was financially independent. To accomplish this dual purpose he instructed Stalin to rob the Tiflis Bank. Stalin picked as his accomplice an Armenian named Petroyan, who afterwards changed his name to Kamo. They discovered the Bank was going to transfer a large sum of money from one place to another by public conveyance. They waylaid the conveyance. Petroyan tossed a bomb. Everything, and everyone, in the conveyance was blown to smithereens, except the strong box containing the cash — 250,000 rubles. Thirty people lost their lives. The loot was turned over to Lenin. Stalin had proven himself as a potential leader.

The Bolsheviks encountered difficulty using the stolen rubles for party purposes because most of the currency consisted of 500 ruble notes. Lenin conceived the idea of distributing the 500 ruble notes among trustworthy Bolsheviks in various countries. They were instructed to get rid of as much of the money as they could on a given day. This directive was carried out, but two of Lenin's agents fell afoul of the police during the transaction. One was Olga Ravich, who afterwards married Zinoviev, Lenin's great friend. The other was Meyer Wallach, whose real name was Finklestein. He afterwards changed his name again to Maxim Litvinov. He became known throughout the world as Stalin's Commissar of Foreign Affairs from 1930 to 1939. [9]

After the revolution of 1905 had ended, Tzar Nicholas II set about making many radical reforms. He planned turning the Russian absolute monarchy into a limited monarchy such as is enjoyed by the British people. After the Duma began to function the Premier, Peter Arkadyevich Stolypin became a great reformer. He dominated Russian politics and drafted the "Stolypin

Constitution" which guaranteed civil rights to peasants who were about 85 per cent of the entire Russian population. His land reforms granted financial assistance to the peasants so they could purchase their own farms. His idea was that the logical way to defeat those who advocated the communal way of life was to encourage individual ownership.

But the revolutionary leaders wanted to usurp political and economic power. They were not the least bit satisfied with reforms. In 1906 the Terrorist Group attempted to assassinate Stolypin. They destroyed his home with a bomb. Several more plots were hatched to do away with the most progressive premier the Russians could have hoped to have. On a dark September night, in 1911, the Great Emancipator was shot to death, in cold blood, while attending a gala performance at the Kiev theatre. The assassin was a Jewish lawyer named Mordecai Bogrov.

In 1907 the International Bankers organized the Wall Street Panic in order to reimburse themselves for the money spent in connection with the Russian wars and revolutions. They were also financing the preliminary stages of the Chinese revolution which broke out in 1911.

Many of Stolypin's proposed reforms were carried out after his death. In 1912 an industrial insurance law gave all industrial workmen compensation for sickness and injury to the extent of two-thirds of their regular pay for sickness, and three-fourths, for accidents. Newspapers of the revolutionary parties were given legal status for the first time since they had been printed. Public schools were expanded. The election laws were revised in order to give more representative government. In 1913, the government of the Tzar of Russia granted a general amnesty for all political prisoners. Immediately they were released from prison they began to plot with renewed energy the overthrow of the Russian Government. Terrorists advocated the liquidation of the Royal Family. But the reforms had appealed to the vast majority of the Russian people. The revolution in Russia looked like a dead issue for the time being. Those who directed the World Revolutionary Movement decided they would give Russia a rest for the time being. They concentrated their efforts in other countries. Portugal and Spain came in for attention.

Because of the Red Fog created by Communist propaganda, and an organized campaign of "L'Infamie" carried on in Russia, as it had been carried on in France and England prior to those revolutions, it is difficult for the average person to believe that the Russian Tzars and Nobles were anything else than big bearded monsters who enslaved the peasants, raped their young women, and speared babies on the points of their swords while galloping through villages on horseback. In order to prove that the last of the Tzars was a reformer we will quote Bertram Wolfe, because Bertram Wolfe was anti-Tzarist and pro-revolutionary. Wolfe says on page 360 of his book *"Three who made a Revolution"*:

"Between 1907 and 1914 under Stolypin's land reform laws, 2,000,000 peasants and their families receded from the village mir and became individual proprietors. All through the war (1914 -1917) the movement continued so that by January 1st, 1916, 6,200,000 peasant families out of approximately 16,000,000 who had become eligible, had made application for separation. Lenin saw the matter as a race with time between Stolypin's reforms and the next revolutionary upheaval. Should the upheaval be postponed for a couple of decades the new land measures would transform the countryside so it would no longer be a revolutionary force. How near Lenin came to being right is proved by the fact that in 1917, when he called upon the peasants to Take the Land they already owned more than three-fourths of it."

It is unfortunately true that Rasputin did exert an evil influence upon certain men and women of the Russian Imperial Court. I know, from ladies attached to the Court at that time, that Rasputin exercised a tremendous influence over the Empress because her young son suffered from hemophilia and Rasputin was the only man who could stop the bleeding.

Rasputin definitely had mesmeric powers which are not uncommon amongst certain of the Russian people. He seemed able to place the Empress under his influence, not as a lover, but for the purpose of making her force the Tzar to do what Rasputin decided he wanted him to do. It is not an exaggeration to say that Rasputin, because of the power he exerted on the Tzar through the Queen, virtually ruled Russia to the dismay of the Russian people.

It is also true that Rasputin introduced into Court Circles men and women who practiced the pagan rites which were secretly carried on in the Palais Royal prior to the out-break of the French Revolution in 1789. These ritualistic orgies were based on the ridiculous assumption that people could not be saved until they had plumbed the depths of degradation in sin. He introduced subversives right into the Royal Household and they obtained information that enabled their masters to blackmail many influential people into doing their bidding. Rasputin was undoubtedly of the Illuminati and the Synagogue of Satan.

NOTES:

1   This fact had a great deal to do with the eventual destruction of Tzarist power which ended with the murder of Tzar Nicholas II, and his whole family, in the house in Ekaterinburg on July 17th, 1918 by a man named Yorovrest. Ekaterinhurg was afterwards renamed Sverdlovsk in honor of the Jew Yakov Sverdlov who was president of the Soviet Republic at the time of the executions. Illuminati symbols were formed on the walls of the death cellar.

2   This is another illustration of how even a Professor of History can fall into the Anti-Semitic pitfalls set by the conspirators. Admittedly the majority of people believe that all the International Bankers and Tycoons are Jews, but this is incorrect. The majority are not Jews, either by blood, racial descent

or religion. They actually foster Anti-Semitism because they can use all Anti-movements to further their diabolical plans.

3   Ginzberg was the official representative in Russia of the House of Rothschild.

4   The Zionist Movement was in turn controlled by the International Bankers and also used to further their secret plans and ambitions. Read The Palestine Plot by B. Jensen.

5   My farther, Captain F.H. Carr, was one of the British officers who served with the Japanese in 1904 and 1905. I have in my possession a very beautiful ivory carving of a Japanese wood-cutter enjoying a smoke after his lunch. This museum piece was presented to my father by the Japanese government in appreciation of services rendered. My father gave me a great deal of valuable information regarding the behind the scene intrigue which led to the Russian-Japanese War.

6   François Coty in Figaro Feb. 20th, 1932 said: The subsidies granted the Nihilists at this period (i.e. 1905 to 1914 – author) by Jacob Schiff were no longer acts of isolated generosity. A veritable Russian Terrorist organization had been set up in the U.S.A. at his expense, charged to assassinate Ministers, Governors, Heads of Police, etc.

7   Because the Rothschild's influence was so great with the Bank of England's directors, and because the directors of the Bank of England could control the policy of the British government, revolutionaries have always been able to find asylum in England when barred by every other country. Karl Marx and Engels are typical examples.

8   Had Lenin and the International Bankers intervened on behalf of the Mensheviks at this time nothing could have defeated the revolutionary efforts. There is no possible explanation for them allowing the Government Forces to regain control except that they had secret plans which they were not then ready to put into effect. That they were preparing for World War One and wished Russia to remain a Monarchy until after the war broke out seems to be the only logical conclusion, and future events would indicate this was their plan.

9   This "Gangster" played an important part in International affairs in England and Germany, in the League of Nations and the United Nations right up to the time of his death.

Chapter Eight
The Russian Revolution - 1917

In January, 1910, nineteen leaders of the World Revolutionary Movement met in London. This meeting is recorded as "The January Plenum of the Central Committee". Ways and means were discussed to bring about greater unity. Lenin was again pressed to give up his policy of financial independence. He responded by burning the Five Hundred Ruble notes left over from the Tiflis bank robbery. Lenin was convinced it was just about impossible to cash the notes without getting caught by the police.

The Plenum decided to accept the newspaper "Sotsial Demokrata" as the general party publication. The Bolsheviks appointed Lenin and Zinoviev, and the Mensheviks, Martov and Dan as editors. Kamenev was appointed to assist Trotsky edit "Vienna Pravda". The Plenum also discussed the pattern the world revolutionary effort should take. The delegates considered the possible repercussions certain contemplated political assassinations would bring about. The policy of the party was set. The Central Committee was ordered to prepare the Temples and Lodges of the Grand Orient for action. The members were to be made active proselytizing their revolutionary and atheistic ideology. [1

The Party Line was to unite all revolutionary bodies for the purpose of bringing all the big capitalistic countries into war with each other so that the terrific losses suffered, the high taxation imposed, and the hardships endured by the masses of the population, would make the majority of the working classes react favorably to the suggestion of a revolution to end wars. When all countries had been sovietized then the Secret Powers would form a Totalitarian Dictatorship and their identity need remain secret no longer. It is possible that only Lenin knew the secret aims and ambitions of the Illuminati who molded revolutionary action to suit their purposes.

The revolutionary leaders were to organize their undergrounds in all countries so as to be ready to take over their nation's political system and economy; the International Bankers were to extend the ramifications of their agencies right around the world. It has been shown that Lenin became active in revolutionary circles in 1894. It has also been stated that he decided to throw in his lot with the International Bankers because he doubted the ability of the men who led the Jewish dominated national revolutionary parties to consolidate their victories when gained. In view of these statements it is necessary to review revolutionary events from 1895 to 1917.

The Empress of Austria was assassinated in 1898; King Humbert in 1900; President McKinley in 1901; the Grand Duke Sergius of Russia in 1905, and the King and Crown Prince of Portugal in 1908. To prove that the Illuminati acting through the Grand Orient Masons were responsible for these political assassinations the following evidence is submitted.

The leaders of the World Revolutionary Movement, meeting in Geneva, Switzerland, thought it was necessary to remove King Carlos of Portugal so they could establish a Republic in Portugal so, in 1907, they ordered his assassination. In December 1907, Megalhaes Lima — the head of Portuguese Grand Orient Masonry went to Paris to lecture to the Masonic Lodges. His subject was "Portugal, the overthrow of the Monarchy, and the need of a republican form of government". A few weeks later King Carlos and his son, the Crown Prince, were assassinated.

Continental Masons boasted of this success. Furnemont, Grand Orator of the Grand Orient of Belgium, said on February 12, 1911: "Do you recall the deep feeling of pride which we all felt at the brief announcement of the Portuguese Revolution? In a few hours the throne had been brought down, the people triumphed, and the republic was proclaimed. For the uninitiated, it was a flash of lightning in a clear sky... But we, my brothers, we understood. We knew the marvelous organization of our Portuguese brothers, their ceaseless zeal, and their uninterrupted work. We possessed the secret of that glorious event."[2]

The leaders of the World Revolutionary Movement, and the top-level officials of continental Freemasonry, met in Switzerland in 1912. It was during this meeting that they reached the decision to assassinate the Archduke Francis Ferdinand in order to bring about World War One. The actual date on which the murder was to be committed was left in abeyance because the cold blooded plotters did not consider the time was quite ripe for his murder to provide the maximum political repercussions. On September 15th, 1912 the "Revue Internationale des Sociétés Secretes" edited by M. Jouin, published the following words on pages 787-788 "Perhaps light will be shed one day on these words spoken by a high Swiss Freemason. While discussing the subject of the heir to the throne of Austria he said: 'The Archduke is a remarkable man. It is a pity that he is condemned. He will die on the steps of the throne.'"

Light was shed on those words at the trial of the assassins who murdered the heir to the Austrian throne, and his wife, on June 28th, 1914. This act of violence committed in Sarajevo, was the spark that touched off the blaze that was developed into World War One. Pharos' shorthand notes of the Military Trial is a most enlightening document. They provide further evidence that the international bankers used the Grand Orient Lodges to bring about World War One, as they used them in 1787-1789 to bring about the French Revolution. On October 12, 1914, the president of the military court questioned Cabrinovic, who threw the first bomb at the Archduke's car.

The President: "Tell me something more about the motives. Did you know, before deciding to attempt the assassination, that Tankosic and Ciganovic were Freemasons? Had the fact that you and they were Freemasons an influence on your resolve?" [3]

Cabrinovic: "Yes".

The President: "Did you receive from them the mission to carry out the

77

assassination?"

Cabrinovic: "I received from no one the mission to carry out the assassination. Freemasonry had to do with it because it strengthened my intention. In Freemasonry it is permitted to kill. Ciganovic told me that the Freemasons had condemned the Archduke Franz Ferdinand to death MORE THAN A YEAR BEFORE."

Gavrilo Princip was a 19-year-old Bosnian Serb and Yugoslav nationalist who assassinated Archduke Franz Ferdinand of Austria. Princip died in prison three years later.

The pistol which was used in the assassination of Archduke Franz Ferdinand. The Browning FN Model 1910.

Add to this evidence the further evidence of Count Czerin, an intimate friend of the Archduke. He says in "Im-Welt-Krieg" — "The Archduke knew quite well that the risk of an attempt on his life was imminent. A year before the war he informed me that the Freemasons had resolved on his death."

Having succeeded in bringing about a World War, the leaders of the Revolutionary Movement proceeded to use the very fact to convince the industrial workers, and the men in the armed forces, that the war was a capitalistic war. They agitated. They criticized everything possible. They blamed the various governments for everything that went wrong. The International "Capitalists" were directed by the Illuminati who remained discreetly in the background, unsuspected, and unharmed. [4]

Because Russia had only emerged from the disastrous war with Japan a few years previously it was a comparatively simple matter for the trained agitators amongst the Mensheviks to create an atmosphere of doubt, suspicion, and unrest in the minds of the Russian workers, and finally amongst the troops in 1914-1916. By January 1917 the Russian Imperial Armies had suffered nearly 3,000,000 casualties. The cream of Russia's manhood had died.

Lenin and Martov were in Switzerland, the neutral ground upon which all international plots are hatched out. Trotsky was organizing the hundreds of ex-Russian revolutionaries who had found refuge in the United States. He was particularly active in New York's East Side. [5] The leaders of the Mensheviks were carrying on their subversive policy in Russia. Their first objective was to overthrow the power of the Tzar. Their opportunity came in January 1917. Cleverly carried out sabotage in the communication systems, the department of transport, and the ministry of supply, resulted in a serious food shortage in St. Petersburg. This happened at the time when the population was swollen so far above its normal size, due to the influx into the city of industrial workers needed for the war effort. February, 1917, was a bad month. Food rationing was introduced. On March 5th, general unrest was evident. Bread lines were growing. On March 6th, the streets became crowded with unemployed. Cossack troops were brought into the city. The Tzar was still at the front visiting the troops. [6]

On March 7th, the Jewish leaders of the Menshevik party organized the women to put on street demonstrations as a protest over the bread shortage. [7]

On March 8th, the women staged the demonstration. The revolutionary leaders then took a hand. Selected groups staged diversionary demonstrations. Gangs appeared here and there singing revolutionary songs and raising Red Flags. At the corner of Nevsky Prospekt, and the St. Catherine Canal, the Mounted Police and Cossacks dispersed the crowds without inflicting any casualties. The crowds who gathered around those who raised the Red Flags and cried out for revolution weren't even fired on. It looked as if definite orders had been given to avoid, at all cost, a repetition of what happened on Bloody Sunday, 1905. [8]

On March 9th the Nevsky Prospekt from Catherine Canal to Nicolai Station was jammed with milling crowds which became bolder under the urgings of agitators. Cossack cavalry cleared the street. Some were trampled but the troops only used the flat of their sabers. At no time were fire-arms used. This tolerance infuriated the revolutionary leaders and the agitators were directed to increase their efforts to bring the people into physical conflict with the police and troops. During the night the revolutionary leaders set up machine-guns in hidden positions throughout the city.

On March 10th an unfortunate incident provided the tiny spark necessary to kindle the revolutionary tinder which had been piled up, and soaked with inflammable oratory. A big crowd had gathered about Nicholai station. About two in the afternoon a man, heavily dressed in furs to protect himself from the cold, drove into the square in his sleigh. He was impatient. He ordered his driver to go through the crowd. He misjudged the temper of the crowd.

The man was dragged from the sleigh and beaten. He regained his feet and took refuge in a stalled street car. He was followed by a section of the mob and ONE of them, carrying a small iron bar, beat his head to a pulp. This single act of violence aroused the blood-lust in the crowd and they surged down Nevsky smashing windows. Fights broke out.

The disorder spread until it became general. The revolutionary leaders by pre-arrangement fired on the mob from their hidden positions. The mob attacked the police. They blamed the police for firing on them. They slaughtered every policeman to a man. [9] The inmates of the prisons and jails were then released to stir up the blood-lust. Conditions necessary for the Reign of Terror were introduced.

On March 11th the depredations of the recently released criminals led to wide-spread rioting. The Duma still tried to stay the rising tide of revolt. They dispatched an urgent message to the Tzar telling him the situation was serious. The telegram explained at considerable length the state of anarchy which then existed. Communist "Cells" within the communication systems sent another message. The Tzar, upon reading the telegram he did receive, commanded the dissolution of the Duma. Thus he deprived himself of the support of the majority of the members who were loyal to him.

On March 12th, the President of the dissolved Duma sent a last despairing message to the Tzar. It concluded with the words, "The last hour has struck. The fate of the fatherland and the dynasty is being decided". It is claimed the Tzar never received this message. This control of communication systems by "Cells" placed in key positions was used widely during the next few months. [10]

On March 12th, several regiments revolted and killed their own officers. Then, unexpectedly, the garrison of St. Peter and St. Paul fortress surrendered, and most of the troops joined the revolution.

Immediately after the surrender of the garrison a Committee of the Duma was formed consisting of 12 members. This provisional government survived until overthrown by Lenin's Bolsheviks in November, 1917. The revolutionary leaders, who were for the most part Mensheviks, organized the Petersburg Soviet. They agreed to allow the Provisional Government to function because it had the resemblance of rightful authority.

St. Petersburg was only one city in a vast Empire. There was no way of knowing accurately just how the citizens in other cities would behave. Kerensky, the Socialist, was a very strong man. He was referred to as the *Napoleon of Russia.*

Through the good auspices of the international bankers, M.M. Warburg & Sons, Lenin was put in communication with the German military leaders. He explained to them that the policy of both Kerensky's Provisional Government, and the Menshevik revolutionary Soviet, was to keep Russia in the war against Germany. [11]

Lenin undertook to curb the power of the Jewish revolutionary leaders in Russia. He promised to take the Russian Armies out of the war against Germany, providing the German government would help him overthrow the Russian Provisional Government and obtain political and economic control of the country. This deal was agreed to and Lenin, Martov, Radek and a party of 30 odd Bolsheviks were secretly transported across Germany to Russia in a sealed railway compartment. They arrived in St. Petersburg April 3rd. The

Warburgs of Germany and the international bankers in Geneva provided the necessary funds.

The Russian Provisional Government signed its own death warrant in 1917 when, immediately after it was formed, it promulgated an order granting unconditional amnesty to all political prisoners. The amnesty included those in exile in Siberia, and those who had sought refuge in countries abroad. This order enabled over 90,000 revolutionaries, most of them extremists, to re-enter Russia. Many of them were trained leaders. Lenin and Trotsky enlisted this vast influx of revolutionaries into their Bolshevik Party.

No sooner was Lenin back in Russia than he used propaganda to attack the Provisional Government which had granted him and his followers pardon. At

the beginning of April, the Petersburg Soviet (meaning Workers' Council) was dominated by the Mensheviks. The Essars (Social Revolutionaries) came second, and the Bolsheviks, for once, were the minority group. The policy of the Provisional Government was to continue the war effort because the majority of Russians considered the totalitarian ambitions of the German "Black" Nazi War Lords a direct threat to Russian sovereignty. This policy was vigorously supported by Tcheidze who had assumed the presidency of the Petersburg Soviet in the absence of Martov. Vice-president Skobelev of the Soviet, who was also a member of the Provisional Government, also supported the war effort because he thought that if the revolutionaries could help bring about the defeat of Germany's armed forces they might be able to help the German and Polish revolutionary groups overthrow the German Government in the hour of its defeat.

Lenin's one object, at that time, was to obtain leadership. He attacked the policy of the Provisional Government. He accused its members of being instruments of the bourgeois. He openly advocated its immediate overthrow by violent means. He didn't want to antagonize the Menshevik members of the Petersburg Soviet at this time. Lenin instructed his Bolshevik agitators to preach the destruction of the Provisional Government to factory workers and military garrisons but to use the slogan "All power to the Soviets" — meaning all power to the workers' councils.

Amongst the thousands of revolutionaries who returned to Russia, following the general amnesty was Trotsky. He took back with him, from Canada and the United States, several hundred revolutionaries who had previously escaped from Russia. The vast majority were Yiddish Jews from the East End of New York. [12]

These revolutionaries helped put Lenin into power. Once these revolutionaries had served their purpose most of them were condemned to exile or death. It was only a comparatively short time before all original members of the First International were either dead, in prison, or in exile. The history of the Lenin and Stalin Dictatorships should convince any unbiased person that the masses of the world's population, regardless of color or creed, have been used as Pawns in the Game of international chess played by the "Red" international bankers and the "Black" Aryan Nazi War Lords as directed by the Illuminati.

Further proof that the international bankers were responsible for Lenin's part in the Russian Revolution is to be found in a "White Paper" published by authority of the King of England in April 1919 (Russia No. 1), but the international bankers, through the directors of the Bank of England, persuaded the British Government to withdraw the original document and substitute another in which all reference to international Jews was removed. [13]

François Coty in "Figaro" February 20th, 1932 states:

"The subsidies granted to the Nihilists in Russia and elsewhere at this period by Jacob Schiff were no longer acts of isolated generosity. A veritable Russian Terrorist organization had been set up in the U.S.A. at his expense, charged to assassinate ministers, governors, heads of police, etc." The Illuminati who use Communism and Nazism to further their secret totalitarian ambitions organize revolutionary action in three steps or movements. [14]

1. The change-over of the existing form of government (regardless of whether it is a monarchy or a republic) into a socialist state by constitutional means if possible.
2. The change-over of the Socialist State into a Proletarian Dictatorship by revolutionary action.
3. The change-over from a Proletarian Dictatorship to a Totalitarian Dictatorship by purging all influential people who may be opposed.

After 1918, all Russian Jews were either revolutionary Jews, clinging tenaciously to the Marxian theories, and working for the establishment of an international of Soviet Socialist Republics, (Trotskyites) of they favored returning to Palestine (The Zionists). Miss B. Baskerville in her book "The Polish Jew" published in 1906 has this to say about the Ghettos on pages 117-118 : "Social-Zionism aims at converting the Zionists to socialism before they go to Palestine in order to facilitate the establishment of a Socialist Government ... in the meantime they do their best to overthrow those European Governments which do not attain to their political standard ... their program which is full of Socialistic ideas ... includes the organization of strikes, acts of terror, and the organizers being very young, acts of folly as well ... "

The *Secret Power* behind the W.R.M. also controls political Zionism, yet the vast majority of the Jews who work for Zionism are absolutely ignorant that they also are being used as "Pawns in the Game", of International Chess.

NOTES:

1 The Atheistic Grand Orient Masons must not be confused with other European and American Freemasons, whose principles are above reproach, work philanthropic, and whose ritual is based on belief in The Great Architect of the Universe.

2 Note: Bulletin du Grand Orient de Belgique 5910, 1910, page 92.

3 Tankosic and Ciganovic were higher Masons than Cabrinovic. It had previously been brought out at the trial that Ciganovic had told Cabrinovic that the Freemasons could not find men to carry out the Archduke's murder.

4 It was indeed a Capitalistic war, but not the kind of Capitalistic war the workers were led to believe it was by propaganda put out by the press the international bankers controlled in every country of the world.

5 Police officials and debates in Congress show this illegal entry is going on today on an ever increasing scale. The underworld characters also find admittance to Canada very easy. The danger lies in the fact that the underworld and the revolutionary underground are interlocked. One could not and never have survived without the other. The men who are The Secret Power direct both. The Aryan War Lords have used the Mafia, The International Tycoons, the Jewish terrorists. This explains gang wars.

6 The troops had 1 rifle to 6 men by Feb. 1917: 1 day's ammunition.

7 This move was almost identical with the plot to use men disguised as women in the march on the Tuileries.

8 One of the best works dealing with the events leading up to the Russian Revolution is "Behind Communism" by Frank Britton.

9 I have definite and authoritative evidence in my possession from people who were in St. Petersburg and in a position to know that the machine guns used were neither placed in their positions, nor fired by the police. The police had received definite orders that they were not to use drastic action.

10 Lenin, in order to break the spirit of the troops fighting the Germans at the front in November 1917, had messages sent to field officers which they accepted as coming from the Russian High Command. One General received orders to advance against the enemy, while two others, one on each flank of the General who was ordered to advance, were ordered to retire. It is little wonder that the troops turned on their own officers.

11 I have evidence to prove that the brother of Paul Warburg of New York was the German Army Intelligence Officer who negotiated with Lenin on behalf of the German High Command and arranged for his safe passage across Germany to Russia.

12 Father Denis Fahey C.S. Sp. in his book *The Rulers of Russia* pages 9-14 gives the names of all these revolutionary leaders, their nationality, racial origin, and the positions they were assigned to immediately Lenin had

83

usurped power and Trotsky consolidated his position in Russia in November, 1917.

13 Captain A.H.M. Ramsay, member of Parliament for Midlothian and Peebleshire from 1931 to 1945, states on page 96 of his book: *The Nameless War* — "I was shown the Two White Papers ... the original and the abridged issue, side by side. Vital passages had been eliminated from the abridged edition."

14 For further details regarding this matter read "The Last Days of the Mevanovs," by Thornton Butterworth; and "Les Derniers Jours des Romanoff", by Robert Wilton, 15 years Russian correspondent for the "London Times".

♟ Chapter Nine

Political Intrigue 1914 - 1919

The way international intrigue was used to depose the Right Honorable H.H. Asquith when he was Prime Minister of Great Britain in 1916 was explained to me by a man who was extremely well informed. I met him while serving as King's Messenger in 1917. We were in my room, in a hotel when, during the course of conversation, I mentioned that I strongly suspected that a comparatively small group of extremely wealthy men used the power their wealth could buy to influence national and international affairs, to further their own secret plans and ambitions.

My companion replied: "If you talk about such things it is unlikely that you will live long enough to realize how right you are." He then told me how Mr. Asquith had been deposed in December 1916, and Mr. David Lloyd George, Winston Churchill, and The Rt. Hon. Arthur James Balfour were placed in power in England.

The story he told me had a remarkable similarity to the plot used by the Secret Powers who directed the campaign of L'Infamie immediately prior to the outbreak of the French revolution in 1789. It will be recalled a letter was used to lure Cardinal Prince de Rohan to the Palais Royal where he was involved with a prostitute disguised as Marie Antoinette. The alleged modern method is as follows:

Shortly after the outbreak of the war in August 1914 a small group of wealthy men authorized an agent to turn an old, but very spacious mansion, into a fabulous private club. Those who made it possible to finance such a costly undertaking insisted that their identity remain secret. They explained that they simply wished to show their deep appreciation to officers in the Armed Forces who were risking their lives for King and Country.

The club provided every kind of luxury, entertainment, and facilities for pleasure. The use of the club was usually restricted to commissioned officers on leave in London from active service. A new member had to be introduced by a brother officer. My companion referred to it as the "Glass Club". [1]

Upon arrival, officer guests were interviewed by an official. If he was satisfied with their credentials they were told how the club functioned. The officer applying for admission was asked to give his word of honor that he would not mention the names of any persons he met during his stay at the club, or reveal their identity after he left the club. Having given this solemn promise, it was explained to the guest that he would meet a number of women well known in the best of London's society. They all wore masks. The officer was asked not to try to identify any of the ladies. He was sworn to keep their secret should he happen to identify any of them accidentally.

With the preliminaries over, the officer was shown to his private room. It was furnished in a most luxuriant manner. The furnishings included a huge double bed, dressing table, wardrobe, cabinet with wines and liqueurs, a smoking humidor, and private toilet and bath. The new guest was invited to make himself at home. He was informed that he would receive a lady visitor. She would wear a brooch of costume jewelry with the number of his room. If, after getting acquainted, he wished to take her down to dinner that was his privilege.

The reception room, where guests and their hostesses mingled over cocktails before dinner, was like that of a King's palace. The dining room was large enough to accommodate fifty couples. The ballroom was such that many people dream about but few seldom see. Costly decorations were set off by luxurious drapes, subdued lighting, beautiful women gorgeously dressed, soft dreamy music, and the smell of rare perfumes, made the place an Arab's dream of heaven. The whole atmosphere of the club was such that the officers' home on leave relaxed at first and then set out to have a real Roman holiday. There was nothing gross or vulgar about the "Glass Club". Everything about the place was beautiful, delicate, soft, and pliant ... the exact opposite of the horrors, the violence, the brutality, of a modern war. Between dance numbers entertainers gave performances which brought out the feelings of joy, fun and laughter. As the evening progressed, a long buffet was literally loaded with luscious dishes of fish and game. A bar provided every kind of drink from champagne to straight whisky. Between midnight and one a.m. five beautiful girls performed the Dance of the Seven Veils. The dance depicted a scene in a Sultan's Harem. The girls started the dance fully clothed, (even to the veil they wore to conceal the facial features) but, when the dance ended the girls were entirely naked. They danced the final act in their lithe-nakedness, waving the flimsy veil around and about them in a manner which extenuated, rather than concealed, their physical charms. Couples, when tired of entertainment, dancing, and other people's company, retired to their private rooms.

Next day they could enjoy indoor swimming, tennis, badminton, billiards, or, there was the card room which was a miniature Monte Carlo. About November 1916 a very high personage was lured into visiting the Club when he received a note saying that he would obtain information of the greatest importance to the British Government. He drove to the Club in his private car. He instructed his chauffeur to wait for him. After being admitted, he was taken to one of the luxuriously furnished bed-sitting rooms. A lady joined him. When she saw him she nearly fainted. It was his own wife. She was much younger than her husband. She had been acting as hostess to lonely officers on leave for a considerable time. It was a most embarrassing situation.

The wife knew nothing of the plot. She had no secret information to give. She was convinced that both she and her husband were philandering. She thought it was only this unfortunate chance meeting which had brought them face to face. There was a scene. The husband was informed regarding the part hostesses played at the Club. But his lips were sealed as if in death. He was a member of the Government. He couldn't afford to figure in a scandal.

Every employee in the club, both male and female, was a spy. They reported everything that happened at the club to their masters. The identity of those involved became known. The information thus obtained was printed for the record in what became known as "The Black Book". "The Black Book" recorded their sins of omission and commission, their peculiar vices, their special weaknesses, their financial status, the condition of their domestic relations, and the degree of affection they had for relatives and friends. Their connection with, and their influence over, influential men in politics, industry, and religion was carefully noted.

In November 1916, a member of Parliament tried to expose the real character of the "Glass Club". Three army officers, who had patronized the club, became suspicious that it was a vast espionage system, after an attempt had been made to blackmail them into giving information that would have been valuable to the enemy. Their adventure involved an Australian lady, her chauffeur, and the wives, and daughters of several highly placed government officials. [2]

The effort to make known the true facts was suppressed, but mention of "The Black Book" was made in Parliament, and in the public press. The government's policy was said to be based on the contention that a scandal of such magnitude could prove a national calamity at a time when the armed forces at sea, on land, and in the air, were meeting severe reverses.

The *Liberal* press began to attack the Prime Minister. He was accused of harboring men within his government who were unfit to hold office. He was accused of having had extensive dealings with German industrialists and financiers prior to the war. He was accused of being friendly towards the Kaiser. He was accused of being unable to make prompt and firm decisions. He was ridiculed as "Wait-and-see-Asquith". My companion told me that evidence against high officials involved in the "Glass Club" scandal caused the Government to resign. Thus, according to my companion, the British Empire was forced to change political Horses in the middle of a World War. When Mr. Asquith did resign in December 1916 he was superseded by a coalition government headed by David Lloyd George. Winston Churchill and Mr. Balfour were two of the more prominent members.

Shortly after hearing the above story, I was struck by the fact that the three army officers mentioned were reported in the official lists as "Killed in action". In war-time such a thing is quite possible. Next came a brief notice that the Australian lady, and her chauffeur, had been imprisoned under the Defense of the Realm Act. Then came an announcement that the member of Parliament involved in the case had retired from public life. A few weeks later I was taken off duty as King's Messenger and appointed as Navigating Officer of British Submarines. We did lose 33% of our officers and men but I was one of those to survive.

It was not until long after the war, when I was studying modern history and comparative religions that I began to realize the vast importance of political Zionism to those who planned to obtain undisputed control of the world's economy. The following historical events speak for themselves.

When war broke out in 1914 the Rt. Hon. H.H. Asquith was Prime Minister. He was an Anti- Zionist. The International Bankers decided that Asquith's Government had to go and be replaced by a coalition government in which David Lloyd George and Winston Churchill would wield great influence. Lloyd George had for years been Solicitor for the Zionist movement as planned and financed by the Rothschilds. Winston Churchill had been a supporter of political Zionism from the time he first entered politics.

In 1917 the International Bankers were supporting both the Bolshevik and Zionist movements. It would seem incredible that the British Cabinet didn't know what was going on, particularly when the British Government had had to intervene to get Trotsky and his revolutionary leaders released after they had been detained in Halifax while on their way from New York to Russia.

The overthrow of the Russian Empire was bound to cause the withdrawal of the mighty Russian Armies from the war on the side of the Allied Powers. The German Armies, which had been engaged on the Eastern Front, would be free to reinforce the Armies fighting against the allied forces on the Western Front.

Despite this knowledge, nothing was done to prevent the plans of the International Financiers reaching maturity.

The British Government was aware of the serious conditions brewing in regard to Russia. This is proved by the fact that the matter was discussed by the cabinet and a decision was reached to send Lord Kitchener to Russia for the purpose of re-organizing the Russian military forces. Lord Kitchener sailed from Scapa Flow aboard the H.M.S. Hampshire. She was mysteriously sunk during the night of June 5th, 1916. Lord Kitchener was lost with all but a dozen of the crew. The survivors drifted ashore on a life-raft. The British Government announced H.M.S. Hampshire was sunk by a German U-boat or a German mine. This has been proved to be a lie.

I investigated this incident very thoroughly. In a previous book *Hell's Angels of the Deep* published in 1932, I PROVED H.M.S. Hampshire had not been sunk by an enemy torpedo or mine. H.M.S. Hampshire was sunk by either sabotage or due to an error of judgment on the part of her navigating officer. Judging all evidence available, I was convinced that H.M.S. Hampshire sank after striking the submerged North Shoals Rocks. It is hard to believe that a skilled and experienced naval navigator committed such an error of judgment. I still believe that a saboteur probably tampered with the magnets in the steering compass. Gyro compasses were not then standard equipment and even ships that had them found the Sperry models very unreliable as I know from personal experience.

General Erich Von Ludendorf (who was Chief of Staff and shared with General Hindenburg the leadership of Germany's military might), also studied the circumstances surrounding the loss of H.M.S. Hampshire and Lord Kitchener's death. He states positively "Action by German naval units, either U-boats or mine-layers, had nothing to do with the sinking of the ship." He said he had arrived at the conclusion that the death of Lord Kitchener was an act of God, because had he lived he would undoubtedly have re-organized the Russian Armies and trained them into the most formidable fighting force. The General then remarked "Had he done this the Bolsheviks would have come into possession of one of the most formidable fighting machines the world has ever known. Such a force would have enabled Communism to sweep over the whole world."

I maintain that the International Bankers could not afford to have the Russian Armies re-organized until AFTER the Menshevik uprising, and after Kerensky's provisional government had been overthrown in 1917. It is very doubtful if Lenin and Trotsky could have accomplished what they did if Lord Kitchener had been able to re-organize, discipline, and train, the Russian armed forces in 1916. History also records that Winston Churchill and Lord Kitchener had quarreled seriously over military policy during 1914–1916. Lord Kitchener had bitterly opposed Churchill's idea of sending the Naval Division to Antwerp in 1914. He had also opposed Churchill's plan to capture the Dardanelles. Both ventures proved to be costly mistakes. The Dardanelles venture could have succeeded, and would probably have ended the war in 1916, if Churchill had waited until both army and naval forces were ready to co-operate jointly.

When Churchill insisted that the naval forces attack the Dardanelles alone he notified the enemy of intended strategy. After Churchill had committed the initial blunder the army was ordered to participate. Lord Kitchener's objections were overruled. His advice was ignored. The allied military forces committed to the assault on the Dardanelles were insufficient in numbers, improperly trained, poorly equipped for such a task, and badly supported both in regard to provisions, medical aid, and reinforcements. They were forced to attack first class troops whose leaders had been alerted to their danger. The allied military and naval forces were required to overcome military and naval obstacles that had not been in existence when Churchill ordered the first naval assault. The Dardanelles campaign was doomed to failure from the start.

The more we study the methods employed by the Secret Powers behind international affairs, the more obvious it is to see that they make private assassinations look like accidents or suicides; sabotage look like carelessness, errors of judgment, and unintentional blunders committed due to excusable circumstances.

The only possible consideration that could justify the policy of the coalition government in 1916, in regard to Russia, was the fact that the government knew they could not obtain financial backing, or military aid from America until AFTER the Russian government had been overthrown. Such a statement seems preposterous, but it is supported by the following facts:

- The Mensheviks started the Russian Revolution February 1917. The Tzar abdicated March 15th, 1917.
- Jacob H. Schiff, senior partner of Kuhn-Loeb & Co. of New York, immediately removed the restrictions he had imposed extending financial aid to the Allies. Mortimer Schiff was then ordered by his father Jacob to cable Sir Ernest Cassels — "Because of recent action in Germany and developments in Russia we shall no longer abstain from Allied government financing."
- On April 5th the British government announced that it was sending Rt. Hon. Arthur James Balfour, the Foreign Secretary, to the United States, to notify the American bankers that the British government was prepared to officially endorse their plans for political Zionism provided they would bring America into the war on the side of the Allies. America came into the war.
- On June 7th, 1917, the first American troops landed in France.

On July 18th, 1917 Lord Rothschild wrote Mr. Balfour as follows:

"Dear Mr. Balfour:

At last I am able to send you the formula you asked for. If His Majesty's government will send me a message in line with this formula, and they and you approve it, I will hand it to the Zionist Federation at a meeting to be called for that purpose."

The draft declaration was as follows:

(1) "His Majesty's government accepts the principle that PALESTINE should be reconstituted as a national home for the Jewish people. [3]

(2) "His Majesty's government will use its best endeavors to secure the achievement of this object, and will discuss the necessary methods and means with the Zionist organization."[4]

Mr. Balfour, and the British government, agreed to the terms dictated by Lord Rothschild and his Zionist confreres. This is proved by the fact that on August 28th. Sir Herbert Samuel, (he was subsequently made a Viscount), Sir Alfred Mond, (he was subsequently made a Lord), and Lord Rothschild persuaded the British cabinet to send Lord Reading to the U.S.A. as head of the Economic Mission. Lord Reading, when Sir Rufus Isaacs, had been mixed up in the Marconi scandal.

The details of the deal he negotiated with the U.S.A. government in September 1917 have never been made known. It is known, however, that the deal had to do with the Bank of England because it was completely re-organized, under American supervision, and physically rebuilt after 1919. [5]

In September, Jacob Schiff of Kuhn-Loeb & Co. wrote a long letter dealing with the Zionist question to a Mr. Friedman. In it the following passages occur: "I do believe that it might be feasible to secure the good-will of America, Great Britain and France, [6] in any event, towards the promotion of a large influx, and settlement of our people in Palestine ... further it might be possible to obtain from the Powers the formal assurance to our people that they shall obtain autonomy in Palestine as soon as their numbers become large enough to justify this."

September 26th, 1917 — Louis Marshall, legal representative of Kuhn-Loeb & Co. wrote his friend Max Senior, another leading Zionist, as follows: "Major Lionel de Rothschild, of the League for British Jews, informs me that his organization is in agreement with the American Jewish Committee ... The Balfour Declaration, with its acceptance by the Powers, is an act of the highest diplomacy. Zionism is but an incident of a far-reaching plan: It is merely a convenient peg on which to hang a powerful weapon. All protests they (the opponents) may make would be futile. It would subject them individually to hateful and concrete examples of a most impressive nature. I would shrink from the possibilities which might result."

Here we have a blunt admission from Louis Marshall, that "Zionism is but an incident of a far reaching plan ... it is merely a convenient peg on which to hang a powerful weapon." The far reaching plan referred to cannot be anything else than the Long Range Plan to which continual reference has already been made. It is a plan by which the International Financiers intend to win ultimate undisputed control of the wealth, natural resources, and man-power of the entire world.

A few of the more important historical events which bear out the above statement are as follows:

On January 28th, 1915, Mr. Asquith, Prime Minister of England wrote in his diary: "I just received from Herbert Samuel a memorandum headed *The Future of Palestine*... He thinks we might plant in this territory about three or four million European Jews. It read almost like a new edition of Tancred brought up to date. I confess I am not attracted by this proposed addition to our responsibilities", etc. Thus Asquith proved himself Anti-Zionist.

Prominent Zionists owned most, if not all, of Britain's major war industries. For no good reason, in 1915-1916, Britain suddenly found herself short of chemicals needed in the manufacturing of explosives. Guns and munitions which had been promised our Russian allies failed to materialize. Shells for our guns were so scarce they had to be rationed. The Asquith government was accused of bungling the war effort. But let us examine the facts.

Sir Frederick Nathan was in charge of chemical production. Messrs. Brunner & Mond were credited with doing all they could to correct the critical situation which had arisen. Using GOVERNMENT FUNDS they constructed a large chemical factory at Silverton. Sir Alfred Mond was appointed His Majesty's Commissioner of Works. He afterwards became head of the Jewish agency in Palestine.

Work on the factory was rushed ahead. The factory was brought into production in record time. Bouquets were passed around and honors bestowed upon the wealthy Zionist financiers who were supposedly doing so much for the British war effort. BUT AS SOON AS THE SILVERTOWN FACTORY CAME INTO PRODUCTION IT BLEW UP WITH THE LOSS OF FORTY LIVES. Over eight hundred buildings and homes were demolished. [7]

Because of the failure of Britain to deliver arms and munitions to Russia as promised, severe military reverses were experienced on the Eastern Front. Newspapers reported Russian troops were fighting with sticks and bare fists until slaughtered by well-armed German troops. A letter written by Professor Bernard Pares, (Professor Pares was knighted afterwards) to Lloyd George would indicate that the guns and munitions promised the Imperial Russian government were deliberately withheld to create conditions favorable for the revolution then being planned in Geneva and New York by the international bankers. Professor Pares' letter, written in 1915, reads in part:

"I have to submit my strong opinion that the unfortunate failure of Messrs. Vickers-Maxim & Co. to supply Russia with munitions which were to have reached the country five months ago, is gravely jeopardizing the relations of the two countries, and in particular their co-operation in the work of the present war ... I AM DEFINITELY TOLD THAT SO FAR NO SUPPLIES WHATEVER HAVE REACHED RUSSIA FROM ENGLAND." David Lloyd George, at the time the letter was written was chancellor of the Exchequer and responsible for financing the war. Messrs. Vickers-Maxim & Co. was controlled by Sir Ernest Cassels business associate of Kuhn-Loeb & Co. of New York, who in turn, were affiliated with the Rothschilds, and the international bankers of England, France, Germany, etc.

When Professor Pare's letter was discussed by the cabinet, Lloyd George is alleged to have defended the government's policy by saying "Charity should start at home. Our British soldiers fighting in France have only got four machine-guns to a battalion. They should be better armed before we export arms to Russia.

Lord Kitchener is reported to have replied. "I consider more than four machine-guns per battalion a luxury when our failure to deliver the arms we promised to Russia has resulted in the Russians having only ONE rifle available for every six men."

The agents of the international conspirators were ordered to smear Lord Kitchener and they circulated the story all over the world that Lord Kitchener had stated he considered more than four machine-guns to a battalion of British soldiers, fighting in France, a luxury. This smear and untruth has continued to this very day. It appeared in the biography of David Lloyd George recently published. It appeared in a review of the biography which appeared recently in the Toronto Star Weekly. I sent the editor of the Star Weekly the truth regarding this important historical event. He replied it was too much dynamite for him to handle. He informed me he had handed my correspondence to the

Daily Star. Needless to say the TRUTH was never published.

This is a typical illustration of how the international conspirators smear the reputations of honest men, even dead men, in order to cover up their own wrong-doing. It illustrates perfectly how their agents use the press of the world to misinform the public so they will blame innocent men, and even their own governments, for the harm done as the result of their machinations.

To prove that Vickers-Maxim & Co. were under the influence of Kuhn-Loeb & Co. at this time, Boris Brazel [Brasol] says: "On February 4th, 1916 the Russian Revolutionary Party of America held a meeting in New York which was attended by 62 delegates ... It was revealed that secret reports had just reached the Party from Russia designating the moment as favorable... the assembly was assured that ample funds would be furnished by persons in sympathy with the liberating of the people of Russia. In this connection the name of Jacob Schiff was repeatedly mentioned." [8]

Jacob Schiff was at that time senior member of Kuhn-Loeb & Co. of New York. Approximately 50 of the 62 people attending the meeting on Feb. 4th, 1916 were men who had taken an active part in the Russian Revolution in 1905. Once again they were to be used to foment revolutionary action, but Jacob Schiff had planned that the fruits of victory were to be usurped by Lenin, in the interests of the international bankers.

The Encyclopedia of Jewish Knowledge says of Zionism: "The World War forced the abandonment of Berlin as the center of the organization and all authority was transferred to the Provisional Zionist Emergency Committee established in New York under the leadership of Justice L.D. Brandeis."

Jacob de Haas writing in his book "Louis Dembitz Brandeis" says : "The (Zionist) Transfer Department ... its ramifications extended through all the war-zones occupied by the Allies, and throughout Turkey, Syria, Palestine, to Trans-Jordan and Bagdad; practically not a cent of the millions handled was lost ... Starting by using the good offices of the U.S.A. Dept. of State (Foreign Office) as a means of communication and deposit, it became so successful, and so reliable, it was employed by the Treasury of the U.S.A. to deliver moneys, and messages, which the government could not handle successfully... Embassies in European capitals advanced cash on the requisition of the (Zionist) Executive Secretary in New York."

L. Fry has this to say in "Waters Flowing Eastward", p. 51: "From then on their influence was felt more and more in POLITICAL circles in Europe and America. In particular, the Zionist Transfer Department, as it was called, was in a position to transmit funds, and information, to subversive elements in enemy countries."

Next we find the Grand Orient Lodges back into the Picture of the W.R.M. again. M. Erzberger says on pp. 145-146 of "My Experience in the World War": "On March 16th, 1916, the Alliance Israelite paid the Grand Orient of Paris the sum of 700,000 francs, and in the archives of the Grand Orient of

Rome it can be proved that on March 18, 1916 the transfer of one million lire to the Grand Orient of Rome took place. I am not so naive as to imagine that the 'Alliance Israelite' makes use of two Grand Orients solely for the purpose of sending one million lire to Italian Jews."

Telling of events AFTER Asquith had been deposed in 1916 — A.N. Field says in "All These Things", p. 104: "Jewish influence in British Politics became pronounced after the rise of Mr. Lloyd George". L. Fry on page 55 of "Water Flowing Eastward" says: "The first official London meeting of ... the Political Committee took place on Feb. 7th, 1917, in a house of Dr. Moses Gaster. There were present Lord Rothschild, James de Rothschild, (son of Edmund de Rothschild of Paris, former owner of the Rothschild colonies in Palestine) Sir Mark Sykes; – (whose house in Buckingham Gates was fully equipped as headquarters for the Zionist Cause with telegraphic apparatus, etc.), Sir Herbert Samuel, Herbert Bentwich, (later Attorney-General for Palestine) Harry Sacher, Joseph Cowen, Chaim Weizmann, and Nahum Sokolov.[9] The Zionist program to serve as a basis for official negotiations covering the future mandates of Palestine, Armenia, Mesopotamia, and the kingdom of the Hedjaz, was discussed in detail."

J.M.N. Jeffries op. cit. p. 139 contributes this further information "The minutes of this meeting were communicated forthwith in cipher to the Zionist organization of the United States ... From now on the political Zionist organization in the United States began to take a hand in the shaping of British policy, and the ordering of British affairs."

To illustrate the power the international bankers exercise over the British government's affairs Samuel Landman is quoted.[10] He says "After an agreement had been arrived at between Sir Mark Sykes, Weizmann, and Sokolov, it was resolved to send a secret message to Justice Brandeis that the British cabinet would help the Jews to gain Palestine in return for active Jewish sympathy, and for support in the U.S.A. for the Allied Cause so as to bring about a radical Pro-ally tendency in the United States. This message was sent in cipher through the British Foreign Office. Secret messages were also sent to the Zionist leaders in Russia through General MacDonogh... Dr. Weizmann (one of the founders of political Zionism) was able to secure from the government the service of half a dozen younger Zionists for active work on behalf of Zionism. At that time conscription was in force, and only those engaged in work of national importance could be released from active service at the front. I remember Dr. Weizmann writing a letter to General MacDonogh (director of Military Operations) and invoking his assistance in obtaining the exemption from active service of Leon Simon, Harry Sacher, Simon Marks, Hyamson, Tolkowsky and myself. At Dr. Weizmann's request I was transferred from the War Office (M.I.9) ... to the Ministry of Propaganda ... and later to the Zionist office ...about December 1916. From that time onwards, for several years, Zionism was considered an ally of the British government ... Passport and travel difficulties did not exist when a man was recommended by our office. For instance, a certificate signed by me was accepted by the Home

Office that an Ottoman Jew was to be treated as a friendly alien and not as an enemy, which was the case of Turkish subjects."

Study of the life of Disraeli reveals that he spent many Sunday evenings with the Rothschilds of London. It is revealed that while Kuhn-Loeb & Co. of New York was financing the Jewish revolutionaries in Russia, the London Rothschilds were the managers of the Tzarist administration in London. We also learn that the London Rothschilds were Liberals and that from 1840 to 1917 the Liberal Press controlled by the Rothschilds was consistently Anti-Russian. Disraeli informs us that in Germany the head men in politics and finance were considered reactionaries because they didn't allow the international bankers to do exactly as they wanted to do. Baron von Bleichroeder of Berlin and the Warburgs of Hamburg were the Rothschild representatives in Germany. In Russia the Weinsteins of Odessa assisted the Ginzbergs in St. Petersburg to look after the Rothschild interests.

Another man who was very active on the part of the international bankers was Otto Kahn. He cleverly hid his true colors, as a world revolutionary, behind the national flags of the several countries in which he lived and pretended to be a Patriotic citizen. Mr. Otto Kahn was born in Germany. He migrated to the United States the same as Paul Warburg did. Like Warburg he also became a partner in Kuhn-Loeb & Co. Kahn, upon arriving in America, obtained employment as a clerk with Speyer & Co. so as not to make matters too obvious. He later on married the grand-daughter of Mr. Wolf, one of the founders of Kuhn-Loeb & Co. When Mrs. Kahn visited Moscow in 1931 she was officially received by the Soviet government which gave a grand dinner and several brilliant receptions in her honor. The Red armies of Stalin lined the roads as she passed along, and the soldiers presented arms as she passed by. [11]

On April 2nd, 1934 an article appeared in the Daily Herald in which Mr. Hannen Swaffer wrote: "I knew Otto Kahn, the multimillionaire, for many years. I knew him when he was a patriotic German. I knew him when he was a patriotic American. Naturally when he wanted to enter the (British) House of Commons, he joined the Patriotic Party." Mr. Otto Kahn would have become President of the English-speaking Union if his revolutionary activities had not been accidentally exposed when it was proved that his house was the meeting place for Soviet agents such as Nina Smorodin, Claire Sheridan, Louise Bryant, and Margaret Harrison.

In the summer of 1917 the problem of who was to finance Lenin and Trotsky during their joint revolutionary effort in Russia had to be solved. The international bankers decided that their representatives would meet in Stockholm, Sweden, because that country was neutral, and comparatively free from international spies. Among those attending the meeting were men representing the banking interests in Britain, Germany, France, Russia, and the United States of America. Mr. Protopopoff, the Russian Minister of the interior was there, and so was Mr. Warburg of Hamburg. He was the brother of Paul Warburg who was a partner in the Kuhn- Loeb & Company of New York, who had drafted the legislation for the Federal Reserve System in 1910. It will be seen that in order to decide how finances should be arranged for Lenin and Trotsky to overthrow the Russian government, delegates attended from ALL warring nations. It was finally decided that Kuhn-Loeb of New York should place $50,000,000 to the credit of Lenin and Trotsky in the bank of Sweden.

Both British and American Intelligence officers reported these facts to their respective governments in 1917. Commander E.N. Cromie died fighting off a revolutionary mob which attacked the British Consulate in St. Petersburg. He held them off in order to give his confreres time to burn documents relating to this and other matters. [12]

The American government forwarded to the British government reports they had received from their intelligence officers. Mr. Oudendyke, the Netherlands Minister in Petrograd (who looked after the British interests in Russia after Commander Cromie was murdered also warned the British government. His warning was published in April 1919 as part of a White Paper on the Bolshevik Revolution published by the King's Printer.

The plans Jacob Schiff had made to allow Trotsky, and his band of revolutionary leaders, to return to St. Petersburg from New York went away when Trotsky was detained by Canadian government officials in Halifax, Nova Scotia, while en route. The power the international bankers exercise over constitutional governments is fully illustrated by the fact that immediately they protested to the governments concerned, Trotsky and his whole gang of revolutionary gangsters, were released and given safe conduct through the British Blockade Zone.

Further proof of the British politicians' complicity in the Russian Revolution of 1917 was obtained by D. Petrovsky who explains the part played by Sir G. Buchanan, the Ambassador. [13] Petrovsky proves that, although fully informed of all that was going on behind the scenes, Lloyd George's government aided the international bankers to put Trotsky and his revolutionary leaders into Russia while at the same time the German High Command aided the international bankers to get Lenin and his gang of revolutionary leaders from Switzerland to Petrograd. Lenin and his followers were provided with a private railway coach for their journey across Germany.

Mr. Petrovsky reveals that Milioukoff, who had been appointed Minister for Foreign Affairs by the Russian Republican government in the spring of 1917, was the man who negotiated this intrigue which involved both warring nations. It is also recorded that in appreciation for the cooperation given by the German General Staff the government of Great Britain agreed to Milioukoff's request that M.M. Litvinov be released. He had been arrested by British Intelligence officers as a spy for Germany. The identification of M.M. Litvinov proves of great interest. He was born to parents whose name was Finklestein. When he joined the World Revolutionary Movement he changed his name to Meyer Wallach. When he was closely associated with Lenin and his Bolshevik Party he changed his name once again to Maxim Litvinov. He is the same man referred to as Litvinov the German Spy and he is the same man who had been arrested while trying to cash the five hundred ruble notes Stalin had obtained when he bombed, and robbed, the Tifilis bank.

Following his release by the British authorities Litvinov returned to Russia. He aided Lenin to overthrow the Kerensky Provisional Government, and the Menshevik Soviet established in St. Petersburg prior to October 1917. Litvinov was Stalin's Commissar for Foreign Affairs from 1930 to 1939. He was appointed a member of the Central Committee of the Communist Party in 1935. His ability as an assassin; receiver of stolen money, spy, international gangster, and leader of revolutionary efforts in several countries was acclaimed by the nations of the world when he was appointed President of the Council of the United Nations. Only an international group, such as the international bankers, could have saved this man's life, and assured him his liberty when he was carrying out the criminal aspects of international intrigue. Only the power and influence of the international bankers could have caused him to be elected president of the United Nations Council. This illustrates the fact that the Illuminati control those who control the United Nations.

Other evidence is available to prove that the international bankers of the United Kingdom, the United States, Germany and Russia worked together even after Germany and Britain were at war. It is contained in a pamphlet entitled Trostky (Defender Publishers, Wichita, Kansas) which quotes a letter written by J.M. Dell to Lloyd George, personally. But why go on. It would take volumes to quote all the evidence to prove that the international bankers organized, financed, and directed the Russian Revolution in order to obtain control of a vast territory so that the Illuminati could try out their ideas for totalitarianism. Only by experimenting in an area as vast as the so-called U.S.S.Rs could they find out mistakes and weaknesses by the process of trial and error. Until they had performed this experiment, which cost millions and millions of human lives, it would have been gross stupidity on their part to try to rule the whole world. Theirs has been a Long Range Plan. It started 3,000 years ago. It was revised at the meeting in Bauer's Goldsmith Shop in Frankfort in 1773. *Unless united action is taken, it is likely to end when they take over economic and political control after World War Three.*

It will thus be seen that the Coalition Government which took over the prosecution of the war from Prime Minister Asquith, in December 1916, made no effort to stop the international bankers from proceeding with their plans for the Russian Revolution, even when they knew its success would cause the Russian armies to be withdrawn from the war. Proof that the Zionists in both Britain and the U.S.A. agreed that the Russian Imperial government should be overthrown, is to be found in the fact that immediately Lenin announced he had established his dictatorship in November 1917, Lloyd George also announced that the policy of the British government would be to back the Rothschild plan for the establishment of a national home for the Jewish people in Palestine. This proves Lloyd George held no resentment towards the international bankers for taking Russia out of the war as an ally of Britain.

The Jewish-dominated Menshevik revolutionaries in Russia had fought the abortive revolution in 1905. They also started the revolution in February 1917. Once again they met with great success during the first stages of the revolutionary effort. They actually established a Soviet in Petrograd. The international bankers didn't mind who carried the ball until it was near the goal, but as soon as the ball carrier got into position to score they stepped in and took over the play. Their goal was to bring about a totalitarian Dictatorship operated on the JOINT STOCK COMPANY PRINCIPLE: Lenin was made Dictator. They remained behind the scene. The Communist "Mob" was blamed for their crimes against humanity.

On July 17, 1917 the Bolsheviks under Lenin started an anti-government agitation in Russia. This resulted in an uprising by thousands of the city's inflamed worker-soldier population. This abortive revolt is known as "The July Days". Kerensky dealt with the situation firmly. The mobs were fired upon, several hundred people were killed, but order was restored. The Bolshevik leaders fled. Some were arrested. Lenin and Zinoviev hid in Sestroretsk. Trotsky, Kamenev, and Lunarcharsky were amongst those arrested. Stalin, who was at that time editor of Pravda, was not molested. After the revolt Prince Lvov resigned and Kerensky the Jewish Napoleon became Prime Minister. Kerensky was a great orator. He tried to whip up enthusiasm for the war effort amongst the soldiers and workers. All Kerensky's oral efforts failed.

Kerensky's influence began to decline steadily. Lenin was busy. He called for the Sixth Congress of the Russian Social-Democratic Labor Party to be held August 8th to 16th. He came out of it leader of the unified revolutionary groups. Within a year the united revolutionary party called itself THE COMMUNIST PARTY. At the congress a secret committee was formed called the October Central Committee. It consisted of 26 members who were to plan the October Revolution and then direct the revolutionary effort in all its various phases. Stalin made the grade at last. He was elected to the presidium of the Sixth Party Congress. The majority of students believe Stalin wouldn't even have been given notice if many of the other experienced revolutionary leaders hadn't been in jail, but the truth is, Lenin was acting as Chief Agent for the "Secret Powers". They had plans to use Stalin to supersede others.

The idea of the Central Committee to organize the October Revolution was to anticipate the Provisional Government's intention to call a general election in which the secret ballot would be used to elect a representative constitutional government to rule the Russian Empire. Lenin felt that if his bid for power was to succeed he had to make it before the Constitutional Assembly met in January to arrange the nation-wide election. If this election was ever held the people would have their own representatives in the government. He felt it would be harder to get the support necessary to overthrow a peoples' government than it would to overthrow the Provisional Government. In this he proved right.

Strange as it may seem, in the light of future events, Kamenev was released from prison August 17th, and Trotsky exactly a month later. By September 24th, Trotsky was elected president of the Petersburg Soviet in place of

Cheidze. On September 26th the Petersburg Soviet voted to transfer all military power to a Military Revolutionary Committee under the leadership of Trotsky. The real Lenin revolution was by now only a few days away. Lenin was proving what proper planning and time-table precision, backed by unlimited financial aid, could accomplish. He knew how to use the element of surprise advantageously. He rapidly convinced many leaders of other revolutionary groups that he was the man to direct the revolutionary war. He soon had everyone under discipline. The leaders were required to obey orders efficiently, and without question — or else.

The revolutionary leaders circulated an order that the second All-Russian Congress of the Soviets would meet November 7th. This was a "red" herring, drawn across the trail to make the general public believe that no revolutionary action was pending in the immediate future. On November 4th, however, the Military Revolutionary Committee arranged huge mass meetings preparatory for the actual revolt. The next day, November 5th, the garrison of Peter and Paul declared itself in alliance with the Bolsheviks. On November 6th Kerensky made a desperate effort to forestall the revolution by ordering the arrest of the Military Revolutionary Committee. He banned all Bolshevik publications. He ordered fresh troops to replace the garrison of Peter and Paul. But Lenin had organized his Fifth Column too well. Kerensky's orders were never carried out. Officials he trusted let him down.

Lenin sneaked out of hiding. He joined the Military Revolutionary Committee in Smolny Institute as soon as he knew Kerensky's counterrevolutionary measures had failed. The Institute served as the revolutionary headquarters. At 2.00 A.M. November 7th, the order to begin the organized revolutionary effort was given. By noon, St. Petersburg was largely in Lenin's hands. At 3.00 P.M. he delivered a fiery speech to the Petersburg Soviet. By 9.00 P.M. Bolshevik troops were besieging the Winter Palace headquarters of the Provisional Government. At 11.00 P.M. the Second All-Russian Congress of Soviets met and the Bolsheviks had a clear majority. The Congress thus became the official government of Russia. Kamenev was elected the first president. Lenin became Premier. Trotsky became Commissar of Foreign Affairs. On November 21st a Jew by the name of Sverdlov succeeded Kamenev. He had been in the Bolshevik Party only six months and was considered a very minor figure but, after being elected president, he quickly assumed absolute control of the Russian economy. He was a specially trained financial expert and agent of the Bankers.

Many things happen in revolutionary circles which never come to light. Sverdlov died, a very young man, only two years after he reorganized the Russian internal economy. He had served his purpose. He knew too much, so he died. Thus history repeats itself.

Bloody battles, which might better be described as wholesale massacres, and the ruthlessly conducted "Reign of Terror" proved the theory that utter ruthlessness and organized terror, in which physical sufferings are combined with mental anguish, and moral degradation, have definite economic value, because the Bolsheviks obtained undisputed control of Petersburg within a few days. Lenin didn't allow success to go to his head. The Russian Empire was large. He craftily allowed the elections, for which the Provisional Government had set up the machinery, to be held on November 25th.

The Provisional Government had planned that the convocation of the Assembly of freely elected representatives should be organized by a special commission. Lenin let everything go according to schedule and then he arrested the members of this special commission. He substituted for it a "Commissary for the Constitutional Assembly". The only difference between the one and the other was that Bolsheviks headed by Uritzky dominated the one Lenin had formed. By this move the Bolsheviks were in a position to exert authority over the newly elected Assembly as soon as it convened. When the Assembly did finally convene Sverdlov took charge of the proceedings ALTHOUGH HE WAS NOT A DELEGATE. The Bolsheviks present resorted to tactics which kept the delegates in a constant uproar. They created utter confusion. After ten hours the Bolsheviks all walked out suddenly. Bolshevik troops walked in. They ejected the remaining delegates and locked the doors of the building. This was the end of Constitutional rule in Russia.

In March, 1918, the Bolsheviks, who called themselves "The Russian Social-Democratic Labor Party" moved to Moscow and changed their name to the Communist Party. The second All-Russian Congress of Soviets now became the official governing body.

The Jewish-led Social Revolutionary Party did not want Lenin as Number One man in Russia. On August 30th, 1918 two Jewish members of this group tried to assassinate him. Lenin was wounded and Uritzky, whom Lenin had appointed head of his Cheka organization, was killed.

This incident gave Lenin the excuse for pulling out all stops. He turned on terrorism at full blast. Night raids became regular occurrences. No person knew when he went to bed, if he would be alive in the morning. David Shub in his Pro-Marxist book "Lenin" says : "Little time was wasted sifting evidence, or classifying people rounded up, in these night raids ... The prisoners were generally hustled to the old police station, near the Winter Palace and shot." Murder, torture, mutilation, rape, burning; these and all other outrages against human sentiment and decency, were the impregnable rocks upon which the so-called Soviet Socialist Republic was founded. Millions of Russian citizens died. It is estimated that more than 12,000,000 others were condemned to serve the State at Forced Labor until they were released by death.

And while the allies were half-heartedly fighting Bolshevism on four fronts, Lenin re-organized the W.R.M. In March, 1919, he convened the Third International. He presided. Zinoviev was elected president. The purpose of the meeting was to consolidate the revolutionary parties in every country in the world, and to arrange to provide the leaders with advice, financial aid, and any other assistance considered necessary to the success of Popular World Revolution. [14]

NOTES:

1   An exact duplicate of this club was organized just outside Montreal during World War Two.

2   This was in keeping with paragraph 8 of the plot exposed in Chapter 3.

3   Note the word used is "Palestine" not "Israel".

4   This letter was quoted by Mr. Stokes, M.P. in the British Parliament during the Palestine Debate December, 11, 1947.

5   Read *"Programme for the Third World War"*, by C.H. Douglas, Liverpool, 1944.

6   Mr. Cambon of the French Ministry of Foreign Affairs accepted the Balfour Declaration in regard to supporting Zionism at this time.

7   For further details of this aspect of the war read "The Brief for the Prosecution", by C.H. Douglas.

8   Boris Brazel was author of "World at the crossroads" see p. 69.

9   This is the Sokolov who afterwards wrote "History of Zionism".

10   He wrote "World Jewry" (London) February 22nd 1936. It will be seen that a very similar situation was created by international intrigue at the beginning of World War II.

11   Read "All These Things" — A.N. Field.

12   Comdr. Cromie served in British Submarines at the same time as the author. His exploits on behalf of the Russians are recorded in "By Guess and by God" — a book published by the author in 1931.

13   Read — *La Russie sous les Juifs*, pp. 20-28 and 34-35.

14   A great deal more information on the Russian angle can be obtained by reading "Behind Communism" by Frank Britton.

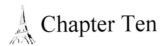 Chapter Ten

The Treaty of Versailles

It has been previously stated that the treaty of Versailles was one of the most iniquitous documents ever signed by the representatives of so called civilized nations. The injustice perpetrated upon the German people by the terms of the *Peace Treaty* made another world war inevitable. [1]

The circumstances surrounding the signing of the Armistice on November 11, 1918 must be understood. The German High Command did not ask for the Armistice because their armies were in danger of defeat. When the Armistice was signed the German armies had never been defeated on the field of battle. The German High Command asked for an Armistice so that they could devote their efforts towards preventing a Communist Revolution. Rosa Luxemburg, and her Jewish dominated Spartacus Bund, had planned to duplicate in Germany what Lenin had achieved in Russia exactly one year previously.

The Armistice was signed as a prelude to a negotiated Peace. It is of the utmost importance to remember this fact because an Armistice entered into under those conditions is far different from unconditional surrender.

The events which caused the German High Command to realize their danger on the home front were as follows:

Rosa Luxemburg's revolutionaries infiltrated into the German High Seas fleet. They became very active in 1918. They spread rumors that the ships, and their crews, were to be sacrificed in an all-out battle with the combined British and American navies. The rumor-mongers stated that the purpose of the battle was to cripple the combined allied fleets to such an extent they would be unable to defend the British coasts against a military invasion planned to bring the German Warlords Victory. The Communist 'Cells' exhorted the German seamen to mutiny because they claimed that the planned invasion of Britain was doomed to failure due to the fact that British Scientists had developed a secret weapon. According to the rumor-mongers invading craft could, by the use of chemicals fired from guns ashore or dropped from planes, be surrounded by a sea of flames. Fire, heat, and lack of oxygen would create conditions in which nothing human could survive. The subversives argued that the only way to avoid such a fate was to bring about a revolution to end the war. The German seamen mutinied the 3rd of November, 1918.

On November 7th, a large body of marines deserted while on their way to the Western Front. They had been told that they were going to be used to 'Spear-head' the rumored invasion of Britain.

Meantime, uprisings had caused shut-downs in many German industrial centers. Subversives talked defeatism. Conditions deteriorated until, the Kaiser abdicated on November 9th.

The Social Democratic Party immediately formed a Republican Government. The Armistice was signed November on 11th, 1918. The Communist leaders of the Spartacus Bund had placed their 'Cells' in key positions within the new government and throughout the armed forces. Their combined efforts created chaotic conditions everywhere. Rosa Luxemburg then played her trump card. She forced the Socialist government to order the immediate demobilization of the German armed forces. This action prevented the German High Command from using their well-disciplined troops to prevent the pending revolution which broke out in January 1919.

Before she usurped power in Germany, Rosa Luxemburg was promised the same financial assistance and military aid the international bankers had given to Lenin and Trotsky a year before. The initial stages of her revolutionary effort were financed by the fund they made available through the Soviet Ambassador Joffe. The revolutionary effort only failed to accomplish what Lenin had achieved in Russia when the promised aid failed to materialize after Rosa had launched her initial onslaught. Then she realized her Jewish Spartacus Bund had been betrayed by the very men she considered her friends and supporters. This incident alone should prove that "The Secret Power", behind the world revolutionary movement, is not concerned about the welfare of the Jews any more than it is about the Gentiles. The majority of the Directors of the W.R.M. are men who descended from the Khazars, Tartars, and other Mongol- Asiatic non-semitic races. They adopted the Jewish religion to suit their own selfish purposes between the 7th and 8th centuries. [2] They have used Jews exactly as they have used Gentiles as "Pawns in the Game".

The purpose of the double-cross was two-fold. The men who plot and plan the World Revolutionary Movement did not want Germany sovietized until after they had used the German people to fight another war against Britain. They calculated a Second World War would render both Empires so utterly exhausted that they could then be easily subjugated by the resources of the U.S.S.R.s they controlled under Lenin's dictatorship. In order to start a Second World War, they considered it was necessary to build up within Germany an intense anti-semitic hatred for the purpose of dividing Europe into two opposing camps — Fascist and Anti-Fascist. The plan required all communized countries to remain neutral, in a military sense, while their agents did everything possible to aggravate the adverse conditions the master-minds created.

After the Jewish-dominated revolution collapsed for want of aid, the German Aryan people took a full measure of revenge on the Jewish people. Thousands of Jews, men, women and children, were rounded up during the night and executed. Rosa Luxemburg, and her right hand man Karl Liebknecht, were captured and shot in the head like mad dogs by a German lieutenant. Thus, once again, a large number of Jews were made to pay the penalty for the crimes of a small group of international gangsters who used them as pawns in the game of international intrigue.

To prolong and intensify the hatred of the German people for the Jews,

103

propaganda blamed the Jews for bringing about the military defeat of Germany's armed forces; and the unjust and humiliating terms enforced by the Treaty of Versailles. Propaganda strengthened the trend towards National-Socialism in Germany by representing Britain, France, and the United States as selfish capitalistic countries influenced and controlled by the international Jewish bankers. Thus the way was prepared for the advent of Hitler.

Soon after the Armistice was signed the international bankers instructed Lenin to consolidate the Communist gain and to prepare to defend the Soviet States against capitalistic aggression. Lenin announced this as his policy. Trotsky disagreed bitterly. He advocated immediate revolution in all European countries which remained to be subjugated. He wanted to help Germany's Spartacus Bund in order to keep the revolutionary spirit alive.

Lenin insisted that their first duty was to establish the Communist sphere of influence in all countries of the world located between the 35th and 45th parallels of latitude in the Northern Hemisphere. Lenin stated he would only countenance revolutionary action in countries within those limits. The most important countries were Spain, Italy, Greece, certain sections of Asia- Minor including Palestine; certain sections of China, and the area both sides of the border in Canada and the United States. Lenin warned the Third International that it was the duty of the revolutionary leaders in all those countries to organize their parties so as to be ready to take over their governments when outside forces created favorable conditions to revolt. Rosa Luxemburg's failure was cited as an example of what would happen if revolutionary action was taken independently.

Lenin's strategic plan is known in military circles as 'The Musk Ox Plan' because these northern animals have been able to survive against the attacks of all their enemies by the simple expedient of forming a circle with their heads pointing out and their tails in. Calves are placed inside the circle. Wolves and bears could not attack the herd from flank or rear. If they attacked head-on they were gored to death, or cut to ribbons, by the razor-like hooves of the oxen. [3]

Lenin justified himself for abandoning Rosa Luxemburg on the grounds that he had thus been able to organize the Soviet armies to withstand the combined onslaught of the Capitalistic countries from 1919 to 1921. In 1921 Lenin informed the members of the Third International that Spain was to be the nest country sovietized. He blamed Rosa Luxemburg as being responsible for the wave of anti-Semitism which had swept over Germany. The Third International then dispatched Karl Radek to lead Communism in Germany. He was instructed to use his own initiative as far as recruiting, organizing, and training the party was concerned, but he was warned not to take revolutionary action until ordered to do so by the Comintern. The Comintern was under control of Lenin, and therefore the international bankers.

Having settled internal conditions in Germany to suit their Long Range Plans the international gangsters next turned their attention to Palestine.

Palestine occupied a central geographical position in their overall plans for world conquest. In addition to that, they knew that world famous geologists [4] had located vast deposits of mineral wealth in the area around the Dead Sea. They therefore decided to sponsor Political Zionism to further their two-fold purpose.

One. To force the nations of the world to make Palestine a National Home for the Jews so they would have a sovereign state which they would control by reason of their wealth and power. If their long-range plans matured to the extent of a third world war they could use their sovereign state to extend the control they exercised over the communized nations throughout the whole world. When this was accomplished they would be able to crown the head of the group 'King of the Universe', and 'God upon this Earth'. [5]

Two. They had to secure control of the five trillion dollars' worth of mineral wealth they knew was hidden in and around the shores of the Dead Sea. Events will show how they went about their dual purpose. After Britain, France, and the United States, had been committed to form a national home for the Jews in Palestine, by the Balfour Declaration in April 1917, Lord Allenby was ordered to drive the Turks out of Asia-Minor and occupy the Holy Land. The fact that Palestine was to be turned over to the Jews was not made known until after the Arabs had helped Allenby accomplish this task. The general impression was that Palestine would be a British Protectorate.

Immediately after Lord Allenby's triumphant entry into Jerusalem the international bankers 'persuaded' the allied governments to appoint their political emissaries as a Zionist Commission. Officially, the members of this commission were sent to Palestine to act as liaison between the military Administration and the Jews. Their real purpose was to 'advise' General Clayton so his military administration would further their secret plans. The Zionist Commission went into effect in March 1918.

Members of the Zionist Commission included Major Ormsby-Gore. He afterwards became Lord Harlich. He was a director of the Midland Bank; the Standard Bank of South Africa; and the Union Corporation. [6]

Major James de Rothschild, the son of Edmund de Rothschild of Paris, who had formerly owned the Rothschild Colonies in Palestine. Major de Rothschild afterwards became a Liberal member of the British parliament. He served in this capacity from 1929 to 1945. He was appointed parliamentary secretary in the Churchill-Labor Coalition Government.

Lieut. Edwin Samuel — afterwards became Chief Censor for the British government during the Second World War. He was appointed Chief Director of Palestine Broadcasting after the State of Israel was established in 1948. [7]

Mr. Israel Sieff — He was a director of Marks and Spencers, the huge British departmental stores. He was a close associate of all the international bankers. He was appointed Chairman of the Political and Economic Planning Committee. He was a permanent member of the 'Brain Trust' which 'advised' successive British governments. His standing in Great Britain was very similar to that of Bernard Baruch in the United States of America from 1918 to date. Mr. Sieff rendered the international bankers such outstanding service that he was made a commander of the Order of Maccabees.

Leon Simon — He was afterwards knighted, and placed in charge of the British General Post Office. He controlled all telegraph, telephone, and cable facilities. The remaining members of the commission were Dr. Elder, Mr. Joseph Cowen, and Mr. Chaim Weizmann; all close friends of wealthy Zionists in America. [8]

Sir R. Storrs says the Zionist Commission was sent to Palestine before the Peace Conference started, in order to create an atmosphere favorable to establishing a national home for the Jews; and also to stimulate its financial supporters.

The international bankers dominated the conference which culminated in the Treaty of Versailles. This is proved by the fact that in January 1919 Mr. Paul Warburg (who drafted the Federal Reserve System in the U.S.A.), arrived in Paris to head the American delegation. His brother Max arrived to head the German delegation. Comte de St. Aulaire says: "Those who look for the truth elsewhere than in the official documents know that President Wilson, whose election had been financed by the Great Bank of New York (Kuhn-Loeb & Co.) rendered almost complete obedience to its beck and call."

Dr. Dillon states "The sequence of expedients framed and enforced in this direction were inspired by the Jews (i.e. representatives of the international bankers) assembled in Paris for the purpose of realizing their carefully thought out programs which they succeeded in having substantially executed."

The Mandate of Palestine was drafted by Professor Felix Frankfurter, the eminent American Zionist, who afterwards became Chief Adviser in the White House to President Roosevelt. He was assisted by the Right Honorable Sir Herbert Samuel, Dr. Jacobson, Dr. Fiewel, Mr. Sacher, Mr. Landman, Mr. Ben Cohen, and Mr. Lucien Wolfe who exercised tremendous influence over Mr. David Lloyd George. [9] He was said to possess all the secrets of the British Foreign Office. [10]

At the preliminary conferences M. Mandel (whose real name was Rothschild \) was private secretary to Mr. Clemenceau of France. Mr. Henry Morgenthau was on the U.S. delegation in a general supervisory capacity. He was the father of the man who afterwards became President Roosevelt's Financial Secretary. Another man affiliated with the international bankers was Mr. Oscar Strauss who took a leading part in forming the League of Nations and molding its policies so that they fitted in with the International Gangsters' Long Range Plan for ultimate world domination.

Mr. Lucien Wolfe says on page 408 of his "Essays in Jewish History" "A small group of other distinguished Jews appear as signatories of the Peace Treaty. The Treaty of Versailles is signed for France by Louis Klotz. (He was afterwards implicated in shady financial transactions and retired from public life. Ed.) Baron Somino for Italy, and Edwin Montague for India."

Mr. Harold Nicolson, author of "Peace Making 1919-1944" p. 243 states that Wolfe suggested to him that all Jews should have international protection while retaining all national rights of exploitation. M. Georges Batault says in "Le Problème Juif", p. 38, "The Jews who surrounded Lloyd George, Wilson, and Clemenceau are to blame for creating a 'Jewish Peace'." Once again the Jewish race is blamed for the sins of a few ruthless financiers.

In the spring of 1919 Béla Kun usurped power in Hungary. He tried to put Lucien Wolfe's ideas into practice. Béla Kun's dictatorship lasted only three months, but during that time tens of thousands of Christians were dispossessed and ruthlessly murdered. The victims included working men, army officers, merchants, land-owners, professional men and women, priests and laymen.

The "New International Year Book of 1919" says in part: "The government of Béla Kun was composed almost exclusively of Jews, who held also the administrative offices. The Communists had united first with the Socialists, who were not of the extremely radical party, but resembled somewhat the Labor Parties, or Trade Union groups, in other countries. Béla Kun did not however select his personnel from among them, but turned to the Jews and constituted virtually a Jewish bureaucracy."

History records that after three months of systematic pillage, rape, and wholesale murder, Béla Kun was deposed. Instead of being executed he was interned in a lunatic asylum. His release was arranged by agents of the powerful group he had served so well. He returned to Russia and was put in charge of the Cheka which terrorized the Ukrainians into subjection when Stalin was ordered to collectivize agriculture in the Soviets. Five million peasants were starved to death for refusing to obey the edicts. Over five million more were sent to forced labor in Siberia.

When Stalin tried to turn Spain into a Communist Dictatorship in 1936, Béla Kun was chosen to organize the Reign of Terror in Spain.

The power of the international bankers is well illustrated by an incident that happened during the preliminary conferences held in Paris in 1919. The negotiations tended to stray away from the policy set by the international bankers. Thereupon, Jacob Schiff, of New York, sent President Wilson, who was attending the Paris conference, a two thousand word cable. He 'instructed' the president of the United States what to do in regard to the Palestine Mandate, German Reparations, Upper Silesia, The Sarre, The Danzing Corridor, and Fiume. The cablegram was dated May 28th, 1919. Schiff sent it in the name of the Association of the League of Free Nations. [11]

Upon receipt of the cablegram President Wilson immediately changed the direction of the negotiations. Of this incident Comte de St. Aulaire said: "The Treaty of Versailles on these five questions was dictated by Jacob Schiff and his co-religionists."[12] It must be pointed out again that the rank and file of

107

the Jewish people had absolutely nothing to do with framing the policy which the international bankers insisted Lloyd George, President Wilson, and Premier Clemenceau carry out.

As soon as the allied governments had been 'persuaded' to make Palestine a British Protectorate, (as demanded in the cable), the international bankers instructed their agents that the terms of the Peace Treaty were to be made so severe that it would be impossible for the German people to tolerate them very long. This was part of the plan to keep the German people hating the British, French, Americans and the Jews so they would be ready to fight again to regain their legal rights.

Immediately the Treaty of Versailles was signed, the phony Capitalist-Bolshevik war was started. This war enabled Lenin to justify his policy, by which he abandoned the German revolutionaries to their fate in order to consolidate the gains he had already made in Russia. The war against Bolshevism was never permitted to endanger Lenin's dictatorship. It was ended in 1921. The net result was that the Bolsheviks gained a tremendous amount of prestige, while the Capitalist countries lost a similar amount. This paved the way for the agents of the international bankers to suggest, in the interests of permanent PEACE, that the Soviet States be admitted to membership in the League of Nations.

The British government, always obedient to the 'wishes' of the international bankers, was the first to comply with the new 'request'. France followed suit on October 28th, 1924. After the infamous Litvinov had worked on Henry Morgenthau and Dean Acheson (who were both dominated by Felix Frankfurter and Louis D. Brandeis), President Roosevelt recognized the Soviets on November 16th, 1933. The League of Nations accepted the Soviet States as members. From that day on, the League of Nations was nothing more or less than an instrument in the hands of Stalin. His agents molded its policy and activities, to suit the Long Range Plans of those who direct the World Revolutionary Movement. [13]

Once the Communist countries had been admitted into the League of Nations, Grand Orient Masons, who were delegates, or on the staff, took charge. [14]

Wickham Steed, former editor of the Times, London, was one of the best informed men in the world. On more than one occasion he discussed the fact that the international bankers dominated international affairs. He made this definite statement just after the Treaty of Versailles was signed: "I insist[ed] that [, unknown to him,] the prime movers (to make the Allied Powers acknowledge the Bolshevik dictatorship) were Jacob Schiff, Warburg, and other international financiers, who wished above all to bolster up the Jewish Bolsheviks in order to secure a field for German and Jewish exploitation of Russia."[15]

Leo Maxse, writing in the August issue of the 'National Review' 1919 stated: "Whoever is in power in Downing Street, whether Conservative,

Radicals, Coalitionist, or Pseudo-Bolshevik, the international Jews rule the roost. Here is the mystery of the 'Hidden Hand' of which there has been no intelligent explanation." Once again the word 'Jew' should have been 'Banker' or 'Gangster'. It would be just as reasonable to blame all Roman Catholics for the crimes of a few Roman Mafia Chieftains who had given up the practice of their religion for many years. [16]

When Mr. Winston Churchill visited Palestine in March 1921, he was asked to meet a delegation of Moslem leaders. They protested that the ultimate objective of political Zionism was to give the natural resources of Palestine to the Jews. They pointed out that the Arabs had occupied Palestine for over a thousand years. They asked Churchill to use his influence to correct what they considered a great injustice. Churchill is recorded as saying in reply: "You ask me to repudiate the Balfour Declaration and to stop (Jewish) immigration. This is not in my power ... and it is not my wish ... We think it is good for the world, good for the Jews, good for the British Empire, and good for the Arabs also ... and we intend it to be so."[17]

When Churchill gave the Arabs his reply he was in all probability thinking of the threat issued by Chaim Weizmann who had been an agent of the international bankers for many years. Just a year before Churchill's visit to Palestine, Weizmann had made an official statement of policy which was published in 'Judische Rundschau', No. 4, 1920 : He said "We will establish ourselves in Palestine whether you like it or not ... You can hasten our arrival or you can equally retard it. It is however better for you to help us so as to avoid our constructive powers being turned into a destructive power which will overthrow the world."

Weizmann's statement must be studied in conjunction with another declaration made by an international banker to a gathering of Zionists in Budapest in 1919. When discussing the probabilities of a super government he was quoted by Comte de St. Aulaire as saying: "In the management of the New World we give proof of our organization both for revolution and for construction by the creation of the League of Nations, which is our Work. Bolshevism is the accelerator, and the League of Nations is the brake on the mechanism of which we supply both the motive force and the guiding power... What is the end? That is already determined by our mission."[18] One world government.

The two statements combined show the international extent of their secret ambitions. Eight years after I had finished this chapter of the original manuscript the following report came into my possession through Canadian Intelligence Service. Because the statements made at the Conference held in Budapest on January 12th, 1952 supports my contentions made in 1944, and confirms the conclusions I had arrived at in 1924, I insert the report of the speech given in 1952 here verbatim. It was originally made available to an American publication 'Common Sense' by Mr. Eustace Mullins, an authority on the Marxist conspiracy. [19]

"A report from Europe carries the following speech of Rabbi Emanuel Rabinovich before a special meeting of the Emergency Council of European Rabbis in Budapest, Hungary, January 12, 1952:

'Greetings, my children: You have been called here to recapitulate the principal steps of our new program. As you know, we had hoped to have twenty years between wars to consolidate the great gains which we made from World War II, but our increasing numbers in certain vital areas is arousing opposition to us, and we must now Work with every means at our disposal to precipitate World War III within five years.

'The goal for which we have striven so concertedly for three thousand years is at last within our reach, and because its fulfillment is so apparent, it behooves us to increase our efforts, and our caution, tenfold. I can safely promise you that before ten years have passed, our race will take its rightful place in the world, with every Jew a king, and every Gentile a slave. (Applause from the gathering). You remember the success of our propaganda campaign during the 1930's, which aroused anti-American passions in Germany at the same time we were arousing anti-German passions in America, a campaign which culminated in the Second World War. A similar propaganda campaign is now being waged intensively throughout the world. A war fever is being worked up in Russia by an incessant anti-American barrage, while a nationwide anti-Communist scare is sweeping America. This campaign is forcing all of the smaller nations to choose between the partnership of Russia or an alliance with the United States.

'Our most pressing problem at the moment is to inflame the lagging militaristic spirit of the Americans. The failure of the Universal Military Training Act was a great setback to our plans, but we are assured that a suitable measure will be rushed through congress immediately after the 1952 elections. The Russian, as well as the Asiatic peoples, are well under control and offer no objections to war, but we must wait to secure the Americans. This we hope to do with the issue of anti-Semitism, which worked so well in uniting the Americans against Germany. We are counting heavily on reports of anti-Semitic outrages in Russia to help whip up indignation in the United States and produce a front of solidarity against the Soviet power. Simultaneously, to demonstrate to Americans the reality of anti-Semitism, we will advance through new sources large sums of money to outspokenly anti-Semitic elements in America to increase their effectiveness, and we shall stage anti-Semitic outbreaks in several of their larger cities. This will serve the double purpose of exposing reactionary sectors in America, which can be silenced, and of welding the United States into a devoted anti-Russian unit.

'Within five years, this program will achieve its objective, the Third World War, which will surpass in destruction all previous contests. Israel, of course will remain neutral, and when both sides are devastated and exhausted we will arbitrate, sending our Control Commission into all wrecked countries. This war will end for all time our struggle against the Gentiles.

'We will openly reveal our identity with the races of Asia and Africa. I can state with assurance that the last generation of white children is now being born. Our Control Commissions will, in the interests of peace, and wiping out inter-racial tensions, forbid the whites to mate with whites. The white women must cohabit with members of the dark races, the white men with black women. Thus the white race will disappear, for mixing the dark with the white means the end of the white man, and our most dangerous enemy will become only a memory. We shall embark upon an era of ten thousand years of peace and plenty, the Pax Judaica, and our race will rule undisputed over the world. Our superior intelligence will easily enable us to retain mastery over a world of dark peoples.'

Question from the gathering: 'Rabbi Rabinovich, what about the various religions after the Third World War?'

Rabinovich: 'There will be no more religions. Not only would the existence of a priest class remain a constant danger to our rule, but belief in an after-life would give spiritual strength to irreconcilable elements in many countries, and enable them to resist us. We will, however, retain the rituals, and customs of Judaism, as the mark of our hereditary ruling caste, strengthening our racial laws so that no Jew will be allowed to marry outside our race, nor will any stranger be accepted by us.

'We may have to repeat the grim days of World War II, when we were forced to let the Hitlerite bandits sacrifice some of our people, in order that we may have adequate documentation and witnesses to legally justify our trial and execution of the leaders of America and Russia as war criminals, after we have dictated the Peace. I am sure you will need little preparation for such a duty, for sacrifice has always been the watchword of our people, and the death of a few thousand Jews in exchange for world leadership is indeed a small price to pay.

'To convince you of the certainty of that leadership, let me point out to you how we have turned all of the inventions of the white man into weapons against him. His printing presses and radios are the mouthpieces of our desires, and his heavy industry manufactures the instruments which he sends out to arm Asia and Africa against him. Our interest in Washington are greatly extending the Point Four Program for developing industry in backward areas of the world, so that after the industrial plants and cities of Europe and America are destroyed by atomic warfare, the whites can offer no resistance against the large masses of the dark races, who will maintain an unchallenged technological superiority. [20]

'And so, with the vision of world victory before you, go back to your countries and intensify your good work, until that approaching Light when Israel will reveal herself in all her glorious destiny as the Light of the World.' Illuminati means 'Holder of the Light'."

This speech also confirms what I have contended in regard to the manner in which the Secret Powers have deliberately stirred up anti-Semitism to suit their purposes and also anti- Communism. It proves my contention that the Illuminati have used Communism, Zionism, and Fascism to further their secret ambitions. And they will, if they can, use Christian-Democracy against Communism to bring about the next phase of their long range plan ... World War Three. But the most illuminating feature of the speech is the fact that it discloses the manner in which the Illuminati use a Jewish Rabbi to convince other co-religionists that they will be the governing class in the New World Order — a fact that past history would indicate is very doubtful. Satanism, not the Jews will rule.

Under the terms of the Treaty of Versailles in 1919 the international bankers obtained control over Germany's military rearmament, and her economic recovery. This accomplished, they entered into the Abmachungen (agreement) with the German High Command. They agreed to have the Soviets secretly supply the German generals with all the arms and munitions they required for a modern army of several million. They also undertook to have the Soviet dictator place complete training facilities at the disposal of the Germans to enable them to train the number of commissioned and non-commissioned officers they would require to officer the new army they planned to bring into being when they considered the time was ripe.

The vast building projects required to put the terms of the Abmachungens into effect were financed by the international bankers. [21] They thus enabled both Communist and Fascist countries to build up their economy and war potentials. The international bankers enabled the German High Command to evade all the military restrictions placed upon them by the Treaty of Versailles. [22]

The vast Krupp Munition and Armaments Plants built in the Soviets behind the Ural mountains were named "Manych". The German armament firms were granted every concession they asked for. International intrigue on such a lavish scale could only mean one thing. Those involved were preparing for World War II. The governments of the so-called allied nations were kept fully informed regarding what was going on behind the scenes, as I found out when I visited London during the conference on naval disarmament in 1930. This is only another proof that Disraeli spoke the truth when he said "The governments elected do not govern."

Thus history reveals that from 1920 to 1934 the Secret Power directed international intrigue in such a manner that the leaders of ALLEGEDLY Jewish dominated Communism in RUSSIA were working hand in glove with the leaders of ALLEGEDLY Aryan dominated Nazism in Germany. This phase of history is most complicated. It is difficult for the average citizen to understand. [23]

Communism and Nazism have several things in common: both are atheistic creeds which deny the existence of Almighty God. They both advocate war, hatred, and force; as opposed to Christ's policy of peace, love, and teaching. The leaders of both atheistic-materialistic ideologies MUST therefore be agents of the Devil. They further the diabolical conspiracy to win the souls of men away from loyalty and obedience to Almighty God. They both use a form of Grand Orient Masonry for proselytizing purposes. [24]

The head of the Council of Thirty Three is the president of the top executive's council of thirteen, previously referred to. Because the initiating ceremonies of ALL Grand Orient Lodges require the candidate to swear he will acknowledge no other mortal as above the head of the organization that head is automatically God on Earth. The international bankers have always been the top executives of the Grand Orient Masonry since 1770. Aryan War Lords have always been the top executive of the German Lodges. They select their own successors.

A review of history, 1914-1934, indicates:

1) That the international bankers fomented World War I to bring about conditions favorable for revolutionary action and thus enable them to obtain undisputed control of the Russian Empire.
2) To remove the Crowned Heads of Europe. These rulers had to be removed before either group could achieve their totalitarian ambitions.
3) To force the British and French governments to agree to establish A National Home for the Jews in Palestine.

The government of Britain was forced to aid the international bankers plan for the Bolshevik revolution in Russia in 1917 in order to obtain their promise that they would bring America into the war on the side of the allies. It can be assumed that S.S. Lusitania was sunk to provide the necessary incident to justify the changer of American policy, just as Pearl Harbor was used as an excuse for America to enter World War II.

The original draft of the mandate on Palestine reads: "TO TURN PALESTINE INTO A NATIONAL HOME FOR THE JEWS". It was altered at the last minute to read "to establish a National Home for the Jew IN PALESTINE". This was done to conceal the secret ambitions of the Zionists.

The international bankers deliberately concealed the truth regarding the vast mineral deposits geologists had discovered in Palestine until AFTER the governments of Britain, France, and the United States had agreed to their Mandate of Palestine. [26] The international bankers used Zionism to obtain control of a centrally located Sovereign State from which they could extend the control they now exert over the U.S.S.Rs. to cover the entire World. The conspirators managed international affairs between 1921 and 1934 so that Europe was divided into two camps — Fascist and Anti-Fascist — in preparation for World War II.

NOTES:

1   The injustice perpetrated at Versailles was only exceeded by the agreements afterwards entered into Tehran, Potsdam, and Yalta. It will be proved that

the same evil influences were at work in all negotiations.

2 See the *Iron Curtain Over America* by Pro. John Beaty. Wilkinson Publishing Co., Dallas, Texas. pp. 15-16.

3 Time has shown how far this long range plan has matured, and it explains why China was turned over to the Communists.

4 This was Conningham-Craig previously mentioned.

5 The Long Range Plans published in Chapter 3 proves this is intended.

6 The directors of the Standard Bank helped bring about the Boer war in order to give them control of the gold and diamond fields in Africa.

7 It might have been more accurate to have given him the title of Chief Director of Propaganda for the International Bankers.

8 The importance of Palestine in the plans of those who direct the World Revolutionary Movement is such that several books have been written on the subject. People wishing to be better informed should read—Palestine, the Reality, by J.M.N. Jeffries; The Palestine Plot by B. Jensen; Zionism and Palestine by Sir Ronald Storrs (who was first Governor of Jerusalem); Geneva versus Peace by Comte de St. Aulaire, (who was at one time ambassador to the Palace of St. James, England); The Paris Peace Conference by Dr. Dillon, London 1919; Brief for Prosecution by Major C.H. Douglas.

9 Mr. L. Wolfe published *Essays in Jewish History* in 1934.

10 See *Jewish Guardian* June issue 1920. Also The Surrender of an Empire by Nesta H Webster, p. 357, 1933; and The Palestine Plot by B. Jensen, p, 60.

11 This league was financed, and dominated, by five American Bankers.

12 See *Geneva versus Peace*, p. 90.

13 For further particulars read Moscow's Red Letter Day in American History by Wm. La Varre, in the August edition of the American Legion Magazine. Also Trotsky's book entitled Stalin.

14 Read *The Hidden Hand*, page 28, by Colonel A.H. Lane. Nahun Sokolov, who was President of the Executive Committee of the Zionist Congress, said on August 25th, 1952, "The League of Nations is a Jewish idea".

15 Read *Through Thirty Years* by Wickham Steed, London. Vol. 2, pp. 301-302.

16 It was the references to The Secret Power and Hidden Hand by Steed, De Poncin, Mrs. Webster, Maxse and others which caused me to investigate the matter in an effort to find the real answer. Author.

17 The full significance of this declaration was not appreciated even by the author until 1954 when Prime Minister Churchill (during his visit to Bernard Baruch) stated "I am a Zionist and have always promoted

Zionism". He then followed this declaration by strongly advocating 'Peaceful co-existence with the Communist Nations'. As the Communist States are actually International Financiers Dictatorships it must be assumed that in 1921 as in 1954 Churchill secretly believed they are best fitted, and most able to rule under present day conditions.

18 Geneva versus Peace, p. 83.

19 Mr. E. Mullins is author of The Federal Reserve Conspiracy. Published by "Common Sense", New Jersey, U.S.A.

20 Study this statement in regard to the meeting of leaders of all 'Dark' and 'Black' races which met in Bandung in April, 1956 and the policy of sending arms to Israel and Egypt.

21 This was prior to the advent of Hitler.

22 It will be proved that the German Generals and top-level officials who negotiated the Abmachungen were the ones condemned to death at the Nuremberg Trials as War Criminals. They knew too much.

23 A great deal of light has, however, been thrown on this subject by Mr. Cecil F. Melville, who made a deep study of this particular phase of the World Revolutionary Movement, and wrote The Russian Face of Germany.

24 NOTE - The German Grand Orient Lodges have never admitted Jews to membership for the obvious reason that the Secret Powers could never have put into effect an international plot of the nature and proportions of the Abmachungen, had their policy been otherwise.

25 NOTE - The truth regarding value of mineral resources was not allowed to leak out until the United Nations had partitioned Palestine in 1948 in such a manner that over five trillion dollars' worth of minerals are now known to be located in The State of Israel. Count Bernadotte of Sweden proposed that the Jews should give up the entire south, and receive West Galilee in the north. His plan was rejected and in September 1947 Count Bernadotte was assassinated by Jewish extremists.

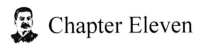

Chapter Eleven

Stalin

Stalin was born Joseph Vissarionovich Djugashvili, in the mountain village of Gori in the province of Georgia in 1879. His father was a peasant from the town Dido-Lilo. His mother, Ekaterina Geladze, was a devoutly religious woman whose forebears had been serfs in the village of Gambarouli.

Not a great deal is known about Stalin's father, except that he sometimes worked as a laborer and sometimes as a cobbler in a shoe factory in Adelkhanov. He is said to have been an easy- going individual who liked to drink a great deal. Stalin's mother, however, was a devoted mother and worked hard. She took in washing to earn extra money for her family's benefit. Her ambition was to see Stalin become a priest. She skimped and saved to provide him with the necessary education. Young Stalin attended the elementary school in Gori for four years and won a scholarship which entitled him to attend the Tiflis Theological Seminary. But Stalin wasn't cut out for a religious life. He was continually getting into trouble with the seminary authorities. He was expelled after completing four years of study. He then joined a group of young revolutionaries.

Stalin first married Ekaterina Svanidze, who bore him a son, Yasha-Jacob Djugashvili. This boy was never very bright. Even after his father became dictator, he worked as an electrician and mechanic.

Stalin's second wife was Nadya. Allilyova who bore him two children, Vasili, a son, and Svetlana, a daughter. Vasili became a major-general in the Soviet Air Force. He usually led the flying demonstrations on special occasions of state after his father became dictator. He was thrown into the discard after his father died.

Stalin and his second wife don't seem to have got along very well together. Stalin had an affair with a beautiful Jewess, Rosa Kaganovich. She is reported to have been living with Stalin when his second wife, Nadya, committed suicide.

It is believed that in addition to Stalin's love affairs, Nadya became more and more depressed as the result of the ruthless way in which Stalin slaughtered so many of her co-religionists whom he accused of being diversionists.

Rosa's brother, Lazar Kaganovich, was a great friend of Stalin's. He was made a member of the Politburo and retained his office until Stalin died. Kaganovich proved his ability as Commissioner for Heavy Industry when he developed the Donetz Basin Oil Fields and built the Moscow subway. Kaganovich's son, Mihail, married Stalin's daughter Svetlana. [1] What became of Svetlana's first husband remains a mystery. It would appear that Svetlana's first hubby removed himself, or was removed, to allow Kaganovich's son to marry Stalin's daughter, just as Stalin's second wife removed herself or was removed, to allow Stalin to marry Kaganovich's sister, Rosa. It is reported that Stalin did marry Rosa after his wife's suicide.

Molotov, vice-premier to Stalin, was married to a Jewess, the sister of Sam Karp, owner of the Karp Exporting Co. of Bridgeport, Conn. Molotov's daughter was engaged to Stalin's son, Vasili, in 1951, so the Politburo was to a certain extent 'A Family Compact'.

As was mentioned previously, Stalin only became a member of the Upper Crust of the Russian revolutionary party because, during the preliminary phases of the Russian Revolution, many of the better known leaders were in jail. Stalin never rose to any very exalted position in the Communist Party during Lenin's dictatorship. It was during Lenin's last illness that Stalin jockeyed for position, and then he moved out in front, to eliminate Trotsky and other Jewish contenders. Once he took over the leadership he never relinquished it until his death.

How Stalin rose to power is an interesting story. Lenin suffered a paralytic stroke in May 1922, and this affected his speech and motor reflexes. In December of that year he appointed a triumvirate composed of Zinoviev, Kamenev and Stalin to share the problems of government. Shortly after Lenin suffered another stroke and died. Trotsky has suggested, and his followers believe, Stalin helped bring about Lenin's death because he was irritated by Lenin's incapacity and prolonged illness.

When the triumvirate started to function in Moscow the Politburo included of Lenin, Zinoviev, Kamenev, Trotsky, Bukharin, Tomsky, and Stalin. Zinoviev and Kamenev had been Lenin's right hand men from the day he became dictator. They naturally regarded themselves as the senior members of the triumvirate and logically his successors. Zinoviev treated Stalin in a circumspectly patronizing manner and Kamenev treated him with a touch of irony. [2]

Zinoviev and Kamenev considered Trotsky as their real competitor for the dictatorship after Lenin died. In Trotsky's book "Stalin" he records that Stalin was used by both Zinoviev and Kamenev as a counterweight against him (Trotsky) and to a lesser extent by other members of the Politburo also. No member of the Politburo at that time thought Stalin would one day rise away above their heads.

Zinoviev was considered senior member of the triumvirate when he was delegated to give the opening address of the 12th Party Congress, a function Lenin had always reserved for himself on previous occasions. Zinoviev didn't go over too well. Stalin was quick to take advantage. Before the congress was over, Stalin had secured control over the Communist Party machine and held a dominant position in the triumvirate. This was the situation when Lenin died in 1924.

117

In April 1925 Stalin had Trotsky removed as war commissar. He then broke relations with Zinoviev and Kamenev and allied himself with Bukharin, Rykov, and Tomsky. Zinoviev, Kamenev and Trotsky then united forces in opposition to Stalin, but they had moved too late. In February, 1926, Stalin had Zinoviev expelled from the Politburo; then from the presidency of the Petersburg (Leningrad) Soviet; and finally from the presidency of the Third International. In October, 1926, Stalin had Kamenev and Trotsky expelled from the Politburo. Next year Stalin had his three enemies removed from the Central Committee of the Communist Party and shortly afterwards he had them read out of the party altogether.

In 1927 Trotsky tried to start a revolt against Stalin on the grounds that he was departing from the Marxian ideology and substituting an imperialistic totalitarian dictatorship for a genuine Union of Sovietized Socialist Republics. What everyone seems to have failed to realize was the fact that Stalin had been nominated to rule the Soviets by the international bankers. He had to purge Russia of all men who might obstruct their Long Range Plans.

During the purge several million people were slain and about an equal number sent to forced labor. Many men, who had been leaders of the revolutionary movement, since the First International was formed, were hounded to death or imprisoned. Amongst the leaders Stalin purged were Trotsky, Zinoviev, Kamenev, Martynov, Zasulich, Deutch, Parvus, Axelrod, Radek, Uritzky, Sverdlov, Dan, Lieber, and Martov. About the only Jews close to Stalin at the time of his death were Kaganovich, his brother-in-law and Rosa, his third wife.

Stalin continued to develop Lenin's policy to establish the Communist sphere of influence between the 35th and 45th parallels of latitude right around the northern hemisphere. Many revolutionary leaders in other countries became convinced that Stalin had developed personal Imperialistic ideas and was intent upon making himself ruler of a world-wide totalitarian dictatorship. They were right. Stalin took his orders, as Lenin had done, from the men who are "THE SECRET POWER" behind the World Revolutionary Movement, until 1936 and then he began to ignore their mandates, as will be proved.

Stalin did not want to involve his armed forces in wars with other nations. His policy was to feed the revolutionary fires in all countries to the south between the 35th and 45th parallels of latitude. His policy paid off exceedingly well. At the time of his death, Communistic control had been established over half the territory in the Northern Hemisphere. About half the world's population had been subjugated.

Lenin had stated in 1921 that Spain was to be the next country Sovietized. Upon his death Stalin accepted the subjugation of Spain as a pious legacy. Once Spain had been turned into a so-called proletarian dictatorship it would be an easy matter to subjugate France and Britain. Germany would then be between the nut-crackers. If by some mischance the subjugation of Spain failed to materialize, then the incident could be used to help bring about World

War II.

While preparing for the Spanish revolution, Stalin was ordered by the international bankers to take an active part in an economic war which was planned in 1918 immediately after the Armistice had been signed. Generally speaking, the people who had not been engaged in the actual fighting became prosperous during World War I. When the fighting ended the people in the allied countries enjoyed two boom years. Then, after speculative investments had just about reached their peak, vast amounts of money were withdrawn from circulation. Credits were restricted. Calls were made on loans. In 1922-25 a minor depression was experienced. [3] This economic juggling was a preliminary experiment before the Powers-That-Be brought about the great depression of 1930.

After 1925 financial policy was reversed and conditions steadily improved until prosperity in

America, Britain, Canada, and Australia, reached an all-time record. Speculation in stocks and bonds and real estate went wild. Then, towards the end of 1929 came the sudden crash, and the greatest depression ever known settled down over the free world. Millions of people were rendered destitute. Thousands committed suicide. Misgovernment was blamed for the economic upset which made paupers out of tens of millions of people, and trillionaires out of three hundred who were already millionaires.

In 1925 Stalin started his five-year industrial plans to increase the so-called Sovietized countries internal recovery. The plan was to exploit the natural resources, manufacture raw materials into useful commodities, and modernize industrial and agricultural machinery. This vast Five Year Plan was financed by loans from the international bankers. This program, when added to the development of the Russian and German war potential under the Abmachungen (agreements) previously referred to, gave a great boost to Soviet economy. The fact that the Rulers of Russia could use millions of men and women as slaves gave those who enslaved them an additional advantage over nations which employ paid labor, and maintain a high standard of living.

The next move was the collectivization of farms. For centuries the serfs in Russia had been little better than slaves of the landed proprietors. Lenin had won their support by promising them even greater concessions than they had been granted under the benevolent rule of Premier Peter Arkadyevich Stolypin from 1906 to 1914, when over 2,000,000 peasant families seceded from the village mir and became individual land owners. By January 1st, 1916, the number had increased to 6,200,000 families.

But, in order to secure the loans they had made for the Abmachungen and industrial development programs, the international bankers insisted that they control the import and export trade of the Sovietized nations. They also demanded the collectivization of farms as the only means to obtain greatly increased agricultural production.

History records what happened when Stalin enforced the edicts. He has always been blamed personally for the inhuman atrocities which made the peasants comply with the laws. Many versions of what happened have been given. The truth, as I reported it to American newspapers in 1930, has never been published to date. It is acknowledged that over 5,000,000 peasants were executed, or systematically starved to death, because they refused to obey, or tried to evade the edicts. Over 5,000,000 more were sent to forced labor in Siberia. What is not generally known is the fact that the grain which was confiscated from the Russian farmers was pooled together with a vast quantity of grain purchased by the agents of the international bankers in other countries except Canada and the United States. In addition to this corner on grain the international bankers bought up huge supplies of processed and frozen meats in the Argentine and other meat producing countries. Canada and the United States could not find a market for their cattle, or their grain.

During the period 1920-1929 the international bankers subsidized shipping in most countries except Britain, Canada, and the United States. As the result of this commercial piracy, it became impossible for ships owned in Britain, Canada, and the United States to compete with ships owned by other countries. Thousands of ships were tied up idle in their home ports. Export trade fell off to an all-time low.

The falling off of exports from the allied nations was accompanied by increasing the importation of cheaply manufactured goods from Germany, Japan, and central European countries. To enjoy reasonable prosperity, five out of every eight wage-earners in Canada must obtain their pay directly or indirectly as a result of the export trade. When the export trade falls off a recession immediately follows, due to loss of purchasing power among five-eighths of the population. This immediately affects those who earn their living by rendering services of one kind or another. If the export trade remains down, then the recession deteriorates into a depression.

To make absolutely sure that the skids were completely knocked from under the economic structures of allied countries, the men who had cornered grain and meats began to dump their supplies on the markets of the world at prices below the cost of production in Canada, America and Australia. This action brought about a situation in which the granaries of the countries allied together in World War I were bursting with grain they couldn't sell, while the people of other countries were starving to death for want of bread and meat. Britain needs to earn £85,000,000 a year from her ocean services in order to offset her unfavorable annual trade balance each year. The British economy was given a severe jolt when unfair competition made it impossible for her to earn this money. The British people were forced to buy their bread and meat in the cheapest markets. This artificially produced economic mess-up was used by the men who master-mind international intrigue to cause grave misunderstanding between different units of the British Commonwealth of Nations and thus weaken the bonds of Empire. [4]

As the result of this economic war, the shipping, industrial, and agricultural activities of the allied or capitalistic countries were brought to a virtual standstill, while the Soviet States and the Axis Powers worked at full capacity. Once again it must be remembered that the men who plot and plan the World Revolutionary Movement always work on the fundamental principle that wars end depressions and pave the way for revolutionary action in countries that still remain to be subjugated. This being a fact, it was essential to the furthering of their Long Range Plans to arrange international affairs so they could bring about World War II when they wished to do so. As Spain had been indicated by Lenin and Stalin as holding a key position, the manner in which Spain was used will be studied next.

NOTES:

1   The marriage of Svetlana Stalin to Mihail Kaganovich was reported in the Associated Press, July 15th, 1951.

2   Note: 'Stalin', by Trotsky, page 337 (ibid page 48).

3   This is explained in Chapters 1 and 2 of "The Red Fog".

4   This phase of history is dealt with more extensively elsewhere.

 # Chapter Twelve

The Spanish Revolution

The Long Range Plan for the ultimate subjugation of Spain started, as in other countries, soon after the death of Christ. In an attempt to crush the power of the Christian Church in Spain, the money-lenders their agents to infiltrate into the congregations and pose as Christians. [1] This placed them in positions to destroy the church organizations from within. This conspiracy became obvious, and in the 13th century Pope Innocence III instituted the Inquisition. The purpose of the Inquisition was to ferret out and question infidels suspected of masquerading as Christians. Spain had been exceptionally kind to the Jews. They were allowed to hold office and acted as tax-collectors. But, as happened in every other country in Europe, the crimes of the atheistic money-lenders, and their agents, were charged against the whole Jewish population. Between 1475 and 1504 during the reign of Isabella and Ferdinand, the Inquisition was used extensively to locate and destroy all traitors who plotted to overthrow the power of the Church and State. The Inquisitors under Torquemada discovered the subversive underground to be so widespread and well-organized that in 1492 Spain followed the example of other European countries and expelled all the Jews. This task provided the opportunity for some extremists to organize mob violence against the Jews and several extensive and regrettable massacres took place. These illegal killings were condemned publicly by the Church authorities in Rome.

After the international bankers re-organized during the 1600s, their agents infiltrated into the Spanish Treasury Department. They were exceptionally active during both the English and the French revolutions, trying to destroy the Spanish economy in order to prepare the way for revolutionary efforts in that country also.

It is worthwhile to study the political intrigue that went on in Spain from 1839 to 1939 because it gives a clear picture of the pattern of the ultimate subjugation of all countries. There are three steps in all revolutionary efforts.

First: Infiltration by the agents of the revolutionary party into the government, civil services, armed forces, and labor organizations in order to be in position to destroy the government from within when the order to revolt is given.

Second: The affiliation of the revolutionary party with the socialist or liberal party left of center in order to overthrow the established government regardless of whether it is a monarchy or a republic.

Third: Subversive activities to bring about anarchy in order to discredit the Popular Front Government and provide the excuse for forming a proletarian dictatorship. Once this is established purges turn it into a totalitarian dictatorship as it happened in Russia in 1917.

Karl Marx's agents organized Spain's first General Political Strike in 1865. In 1868 the Directors of the World Revolutionary Movement (W.R.M.) sent Senor Fanelli to Spain to affiliate the Anarchists with the Marxist revolutionaries. Fanelli was a close friend of Bakhunin who was a close associate of Marx and Engels. In 1870 Bakhunin fell out with Marx over Policy. He was expelled from the First International of the W.R.M. [2]

In 1872 Bakhunin influenced the Spanish revolutionary leaders into forming the Socialist- Democratic Alliance. [3] The Spanish government decreed Bakhunin's extremist organizations illegal, but they continued to exist underground. The Grand Orient Lodges formed convenient headquarters. At a congress held in Zargoza the Spanish section of the Marxist International agreed to ally themselves with the Anarchist International. After its affiliation, both groups concentrated in organizing the various Labor Groups into a vast 'Carnorra.' They crowned their combined efforts with a revolution which produced the first Spanish Republic in 1873.

The effort on the part of the revolutionary leaders was accompanied with the usual Reign of Terror. Anarchy ran wild. All kinds of excesses took place. Finally, General Pavia brought off a 'Coup d'Etat' and the revolutionaries went underground again.

In order to emerge into the open once more, the members of the revolutionary underground supported the leaders of a mild 'liberal' movement to obtain political power. The revolutionary leaders used the quarrel going on between those who claimed the descendants of Don Carlos should occupy the throne, and those who claimed the descendants of Isabella should reign, to start a Civil War. This war ended with the defeat of the Carlist Group in 1876. [4]

The Spanish workers really desired to organize for their own protection, but the majority did not agree with the extreme policy advocated by the Anarchists. The anti-revolutionaries therefore organized the "Workers Association." These moderates were immediately set upon by both revolutionaries and employers of labor alike. [5] This persecution continued until 1888 when, at the suggestion of Pablo Iglesias, the moderate group adopted the name "The Workers General Union" which became known in Spain as the U.G.T. The members of this organization did not get much support until after the government outlawed the Iberian Anarchist Federation.

The syndicalist elements collaborated with the radical republican party until 1908. They then formed the 'Solidaridad Obrera', and, two years later, in 1910, they rounded the Regional Federation of Labor known in Spain as the C.R.T. Immediately afterwards they formed the National Federation of Labor (C.N.T.).

In 1913 both the C.R.T. and the C.N.T. were suspended as the result of a series of strikes. The government did not object to the principles of collective bargaining, but it did object to the extremist policy, and revolutionary actions, of the leaders. So legitimate labor, striving for social justice, found their organizations barred because the radical element always seemed able to work its way into executive positions within the Unions.

The reaction was what the plotters of world revolution expected it would be. Their revolutionary syndicalist movement greatly increased in power and acted against all political parties, and against the State itself. The policy of these extremists was "direct action," advocated with the greatest heat and violence. In 1916 the C.R.T. was reorganized by Angel Pestana and Salvador Segui. In 1918 these two labor leaders were able to form in Barcelona the 'Sole Syndicate' generally known as 'The One Big Syndicate.'

During World War I Spain, as a neutral country, made a vast amount of money but, generally speaking, the laboring classes did not receive anything like a fair share of the national prosperity. This fact was perhaps the deciding factor which drove the majority of the working classes out of moderate labor organizations into the arms of the revolutionary leaders in the extremist labor groups. However, the more moderate and level-headed labor leaders didn't give up the fight against the radical groups and as a result of their efforts, they brought into being a new labor group known as "The Free Syndicate" in 1920. During the next three years there was continuous strife going on between the Right and Left labor organizations. Local strikes, general strikes, destruction of property, private assassinations to remove labor leaders, wholesale murders to reduce the strength of opposing organizations. All these crimes were committed in the name of liberty. By 1923 conditions became chaotic. To prevent the Communist Party bringing about another revolution the king of Spain asked General Franco to become military dictator.

One of the first results of Primo de Rivera's dictatorship was the successful termination of the Moroccan War. It was during the final stages of this war that General Franco greatly distinguished himself in the field. He turned what looked like a complete military defeat into a brilliant victory. By tempering

justice with mercy he won the admiration, and the loyalty, of many of the Moroccan natives. It was thus he came to the notice of the general public in Spain, Rivera is accused by General his enemies of doing everything a man shouldn't do. It is only fair to record that he did restore law and order; he brought about a number of social reforms; he cooperated with Largo Caballero to improve working conditions. He worked so hard that only his breakdown in health in 1929 can explain the errors in judgment he made during 1930.

Tired and worn out, and as if in a hurry to unburden himself of the responsibilities of office, he called in two socialist leaders, Besteiro and Saborit. He charged them with the task of re- organizing the electoral machinery of the nation so the people could decide whether they wanted a monarchy or a republican government. Just why De Rivera appointed Besteiro and Saborit to re-organize the electoral machine of Spain will probably never be known.

The two socialists rigged the election machinery so well a socialist-Republican Government was assured. In Madrid alone the number of fictitious voters exceeded 40,000. [6] Similar corruption existed in all the larger centers of population.

To ensure the end of the monarchy in Spain The Grand Orient Lodges organized a special "Military Brotherly Union" by which they obtained the promise of twenty-one of the twenty- three Spanish generals to support the Republican Cause. General Mola, who was Chief of the Spanish Internal Security, in his book, Tempestad Calma Intriga Y Crisis informs us that the generals were initiated into the Grand Orient and had one and a half million pesetas placed to their credit, to help them escape aboard should the republican movement fail. Franco was one of the two generals who refused to join the "Military Brotherly Union." In support of Mola's statement, Cano Lopez said on the floor of the Spanish Cortes (parliament): "Since 1925 masonry has grouped under the heading 'Military Brotherly Union' most of the high ranking officials of the army. The members include Cabanellas, Sanjurjo, Goded, Mola, Lopez, Ochoa, Queipo de Llana, and others... Of twenty-three divisional generals, twenty-one were masons... All had taken the oath of the Grand Orient." (I swear obedience without limitation to the Head of the Council of Thirty-Three... I swear to acknowledge no mortal as above him.) Lopez added: "Both in 1929, for the abolition of the dictatorship of de Rivera, and in 1931 for the abolition of the monarchy, the Grand Orient issued the orders most of the other generals obeyed." [7]

General Mola tells how he, and most of the other generals, broke their oath to the Grand Orient when they became convinced that they were being used to further the secret plans of Stalin to turn Spain into another Communist dictatorship. [8]

The international bankers helped finance the revolutionary effort in Spain without becoming involved themselves. In February 1932 Le Journal reports that Stalin promised $200,000 to help finance the Revolutionary Training Schools in Spain.

The financial statements submitted to the 1931 congress of the Communist international discloses the fact that £240,000 (English money) had been received to help the Spanish Revolutionaries. [9]

In addition to the above, two and a half million pesetas were made available for the purchase of arms and ammunition.

General Mola says that by 1938 over two hundred revolutionary leaders had arrived in Spain after being trained in the Lenin Institute in Moscow.

From 1930 to the date of the election a campaign of L'Infamie was carried on against the king of Spain and the royal family exactly as it was against Louis XVI and Marie Antoinette. One of the most ridiculous lies ever invented claimed that one Spanish soldier was bled to death every day to keep the Prince of Asturias alive. He was known to be suffering from hemophilia. Other slanders accused the king of being a libertine, just as the Empress of Russia had falsely been accused of being mistress to Rasputin.

The plugged ballots in the large industrial centers wiped out the strong rural vote in favor of the monarchy. After the election had been declared to favor a republican form of government, King Alfonso XIII of Spain issued his last public proclamation. It read as follows:

> "The elections held on Sunday proved to me that I no longer hold the love and affection of my people. My conscience tells me this condition will not be permanent because I have always striven to serve Spain, and my people, with all my devotion. A king may make mistakes. Without doubt I have done so on occasion, but I know our country has always shown herself generous towards the faults of others committed without malice.
>
> I am the king of all Spaniards, and I am a Spaniard. I could find ample means to maintain my royal prerogatives in effective resistance to those who assail them, but I prefer to stand resolutely aside rather than to provoke a conflict which might array my countrymen against one another in Civil War and patricidal strife.
>
> I renounce no single one of my rights which, rather than being mine, are an accumulated legacy of history for the guardianship of which I shall one day have to render strict account. I shall wait the true and full expression of the collective conscience and, until the nation speaks, I deliberately suspend the exercise of my royal powers and am leaving Spain, thus acknowledging that she is sole mistress of her destinies. Also now I believe that I am fulfilling the duty which the love of my country dictates. I pray God that all other Spaniards may feel and fulfill their duty as sincerely as I do." [10]

Many of the Socialists who formed the Spanish republican government in 1931 were sincere in their beliefs. They wanted no part of "Red" Communism or "Black" Nazism. But they were proved to be powerless to prevent the Communists and Anarchists from putting the second part of their revolutionary program into effect.

The tactics the revolutionary leaders employed were to double-cross the Socialists at every opportunity. Red Cells within the government caused the government to commit some foolish mistakes. The Reds outside then damned the government as a lot of incompetent, corrupt, and inefficient nincompoops. The Communists, and Anarchists, claimed only a dictatorship of the proletariat could establish a stable government. The agents of Moscow committed every conceivable kind of crime to bring those responsible for internal security into disrepute also.

General De Rivera had used Largo Caballero a great deal to iron out differences between labor and employers during the years he had been dictator. With the advent of the republican movement Largo Caballero showed his true colors. By 1935 Caballero openly boasted that he had placed "Tens of thousands of Communist Cells throughout Spain."

At the Eleventh Plenum of the Executive of the Communist International, the Spanish delegates were showered with congratulations because "The prerequisites of a revolutionary crisis are being created at a rapid rate in Spain." [11]

At the Twelfth Plenum the wording of the congratulations to the Spanish delegates was as follows: "In Spain, in particular, we have been able to observe such revolutionary strike struggles going on uninterruptedly over period of many months as the Spanish proletariat has never experienced before. What is happening in these struggles is, above all, the further development of a Spanish Revolution."

There is an old saying "When thieves disagree the truth will come out." That is exactly what happened in Spain. The three leaders of Moscow's underground in Spain were Joaquin Maurin, Victor Serges, and Andres Ninn. They were all young men. They had all received special training in revolutionary activities in the Lenin Institute in Moscow before being entrusted with the leadership in Spain. Maurin had been mixed up in the Separatist movement in Catalonia since he was sixteen years of age. At the mature age of seventeen this intellectual thinker had set out to teach the Spanish people the Soviet solution of the world's economic troubles. At the age of twenty-one he was elected head of the Anarchists. He preached and practiced the religion of hate and violence. In 1914 he was condemned to twenty years' imprisonment but he was not of legal age for such a penalty. Maurin was a delegate to the Third Congress of the Communist International held in Moscow, 1921. He attracted favorable attention.

With the fall of Primo De Rivera, Maurin returned to Spain. He had been hiding out in France and Moscow. He had lived a hectic life. He had been in and out of jail; had escaped from prison; been wounded in 1925; confined in Citadel Montjuich, etc., etc. It is said the only period of peace he enjoyed in his life was the three years he and his young wife spent in Paris, 1927-30.

Maurin wrote a book in 1936. Victor Serges wrote the preface to it. In this book *Hacia la Segunda Revolucion* he exposed the fact that Stalin had departed from the Marxian ideology and charged he was using the forces of Communism to forward his own secret totalitarian imperialistic ambitions. [12]

Even after Maurin, Serges, and Ninn broke openly with Stalin in 1936, their power and influence amongst the working classes was so great that Stalin ordered that they should be allowed to live until they had served their purpose. Stalin used them right up to the beginning of the Civil War in Spain. Then he ordered them liquidated. He directed that "Their deaths shall be accomplished in such a manner as to make it appear to the public that all three had died as martyrs to the Communist Cause." Maurin was betrayed to Fraco's forces and after trial was executed. Serges is reported to have been shot by Loyalists while fighting, and Ninn was also disposed of. Their deaths were loudly attributed to acts of violence by the enemies of communism.

Victor Serges wrote "The evolution of Soviet Communism was completed in 1936...from revolutionary internationalism to a nationalism of great military power served, in various countries, by parties which it subsidized. After July 1936 the Stalinites formed the unified Socialist Party affiliated with the Third International... and the object of Stalinism is to establish the new power of a Fascist nature to encircle France, the probable ally of Russia, IN THE WAR THAT IS being prepared."

Then again Maurin says: "The traditional policy of England is to ruin its adversaries, so as then to pose as the Protector and to render impossible the renaissance of the conquered vassal. Spain is primarily the victim of England and, next in order, of France. When Spain hesitates, England and France attack her strongly. If she inclines towards England, France increases the persecution. So long as France and England are capitalistic countries they will not have to be the natural ally to Spain. [13] The Logical line would be the curve through Portugal, Germany, Italy and Russia. A bloc of this nature would neutralize France and England."[14]

Serges explained how so much Loyalist propaganda found its way into the universal press, while so little space was given to Franco's releases. Serges wrote: "Never has there been brought into play, the one against the other, such low and demoralizing methods as those used by Stalin and his instrument, the Third International, in a continuous stream of propaganda at long range and without heed for the truth. The method of repetition and cynicism have become almost mechanical ... The Soviet bureaucracy is plotting this procedure on an international scale. Every infamy given out by a correspondent of Izvestia at Valentia is at once taken up in a chorus by the special papers in Paris, Stockholm, Oslo, Brussels, London, New York, Melbourne and Buenos Aires... Millions of copies of infamous lies are circulated, they are the only information millions of Soviet workers receive. English, American, Chinese, and New Zealand papers reproduce these lies (by order). Advanced intellectuals, who think they are anti- Fascist, will appear to believe them. One sees that a formidable enterprise of demoralization is functioning in the universe, and I find pitilessly just, the words of Trotsky, that the Stalinite Comintern propaganda is a Syphilis of the Workers Movement." [15]

What Maurin and Serges wrote in 1336 only confirms what Pope Pius XI said in his encyclical "Divini Redemptoris" issued in March 1937. One chapter of this famous document reads:

"There is another explanation for the rapid diffusion of Communistic ideas....A propaganda truly diabolical that the world has perhaps never witnessed its like before. It is directed from one common center; it is shrewdly adapted to the various conditions of diverse peoples; it has at its disposal vast financial resources, innumerable organizations, international congresses; and countless trained workers; it makes use of newspapers, and pamphlets, cinema, theatre, radio, and schools and even universities. Little by little it penetrates into the minds of all classes of the people. Another powerful factor is the suppression and silence on the part of a large section ... of the press of the world ... we say suppression because it is impossible otherwise to explain how a press, usually so eager to exploit even the little daily incidents of life, has been able to remain silent for so long about the horrors perpetrated in Russia, in Mexico, and even in a great part of Spain; and that it should have so little to say concerning a world organization as vast as Russian Communism. The silence is due in part to short-sighted political policy and is favored by various occult forces which for a long time have been working for the overthrow of the Christian social order.

The sorry effects of this propaganda are before our eyes. Communism has striven, as its champions openly boast, to destroy Christian civilization and the Christian religion by banishing every remembrance of them from the hearts of men, especially of the young... In Spain, as far as possible, every church and monastery was destroyed and every vestige of the Christian religion eradicated. The theory has not confined itself to the indiscriminate slaughter of bishops, and thousands of priests and religious of both sexes; it searches out above all those who have been devoting their lives to the working classes and the poor. The majority of victims have been laymen of all conditions and classes ... with a hatred and a savage barbarity one would not have believed possible in our age. No man of good sense, nor statesman conscious of his responsibility, can fail to shudder at the thought that what is happening to-day in Spain may be repeated to-morrow in other civilized countries. For man some restraint is necessary, as an individual or in society... But tear the idea of God from the hearts of men, and they are urged by their passions to commit the most atrocious barbarities."

We will proceed to review the conditions in Spain to which Pope Pius XI tried to draw the attention of the Christian world early in 1937, and failed.

NOTES:

1   This refers to the advice sent by the Sanhedrin in Constantinople to Chemor, Rabbi of Arles in Provence in 1489 mentioned previously.

2   For further particulars see Bakhunin by Professor E.H. Carr.

3   For details regarding this period of Spanish History read La Quiebra Fraudulenta de la Republica by C. Domi.

4   This is a typical example of how any situation is used to divide the citizens of a nation and get them fighting each other on the principle that all wars pave the way for revolution.

5   This is a typical example of how the agents of the International Bankers

are placed in private and responsible enterprise for the purpose of helping their revolutionary leaders to oust moderate leaders they cannot buy or otherwise control.

6 See The Spanish Arena, p. 56.

7 See Jean Dauraya L'Oeuvre Latine January, 1937.

8 What General Mola said was confirmed by a broadcast over the radio from Moscow on March 13, 1938. The announcer was explaining why the Civil War wasn't going in favor of the Communists (Loyalists). He said: "The great work in Spain was seriously compromised by the wicked generals breaking their plighted word to the Grand Orient."

9 Evidence is given elsewhere to prove the revolutionary leaders were supplying counterfeit English Bank Notes to finance revolutionary efforts in other countries also.

10 This document proves that the International Press lied to their readers when it reported The King of Spain had abdicated. The King of Spain never abdicated. Franco holds control of Government because the International conspirators are still determined to turn Spain into a Totalitarian Dictatorship to serve their ends).

11 See English edition of report of Eleventh Plenum, p. 11, and Twelfth Plenum, p. 37.

12 Even Maurin and Serges failed to suspect that Lenin and Stalin were only carrying out the orders of the international bankers, who in turn obey the Illuminati.

13 Here again is a typical example of how well the International Bankers kept their secret. Maurin blamed the Governments of England and France for the international crimes perpetrated against humanity by the Bankers, under the direction of the Illuminati.

14 This confirms what has been previously stated, that once the Sphere of Influence was established between the 35th and 45th parallel, the countries within the circle would be subjugated.

15 Victor Serges in Maurin's Revolution et Contre-Revolution en Espagne.

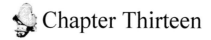 Chapter Thirteen

The Civil War in Spain

General Mola said: "Following the election of the Socialist government in Spain, and the king's withdrawal from the country, there was an absolute avalanche of public officials who rushed to the Grand Orient Lodges to request entry. They thought they could thus be free of the persecution which had been practiced by the majority of Masons in the government. Their purpose was to give evidence of their republicanism and to prevent the certainty of having their careers ruined."

Immediately after the king had left, Franco told the Military Academy, of which he was then in charge, "The republic has been proclaimed in Spain. It is the duty of all at the present time to cooperate with their discipline and allegiance so that peace may reign and the nation be permitted to direct itself through the natural judicial channels. Hitherto, at the Academy, there has always been discipline and exact fulfillment of duty. To-day these qualities are even more necessary; the Army needs, serenely, and with a united spirit, to sacrifice every thought of ideology to the good of the nation and the tranquility of the fatherland." The wording of this proclamation shows Franco to be anything but a "Black" Nazi which Communist propaganda would have the public believe him to be.

But the Secret Powers were not willing to give the republican government a chance to operate in an efficient and democratic way. Churchill wrote: "The Communists helped set it up so they could knock it down again and create more political and economic chaos, until they had the country, and the people, in such a state that the leaders could advocate with reason, that only a proletarian dictatorship could restore law and order and save the day."

Having overthrown the monarchy in Spain, the next logical move was to attack the religion of the people. Secularism was introduced into the schools. A campaign was launched to destroy parental authority and that of the Church. Having created thousands of anti-religious, and anti- social young Bolsheviks, it was only necessary to await the opportunity to turn the masses loose against the forces of law and order in a well-planned revolt.

On May 14th, 1931, a meeting was held in the Ateneo Club, in Madrid, to discuss the new political program.

Its eight points were:

1. Creation of a republican dictatorship.

2. Immediate punishment of all responsible for illegal acts under the dictatorship.

3. Disbanding the Civil Guard, the Army, and the police, etc., and the

substitution of armed republicans chosen from the laboring classes and Republican Clubs.

4. Confiscation of property of religious orders.

5. Nationalization of land.

6. Suppression of all press agencies hostile to the Republican cause.

7. Utilization of technical schools and other buildings for the public good.

8. Postponement of the Cortes until this program had been carried out.

Azana, an intellectual Liberal; Prieto — a socialist; and Caballero, a Communist, were three of the most prominent political leaders at this time. Azana, with his tongue in his cheek, publicly opposed such radical suggestions, although he secretly approved. When elected to power he put the program into effect.

In due course the 'Cortes Constituyentes' was elected. Under the excuse of "Law for the defense of the Republic", a ruthless dictatorship was set up — the only democratic feature about it was its name "the Republic of the Workers". A Moscow trained revolutionary, Jiminez Asua drafted the new Constitution. [1] Azana now concentrated his entire efforts on destruction of the churches and persecution of religious orders. In December 1932, he set up the "League of Atheism". He financed its periodical 'Sin Dios' (The Godless), out of public funds. All these moves were made in the name of democracy. The leaders told the people they were being liberated from the control of the religious orders, and the clergy who, they said, were allied to feudalism and tyrannical monarchs.

In Catalonia the revolutionary activities which General Prime, de Rivera had subdued broke out again. By January 1933, the London Morning Post correspondent reported "Huge stocks of bombs, rifles, and ammunition are being found by the police all over Spain. An enormous amount of money is being spent to foster the revolutionary cause. Many of those arrested, though to all appearances not well paid, carried note-cases full of bank-notes." [2]

Next an uprising in Astoria was organized, and on September 14th, 1934 a report was issued which implicated war officials and army officers in the sale of Arms.

General Franco made a desperate effort to try to re-organize the Spanish Army and put an end to Anarchy, but he obtained little support from government authorities. To indicate how well the Communist underground was organized, over three hundred churches were set afire at exactly the same time in a hundred different cities and towns. The assassination of individuals the revolutionaries wanted removed became so common that 'Professional Pistoleros' became competitive. It was possible to have an enemy liquidated for 50 pesetas (a little more than $5.00 American). The Moscow agents used the confused conditions existing in Spain to carry out Lenin's mandate: "The Communist legal Code is to base terrorism on fundamental principles." [3]

Torture, mutilation, rape, burnings, bloodshed, and death, were the methods by which Communism tried to obtain power. Conditions deteriorated from bad to worse. By the beginning of 1936 the whole country was in a state of turmoil. President Alcala Zamora dissolved the Cortes. February 16th was set as the date for a general election. Gil Robles, and Calvo Sotelo, stamped the country on a straight anticommunist ticket. Bolshevik election propaganda was issued by 'The Friends of Russia'.

Largo Caballero was in prison at this time for the part he had played in a revolutionary uprising. He was interviewed by Mr. Edward Knoblaugh who afterwards wrote "Correspondent in Spain".

Caballero said: "We will win at least 265 seats. The whole existing orders will be overturned. Azana will play Kerensky to my Lenin. Within five years the republic will be so organized that it will be easy for my party to use it as a stepping stone to our objective. A union of the Iberian Republics ... that is our aim. The Iberian Peninsula will again be one country. Portugal will come in peaceably we hope, but by force if necessary. YOU SEE BEHIND THESE BARS THE FUTURE RULER OF SPAIN. Lenin declared Spain would be the second Soviet Republic in Europe. Lenin's prophecy will come true. I shall be the second Lenin who shall make it come true."

After the most completely dishonest election Spain ever endured, President Zamora wrote: "The Popular Front was hoisted into power on the 16th of February, thanks to an electoral system as absurd as it is unfair, which gives an extraordinary advantage to a relative majority though absolutely it may be a minority. Thus in a certain constituency the Popular Front with 30,000 votes less than the opposition was nevertheless able to win ten seats out of thirteen, though in no part of the constituency did the number of votes exceed those of its major adversary by more than 2 per cent. Paradoxical cases of this kind were fairly common."

In spite of the illegal means employed, first count only gave the Popular Front 200 seats out of a possible 465. Thus it became the largest minority group in the parliament, but did not have enough seats to form a government. The next move was for the Popular Front members to join forces with the Basque, and other minority groups. They elected a Committee to verify the election returns in each constituency. They made sure the final returns were favorable to the Popular Front Party. In several cases Rightist candidates were disqualified and Popular Front candidates were elected as deputies in their place. When the "fixing" was all over the Popular Front had the 265 seats Caballero predicted they would have... But even after all this had happened, the final breakdown of the votes showed: —

For 'Centre' and 'Right' parties	4,910,000
For the 'Popular Front'	4,356,000
'Right Centre' majority:	554,000

It must be understood that Popular Front candidates elected to the Spanish Cortes represented every kind of individual from the very mild socialist to the dyed-in-the-wool Bolshevik.

The Stalinites created so much chaos that hellish conditions broke out all over Spain. Previous to the February elections in 1936 the governmental record in Spain was as follows:

From the end of the Prime de Rivera dictatorship in 1931 there had been one revolution with 2,500 persons killed, seven revolts, 9,000 strikes, five prorogations of the budget, two billion pesetas increase in charges, 1,000 municipalities suspended, 114 newspapers forbidden, two and a half years of "States of Exception" (equivalent to our state of martial law). After six weeks of popular front government under Azana, Caballero, and Prieto the record read: —

Assaults and robberies: At Political headquarters, 58; at public and private establishments, 105; at churches, 36. Fires: At political headquarters, 12; Public and private establishments, 60; Churches, 106. Disturbances: General strikes, 11; Risings and revolts, 169; Persons killed, 76; Wounded, 346.

Caballero, speaking at Zaragoza, said: "Spain must be destroyed in order to remake it ours. On the day of vengeance we will leave not a stone upon a stone."

Caballero also declared: "Before the elections we ask for what we want. After the elections we will take what we want by any means. 'The Right' must not expect mercy from the workers. We shall not again spare the lives of our enemies."

Azana declared happily, "Spain has ceased to be Catholic".

Communist leader, Marguerita Nelken, announced "We demand a revolution. But even the Russian kind will not serve us. We need flames that will be seen throughout the planet, and waves of blood that will redden the seas."

The Times correspondent reported conditions in Barcelona. In February 1936, he said: "A vigilance committee warned a number of high officials on February 20th to relinquish their posts. The committee was obeyed." A month later he wrote: "The Dictatorship of the Proletariat is now the open aim of all the Reds." A little later he wrote: "Spanish Socialism had been drifting towards Communism. It is among the younger generation that Marx and Lenin have gained most of their disciples. These young people believe that the conquest of power is the immediate requirement of Spanish Socialism; violence the ultimate means of getting it; and a dictatorship of the proletariat the only way to retain it. The subversive doctrine is preached untiringly." In March 1936 he reported: "Deputies in the Cortes (Spanish Parliament) with clenched fists, in Communist salute, sang the Soviet national anthem, L'Internationale, in the House itself."

Why did the youth of Spain turn in great numbers to Communism? If the technique used by those who direct the W.R.M. is to be understood the answer must be found, because it is from the laboring classes, and the youth of the nation, that the revolutionary leaders draw their shock troops.

Investigation reveals that Azana represented himself as an intellectual with a sincere belief in Socialism. He was openly anti-religious. He protested, however, that he was not in agreement with the terrorism advocated and carried out by the Anarchists and the Communists. Once he obtained the necessary political power, however, he used it to have the republican government abolish religious teaching orders from the schools. He engaged Francisco Ferrer to establish secularism in the schools. Instead of opening the school day with a prayer to Almighty God, the new secular teachers opened the classes by having the pupils sing:

"We are the sons of the revolution
We are the sons of liberty.
With us comes the dawning
Of a new humanity."

A translation of another 'Hymn' sung at the beginning and end of class periods in Barcelona schools is as follows:

"Sling the bomb; place well the mine; grasp firm the pistol,

Pass on the word of revolution ... Help for the Anarchists.

Stand to arms till death; with petrol and dynamite destroy the government."

The news editors of British and American papers refused to publish the truth because it sounded so fantastic. Very similar 'Hymns' were broadcast in English from Moscow for the instruction of English Communists during 1937-38.

The most damning evidence, proving the systematic method used to subvert, and pervert, youth into becoming revolutionaries, was supplied by Francisco Ferrer himself. In a letter to a revolutionary comrade he wrote:

"In order not to scare people and give the government (republican) a pretext for closing down my establishments I call them 'Modern Schools', and not schools for Anarchists. My wish is to bring about the revolution. For the time being, however, one must be content to implant the idea of violent upheaval in the minds of the young. They must learn that against the police, and the clergy, there is only one means of action... bombs and poison." [4]

When Ferrer was captured by Franco's forces during the Civil War he was tried as a traitor to Spain. The above letter was used as evidence. He was found guilty and executed. The High Council of the Grand Orient of Paris protested to Masonic Lodges all over the world claiming that Ferrer had been murdered because of his Anti-Catholic activities.

Investigation into the youth training program revealed the methods used to corrupt the morals of the youth of a nation also. Lenin had said: "The best

135

revolutionary is a youth devoid of morals." His word being law in Communist organizations, all members work secretly to make young people of both sexes anti-social and immoral.

Children up to teen-age are taught to rebel against the discipline of the home. Parents are represented to their children as old-fashioned. Parental authority is scoffed at. The subverters argue that parents have lied to their children since they were old enough to listen, regarding Santa Claus, and where babies come from. The subversives claim parents are the victims of reactionary teachings and capitalistic exploitation. The child is encouraged to educate the parents in regard to modern and progressive ideas. They are warned that, for their own good, they must refuse to be dominated or disciplined by their parents. The purpose of this subversive campaign is to destroy the sanctity, and unity, of the home which is the foundation upon which our civilization is founded.

To rob children of their respect for the ministers of religion the subversives first represent them as being chosen from the less intelligent or physically retarded members of families. They are ridiculed as spineless 'holy joes', 'womanish do-gooders', and servants of the ruling classes. Quoting from Marx, children are told: "Religion is the opium of the people, because it teaches acceptance of poverty, sickness, and hard work as good for the soul."

The Christian child is poisoned against the ministers of his religion by being told the most fantastic slanders against them in connection with their private lives. They are presented as 'sheep in wolves clothing'; as 'black crows' feeding upon the gullibility of their parishioners. If, as often happens, a minister or priest does become involved in a scandal it is played up for all it is worth.

The Christian religion is ridiculed in a most nauseating manner. Christ is represented as the illegitimate son of Mary, a young Jewess, who, in order to save her face, hoaxed Joseph into believing she had been conceived by the Holy Ghost. Christ as an adult is depicted as a faker. His miracles are said to be illusions cleverly performed as magicians perform them to-day. The twelve Apostles are said to have been his accomplices. The so-called comic "Mandrake The Magician" is often used to illustrate how a hypnotist and magician can fool the public.

One favorite story told Christian children is that Christ was a bootlegger at a very early age. Subversives claim he pretended to work a miracle at the marriage feast of Cana in order to sell his bootleg wine. They even accused Christ, and all Roman Catholics, of being cannibals. They support their arguments with the biblical quotation that Christ admonished his followers that unless they ate his flesh, and drank his blood, they could not have eternal life.

Teen-aged youths are introduced to companions who teach them liberalism which is soon turned to licentiousness. They are taught the Anarchist conception of life. The fewer laws, the better. Do as you like. According to subversive teachers, there is only one sin and that is disobedience to orders given by authorized leaders. There are only two crimes — neglect of duty and betrayal of party secrets.

The next step is to lead anti-social youth into actual conflict with the police. They start them off by linking them up with some 'gang'. Young Communist leaders egg the other members on. They dare them to do things outside the law. They force them into fights to prove their physical courage. They inveigle them into petty crime and then lead them deeper into the jungle of the Communist organized underworld. [5]

The publication of Crime and Sex Comics is part of the Communist psychological warfare. These Comics are calculated to awaken in children hidden and suppressed sadistic tendencies and to weaken the moral armor of children who are otherwise normal. Any 'professor' who claims Crime and Sex Comics do not influence children in the way the Illuminati wants them to go is either a fool or a knave.

Toy guns, soldiers, revolvers, movies, with plenty of crime and shooting, are all calculated to break down the finer feelings of normal Christian children and acclimatize them to the use of weapons, scenes of violence, and sudden death.

Pornographic books and magazines are circulated profusely at low prices, because such literature is calculated to destroy the thin veneer of virtue and respectability which civilized Christian moral codes have caused us to develop.

Few people realize the important part modern movies play in subverting youths away from their homes, their country, and their religion. Many movies show an hour of film in which the criminals and bad men and women do everything that is forbidden by our laws and moral code and devote one minute during which the law catches up with them, or they die because of their sins. Films taken of actual fighting during the Mexican revolution in 1913 were shown in Galveston, Texas. The sight of seeing men killed in battle, or being dragged from their homes and slaughtered by revolutionaries caused women to scream and faint, and men to vomit. Public opinion caused the showings, to be prohibited. To-day these scenes are shown on films advertised as "Children's Special" for Saturday afternoon performances. That is just one illustration of how the general public, and particularly the children, have been systematically hardened to accept the sight of violence and bloody death as normal. It supports the revolutionary motto that "Much needed reforms can only be brought about speedily by revolutionary action."

In every country not subjugated to date the directors of the World Revolutionary Movement have set up private Film Agencies which supply the most obscene pictures imaginable for presentation to private parties. These films illustrate every form of sexual depravity known to man. They are used for the purpose of demoralizing youth so they can be recruited into revolutionary organizations. This statement is proved by the fact that the laws barring them in the USSR are strictly enforced.

Youths who prove themselves to be anti-social, anti-religious, hardened, and brutalized, are sent to Moscow and taught "Revolutionary Warfare, and the Art of Street Fighting". This is a different course from that given prospective labor leaders and intellectuals.

Revolutionary psychological warfare is accomplishing its purpose in the Western World as it did in Spain. This is proved by the fact that no person loses any sleep nowadays when the last thing they hear before going to bed is a recital of the details of air disasters, automobile accidents, crimes, and brutal slayings. A night-cap of that kind would have been too strong to induce sleep fifty years ago.

Public opinion is no longer aroused to action when the newspapers blandly report that several thousand Jews were systematically exterminated in gas chambers by anti-Semitics, or that ten thousand Christians were martyred because of their anti-Communist convictions by Béla Kun or Chinese sadists. Such horrors are now accepted as everyday occurrences. We are being rendered immune to the reactions we once experienced when violence of any kind came to our attention. We no longer are disturbed by the overthrow of established governments by force. If we were, we would have done something to stop what has been going on. People listen to those who continually cry, as they did in Spain, "Communism can never cause a revolution here". They listen to those who give them a sense of false security. The majority of citizens are like children, who hide their heads under the blankets when they fear danger. It should be remembered that pulling the bedclothes over one's head never saved a person from an assassin, a rapist, or an exploding bomb.

A few illustrations will show how psychological warfare worked in Spain. We must remember always that Lenin said: "Part of the training of all revolutionary youths must consist of robbing a bank, blowing up a police station and the liquidating of a traitor or a spy." Not until a youth has been drained dry of the milk of human kindness, and all feelings of sympathy, is he considered qualified for party membership. This is a vastly different status from that of a 'Fellow Traveler'.

As the day chosen for the revolt drew near in Spain, the purveyors of pornographic literature and obscene pictures became so bold they took their stand at the entrances to churches and offered their wares to the congregations going in and coming out. The outside covers of these publications usually showed a picture of priests and nuns engaged in sexual high-jinks. Mr. Edward Knoblaugh, [6] who is recognized as an authority on the Civil War in Spain, was so struck by this anti-clerical campaign that he wrote: "Occasionally delegates of Protestant clergymen came to Loyalist Spain to investigate stories they had read of anticlerical activities. These delegations were warmly received. Great pains were taken to convince them they had been badly misled. Special guides were detailed to show them around. They saw only what the Communist authorities wanted them to see. After a day or two they were hustled home, suitably impressed."

But one day there was a slip up. A delegation of clergymen stopped at a book-stall to admire some rare old volumes. Before the guide could prevent it they saw also copies of "La Traca" and "Bicharracos Clericales". The covers portrayed priestly orgies with semi-naked nuns. Both magazines were profusely illustrated with obscene pictures. Mr. Knoblaugh commented: "The delegates left in a huff".

The situation in Spain between 1923 and 1936 was very similar to that which exists in Canada between the French and English speaking population to-day. The Basque people have their own language, culture, and traditions, which date back into antiquity. They are deeply religious and very proud. Like many French Canadians they believed they deserved National Independence. To achieve this objective they organized a separatist movement to liberate the Basque people from the rest of Spain. As was only natural, the plotters of the revolutionary movement in Spain didn't overlook such a situation. The Basque people were devout Roman Catholics. They believed they were justified in fighting for political independence if necessary. The vast majority however, would never have knowingly affiliated with the Communist Party to achieve their goal. Yet that is exactly what happened. Marxist 'Cells' infiltrated into Basque society. They hid their real identity so well, they became the leaders of the "Separatists". Then, like the Judas Goat, they led the Basques to slaughter. Operating under the banners of intense patriotism and religious fervor, the Basque leaders, President Aguirre, Gird, and Negrin, blended and beat into an unbelievable mass, Christ's cross, the pistol of Anarchism, and the sickle and hammer of Communism. Then, when the revolt started, the masses were abandoned to their fate. Aguirre was head of the Basque State and generalissimo of the Basque armies. He sat in his office in Bilbao, while hundreds of Catholic priests and other leaders of Basque society were systematically murdered. Their martyrdom naturally increased the hatred existing between the Basques and Spain.

F.J. Olondriz wrote the foreword to the book The Red Persecution in the Basque Country, written by José Echeandia. He said: "When the day arrived, the Basque separatists, blind with passion, many of them forgetting their faith, and their Catholic sentiments, felt closely and firmly united to the Communists, to the Atheists, and to the Anarchists ... and they launched into a war, and made themselves responsible for slaughter, and believed all means were licit, rebelliously ignoring the peremptory words of their religious leader, Pope Pius XI, as contained in his encyclical 'Divini Redemptoris' — Communism is intrinsically perverse, and it cannot be admitted that those who wish to serve the Christian civilization may in any way co-operate with it." How well some of our top-level statesmen should have remembered those words of wisdom when they tried to co-operate with Stalin during World War II. Another truth Government leaders must never forget is the fact that Communists, and all other international groups, are used by the Illuminati to further their own secret plans and ambitions.

NOTES:

1   Exactly as agents of the W.R.M. drafted the Federal Reserve Banking legislation in the U.S.A. 1910 and 1913 and the 'Palestine Mandate' in England in 1916.

2   Police seized 90,000 rifles; 33,000 revolvers; and 500,000 rounds of ammunition and a tremendous amount of counterfeit money.

3   See The Bolshevik, October issue, 1930.

4   It was to finance Ferrer's 'Training Schools' for youth that Moscow subscribed the $200,000 previously mentioned. In Toronto in 1954 there were seventeen such 'Training Schools'. There were several in Sudbury. All big cities of population have them.

5   The sex orgy that took place in the Ford Hotel in Toronto, October 23, 1954, after the Red Feather Football game, involved dozens of teen-agers of both sexes. It was a typical example of what Communist influence, secretly exerted, can have on the youth of any nation.

6   Mr. Knoblaugh was a 'Correspondent in Spain'. He published a book with that title.

Chapter Fourteen

Franco

To understand what happened in Spain in 1936, one must have at least a general idea of the type of man Franco really is. Franco entered the Spanish army seriously intending to make it his career. His life in the army reads like a romance. He distinguished himself after he was appointed to the Spanish Legion. He turned the defeat inflicted on General Sylvestre by the Moors, into final victory. Not only did he lead his troops fearlessly, but he inspired in them great confidence because of his genius regarding strategy. He also earned the respect of his foes, because of his military progress, and his sound administrative policies in Morocco. The Moors finally looked upon him as almost divine. They came to call him "The Victorious"; "Chief of Chiefs"; "Brave as a Lion". The above facts explain why they rallied around him when he asked for their loyalty in July 1936.

Franco is not spoken of as being popular with his brother generals. He did, however, have the respect of most of them. It was this fact that prevented the Popular Front Government being turned into a totalitarian dictatorship.

Azana, Caballero, and Carlos Prieto, dominated the Popular Front Government. Senor Gil Robles, and Calvo Sotelo, led the Rightist opposition.

When Sotelo revealed in the "Cortes" that between February and June 1936 there had been 113 general strikes, 218 partial strikes, 284 buildings, 171 churches, 69 clubs and 10 newspapers offices burned, and over 3,300 assassinations committed, Casares Quiroga, Premier at the time, jumped to his feet and angrily retorted "You will be held personally responsible for the emotion your speech will cause."

Dolores Ibarruri, a Communist, named "Pasionaria" because of her inflammatory speeches and fanatical actions, was a member of the Spanish Cortes. She jumped to her feet and, pointing her finger at Sotelo, literally screamed: "That man has made his last speech." She proved to be right. On July 13th, 1936, Senor Calvo Sotelo was dragged from his home by fifteen Assault Guards under command of Captain Don Angel Moreno. He was taken to a near-by churchyard and murdered. It was this event that caused many of the Spanish generals to break their oath to the Grand Orient and ask Franco to take over leadership in Spain. Dolores Ibarruri was a Stalinist agent in Spain. She had been entrusted with the task of corrupting army officials, organizing and directing raids on government armories, and arming the revolutionary forces in Spain. She performed her various tasks most efficiently.

Assault Guards raided the houses of many other prominent anti-communists following Sotelo's murder, but most of them had been warned and made their escape.

On the day of the elections in February 1936, General Franco telephoned General Pozas, who was then in charge of the Civil Guard. He warned him that the Communists elected to the Cortes planned to stir up mob violence in the hope that they could develop a revolutionary effort for the purpose of overthrowing the republican government. General Pozas informed General Franco that he thought his fears were exaggerated. General Franco next telephoned General Molero, the Minister for War. He informed him of the threatening danger. Franco suggested that he be allowed to declare Martial Law, Franco drew up the necessary orders which would give him the authority to prevent excesses and mob violence. Only the signatures of the Council of Ministers were necessary to enable him to preserve law and order, and protect the republican government from revolutionary action. But Portela, who was then acting as premier, pleaded that he was too old to put the Cabinet's decision into practice. Franco retorted "You have brought Spain to this sorry pass. It is your duty now to try and save her."

General Franco was given orders to proceed to the Canary Islands. The order actually meant his virtual exile from Spain.

Before he left, General Franco had a conference with Generals Mole, and Varela. They assured him, they felt certain, that once the other generals who had joined the Grand Orient Military Lodges, knew the truth, most of them would break with the Grand Orient and accept his leadership. Before the meeting broke up a secret means of communication between Mola and Franco had been arranged. Immediately Franco departed for the Canary Islands Stalin's agents renewed their activities.

On June 23rd, 1936, Franco wrote a long letter to the Minister for War in which he once again pointed out specific dangers. [1] But these warnings were ignored as the others had been. It was obvious that the Communist members of the republican government were able to dominate its policy and actions.

The murder of Calve Sotelo on July 13th decided Franco. He sent a coded message to the generals who were sworn to fight to save Spain from becoming a Russian satellite state. Amongst those Franco contacted were Mola, Goded, Fanjul, Sanjurjo, Saliquet, some officers of the Spanish Navy, and Queipo de Llano. After the message was sent Franco flew from the Canaries to Tetuan where he knew he could rely upon the loyalty of the Moroccan troops.

On July 21st, 1936 Franco issued his proclamation which defined the issue at stake in the least possible number of words. It read: "It is the duty of every man to enter this definite struggle between Russia and Spain." Thus started the civil war. Professor Unamuno explained the issue in even fewer words. He said: "It is a struggle of Christianity against barbarism." He should have said "Against Illuminism".

Other evidence was obtained to prove that Stalin's Comintern plotted to subjugate Spain to bring about a total war between Britain and her allies, on the one side, and Germany and her allies on the other. There is the report of the meeting of the Political Secretariat of the Comintern which took place January

25, 1938. The purpose of the meeting was to discuss ways and means to develop the revolutionary effort in Spain and North Africa. Attending the meeting were representatives of the Profintern, and the Foreign branches of the G.P.U. (The Secret Police). All of Moscow's most experienced revolutionary leaders were present; Iejov, head of the secret section of the Comintern; Georges Dimitrov of the Reichstag Fire infamy; head of the League of the Godless, and the Free Thinkers League; the then Secretary of the Communist International; Schick, Manuilsky, and Lozovsky of the Profintern; Popescu, Weintrauben, Gourovitch, Liemann, Turrini, Adami, and Valdez, who represented the Soviet of Foreign Affairs in the political bureau of the Comintern (These are the names of men who all took an active part in spreading the sphere of Communist influence around the world in later years). After the meeting opened Dimitrov gave a fiery speech. He denounced the lack of missionary vigor among the special military envoys who had been sent to Spain to help corrupt the Popular Front Government and direct the military operation of the Loyalist armies. Their action he said: "Has not had sufficient stimulus, and revolutionary elan, on the general European masses. The results obtained have not justified the heavy risks taken. THE PRINCIPAL STRUGGLE, WHICH IS TO BRING ABOUT AN ARMED CONFLICT BETWEEN TWO GROUPS OF CAPITALISTIC STATES, HAS NOT BEEN REACHED." Then he went on to advocate "The Soviet military commandant in Spain should pass under the control of the Comintern emissaries, like the ambassadors, who know how to impregnate him with the necessary revolutionary feeling." [2]

In the Civil War in Spain the propaganda issued at the time convinced the average person that a small group of generals in Spain had organized a revolt to overthrow the Republican Popular Front Government and establish a military dictatorship. The Popular Front Forces named themselves Loyalists. Franco Forces called themselves Nationalists. The Loyalists were comprised of all political factions Left of center. The Nationalists contained all political factions Right of Center.

The Communists were divided into two groups ... those who intended to turn the Proletarian Dictatorship into a Stalinist Totalitarian State, and those who wished to make the Spanish Soviet a unit in the International of Soviet Republics as advocated by the Marxism theory. The Nationalist Forces included men who had sponsored the Carlist movement which, ever since 1837, had had as its cause the restoration of the Spanish Throne to the descendants of Don Carlos. The Carlists were located in the Navarre province and they supported Franco's Nationalist Army simply because they didn't intend to tolerate Communism in Spain.

On the Right also were the Falangists, the extreme Rightists among whom there were undoubtedly quite a number of the German type of Nazi who believed in using Total War to subdue their Leftist enemies. With a situation of this kind it is understandable that those on the Right accused all those on the Left of being Communists, while all those on the Left accused all those Right of center of being Fascist.   Most horrible atrocities, including torture, mutilation, rape, and the execution of thousands of innocent victims, were committed by the Communists as part of the accepted pattern of the Reign of Terror.   A few extremists on the Franco side committed atrocities also.   All civil wars seem to turn a great number of men into inhuman brutes who descend below the level of brute beasts once the blood lust has been aroused in them.   Civil War cannot be justified.   Those who advocate revolutionary wars should be executed.   The evidence goes to show that the king of Spain in 1931, and General Franco in 1936, did everything in their power to avoid fighting a civil war.

Franco did not call upon the citizens of Spain to rally around him until he had exhausted every other means of preventing the Communist coup taking place on July 26th, 1936.   The professional Army in Spain had been reduced greatly in numbers.   It had been replaced by a National Police Force controlled by the Leftist government.   It is extraordinary that Franco's bid to defeat the Communist plot did not fail, because post-war investigations revealed that in 1936 the armed forces were riddled with traitors, both officers and men, who had been placed in key positions by the agents of Moscow working within the Popular Front Government in Spain.   On July 21st, 1936, the Moscow directed organization for taking over the government in Spain was complete.

Franco knew that in one day Julio Alvarez del Vayo, who was Foreign Minister in the republican government, and Commissar-General, appointed hundreds of political commissars to the republican army.   The majority of these men were Communists.   Vayo did this without consulting the Premier.   The commissars compelled soldiers to join the Communist Party, offering them advantages, and promotion, if they did, and they threatened persecution by every means in their power if they did not.   Luis Araqistain, ex-ambassador of the Spanish Republic in Paris, published this fact in the New York Times May 19th, 1939.   It was proved to be true.

Indalecio Prieto was Spanish Socialist deputy, and minister of National Defense, during the Spanish Civil War.   He helped direct the war against Franco.   In a report published in Paris in 1939 entitled : "How and Why I left the Ministry of National Defense", he said : "It is difficult to be on guard because there are Communists occupying confidential positions who, so as to avoid suspicion, are ordered to hide their affiliation, and sometimes ordered to conceal it by joining other parties. Dr. Juan Negrin was one of these. He was one of the most powerful men in Spain during the Civil War." Prieto wrote of him: "Because I refused to obey orders from Moscow, Juan Negrin expelled me from the government over which he presided on April 5th, 1938.   I occupied the post of Minister of National Defense in his government. Two simultaneous actions were initiated against me; one was entrusted to the Russian secret police, and military men who operated in our country and the other to the Spanish Communists ... The Russians ordered and the Spanish Communists obeyed."

Dr. Juan Negrin claims he was, and is, not a Communist, but it was he who ordered that 7,000 boxes of Spanish gold be delivered to Stalin. The boxes were loaded in the ships "Kine", "Neve", and "Volgiles" — All three displayed the Soviet Flag. Jose Velasco, and Arturo Candela, accompanied the shipments as persons of trust to Odessa. Everything was done undercover and other members of the Popular Front government were not cognizant of the situation. During Negrin's term of office three Communists were appointed as under-secretaries of defense, and thus were the true masters of the republican army, navy, and air force. [3]

Largo Caballero was a Communist but, when he refused to obey the order given him by Moscow's emissaries they overruled his orders even when he was serving his presidential term. When he tried to rectify his own mistakes, he found it was too late. How Moscow's agents in foreign lands obtain such an absolute control of Leftist leaders is explained by Prieto. He wrote: "The majority of the military commands of the Popular Front government were finally occupied by Communists, and in their hands were the most important reins of power. How could that phenomenon happen? Through a system of coercion graduated between personal advancement for those who bowed their heads, and the murder of those who rebelled."

Theo Rogers in his "Spain; a Tragic Journey" makes reference to the capture of documents which proved beyond doubt that a full scale revolution had been planned to break out in July 1936. Rogers wrote: "Discovery amongst militant Communists, and Anarchists, of documents and plans, showed that a carefully schemed plot had been matured for an outbreak which would upset even the central government in Madrid and establish a Soviet Dictatorship." The Work of the Illuminati.

Roger's statement was proved to be true. Evidence was produced to prove that both General Franco, and General Mola, knew as early as April 1936 that a Communist coup was planned first for May 1st; then set back to June 29th; and then set back again to July 22nd. The delays were ordered to give those who were entrusted with putting the plan of revolt into effect, more time to complete the final necessary details.

The whole world should have known of the Moscow directed plot against Spain because the final orders were intercepted while being passed by the Comintern to the leaders of the revolutionary movement in Spain. The documents were given to the Echo de Paris, which published them in April 1936. The Echo de Paris article reads:

"TEXT OF INSTRUCTIONS FOR THE RED MILITIA"

"These instructions to the heads of the Spanish Red Militia ... do not emanate from a Spanish Central Organization, but from the Technical Services in Paris, which sent them to Spain at that date. These Technical Services are those of the French Communist party, working in close co- operation with the Comintern, and its delegates in France. The document, which we are publishing, is in the hands of the government; we were not the parties who communicated it to them. We are convinced that M. Daladier, Minister of War

145

and Defense, has given orders for preventive measures of defense, and protection, to be taken."

The abbreviated text is as follows:

1. Reinforce shock troops and guards in barracks, and supply them with automatic pistols. These shock troops and guards are members of the Communist party serving in the permanent forces and reserves.

2. These troops will be placed in communication with the Groups who are to break into the barracks. The latter will be in uniform, and under the orders of our officers in whom we have complete confidence.

3. When the fight starts our officers will be given admittance with their groups secretly. They will contact the respective committees and carry out the pre-arranged plan of attack inside the barracks.

4. The provisional committees, in the barracks, shall renew every two days, their lists of enemies, neutrals, sympathizers, and experts. When the barracks have been taken over, those classed as enemies, including in particular all commanders and officers, shall be rapidly eliminated, and without hesitation.

5. Each member of the committees shall be provided with a list of the names of individuals who are to be murdered by himself personally.

6. After the enemies have been disposed of, neutrals shall be subjected to severe teats in order to kill in them any hesitation habitual in such undecided characters.

7. The committees handling the neutrals will make the necessary arrangements for the vigilance groups outside to enter the barracks on the pretext of assisting to put down the rebellion.

8. This has little importance.

9. Those detailed to liquidate generals on the active list shall consist of ten men with revolvers. The generals have two adjutants, and a secretary, who must be murdered in their own homes. Those detailed to perform these killings shall not withdraw in face of any obstacle or opposition, and they shall eliminate anyone who opposes them regardless of sex or age.

10. Those detailed to eliminate generals not holding command shall consist of three men groups and shall carry out their duties as outlined in preceding paragraph.

11. and 12. Details how houses and sites, in strategic positions, must be procured by Communist militants, and secretly armed and fortified in order to ambush troops who may succeed in escaping from barracks. The instructions read : "As military officers have protected cars, groups of our militants must proceed to strategic points such as cross-roads, in cars and trucks; armed with machine guns so as to prevent help reaching those inside the cities. Lorries shall carry supplies of grenades."

13. Our militants shall quickly put on the uniform previously obtained and they shall be served with rifles.

14. When the rebellion breaks out our militant groups, wearing uniforms of the Civil Guards, and of the Assault Guard, and equipment already prepared for them, shall arrest all heads of all political parties under pretext of the necessity of doing so for their personal protection. Once in custody the procedure for the elimination of generals not holding command shall be carried out. Uniformed groups shall also arrest and detain important capitalists whose names appear in appendix "B" of Circular No. 32.

15. Violence shall not be used against these capitalists except if they resist; they shall however be forced to hand over the balance of the current accounts at the banks, and their securities. In the event of concealment they shall he completely eliminated, including their families, without exception. It is desirable that Cells shall be worked in on their staffs as domestics, or mechanics, as they can be very useful. [4]

16. Can be skipped.

17. With regard to members of the armed forces who claim to be sympathizers the same tactics shall be followed as was done in Russia. First use their services and then eliminate them as enemies. For our effort to be successful, and permanent, a neutral officer or man is better than one who has betrayed his uniform because his life was in danger. It is likely he would betray us also if provided with the opportunity.

18. Instructions to our militia regarding mobilization, movements of transportation, use of arms, and marksmanship, must be intensified. [5]

19. Militia posted at cross roads must eliminate all defeated troops trying to escape.

20. Machine gun posts shall be located in premises which cover the front and rear of all armories, police stations, and fire halls and all approaches to, and exits from, the cities, and if, in spite of this, the enemy is able to get out, they shall be attacked with hand-grenades.

21. Other militia shall be placed in armored lorries in strategical positions within the cities not more than one kilometer apart, they also shall be armed with machine guns.

22. Liaison shall be by light cars, and cyclists, who shall be armed with revolvers.

23. Is of no special importance.

24. The most intimate details concerning the lives and characters of all neutrals and sympathizers must be obtained and carefully recorded, including their family requirements, and the influence which love of their children, and desire for these necessary requirements, may exercise over them. If any of our militia, or any of the neutrals, and sympathizers, show any kind of

weakness, or resistance to orders, they must be denounced to the highest committee of the organization as being guilty of complicity and/or reaction.

25. Our militia must be organized to work away from their own homes and localities because experience has taught us that at the last moment, through sentimentalism, men working in their own localities, and amongst their families, and friends, have failed to carry out our plan with proper enthusiasm.

26. All owners of depots of goods and merchandise shall be regarded as important capitalists. These depots must be organized to serve the proletariat through the administrative groups. [6]

27. Deals with the question of using STARVATION as a means of reducing opposition quickly, and confirms what has been said regarding the use of this weapon in national disputes, and international warfare. It reads: "During the first week, and until the constitution becomes normal the supply of food and drink to the bourgeois is prohibited."

28. Reads – Stock of foods in barracks, and in the hands of our enemies, which cannot be captured, must be rendered useless by mixing paraffin or other substances with them.

Since these orders were issued the revolutionary leaders in all countries have been given special instruction to make careful plans to deal with the members of the police and fire-departments because experience has shown that the majority of these civic employees "remain loyal to their bourgeois bosses". The action recommended is to:

1. Infiltrate into the two forces.

2. Corrupt the rank and file.

3. Party members are urged to purchase or rent properties covering the approaches to both back and front of police stations, and fire halls, so the member, can be eliminated as they change shifts. The hour to revolt is to coincide with the time the police change shifts.

The orders which were given to the leaders of the Communist party in Spain detailed how they were to take over all public utilities and public services as well as civic administration. The objective was to obtain, in the shortest possible time, full and absolute control of all food supplies, and communication systems.

Revolutionary Orders seized at Majorca in October, 1936 were translated by Jacques Bardoux who afterward wrote "Chaos in Spain". They were on their way to revolutionary leaders in Spain.

148

With the object of being able to control the smallest details of the movement, from the 8th of May, only the link agents will be able to give orders and they will communicate with each other by means of the Cypher E.L.M. 54-22. The local leaders must give verbal instructions to the committee with the help of the following code:

1.2.1. Order to begin mobilization.

2.1.2. Order to begin the revolt.

2.2.1.1.1. Order to attack at pre-determined points.

3.3.3. Provide for counter-revolutionaries.

2.4.3. Mobilization of trade unions.

2.5.5. General strike.

2.6.5. Acts of sabotage, i.e. blowing up railway lines, etc.

1.3.2. Signal to put off the revolt.

1.1.0. Order to provision.

1.0.0. Reorganization is ready.

0.0. Close frontiers and ports.

1.1. Execution of those whose names are on the black list.

All these orders will be given on the day before the revolt, 1st May or 29th [7], at midnight, from the transmitter installed in the Casa del Pueblo at Madrid, the wave-length of which is nearly the same as that of the Madrid Union Radio.

Organization of Madrid:

To be divided into the following sections:

A.B. Chamartin de la Rosa, H.Q. at the Casa del Pueblo of this district.

C.D. Cuatro Caminos, H.Q. at Socialist Club of the district.

E.F. Palace District, H.Q. at the printing works of Mundo Obrero.

G.H. University District, H.Q. at editorial offices of El Socialista.

I.J. Latina District, H.Q. at Casa del Pueblo.

M.N. Inclusa District, H.Q. at Socialist center.

N.O. Pardinas District, H.Q. at Garage, at Castello 19.

P.Q. Southern District, H.Q. at Socialist Centre of Vallecas.

R.S. Carabanchel District, H.Q. at Socialist Club.

T.U.V. Centre of Madrid, H.Q. at Casa del Pueblo, Secretary's.

X.Y.Z. Offices Nos. 2, 3, 4, 6, 8, 10, 12 (balcony room).

Plan of Campaign in Madrid:

The revolt will be announced by five bombs let off at dusk. Immediately a Fascist attack on one of the C.N.T. (labor) centers will be faked; then a general strike will be declared and the soldiers and chiefs who support us will rise in revolt. The groups will come into action.

Those designated in T.U.V. will take over the Bureau of Communications, the Presidency, and the Ministry of War. Those belonging to the district will attack the Commissariats, and those belonging to the X.Y.Z. Section will take the Bureau of Public Safety.

A special group composed exclusively of machine-gunners with hand-grenades will go to the headquarters of the government and attack it by the following routes: Carretas, Montera, Mayor, Correos, Paz, Alcala, Arenal, Preciados, Carmen and San Jeronimo. The groups, composed of fifty cells of ten men each, will act in streets of the second and third order, and of two cells only in those of the first order and in the avenues.

The orders are for the immediate execution of all the counter-revolutionaries who have been detained.

The republicans of the Popular Front will be asked to support the movement, and in ease of refusal they will be expelled from Spain.

FRENCH DOCUMENT

Secret.

To the Leaders of Groups and Sections:

Cell of St. George du Bois, Look-out Station.

FIRST GROUP: H.Q. Town Hall. Leader of Group, A. President.

First Section: B.

4 volunteers

5 rifles, 1 revolver, 70 rounds of ammunition for rifle, 20 for revolver, 15 grenades.

Second Section: C.

6 volunteers

4 rifles, 3 revolvers, 70 rounds of ammunition for rifle, 20 for revolver.

Third Section: D. Leader, C.

4 volunteers for distributing arms and ammunition and for making ammunition. 6 revolvers, 15 cans petrol, 25 cans (5 liters each) reserve, issued to Comrade C.

SECOND GROUP: H.Q. Railway Station. Leader, D.E.P.

7 volunteers, 8 rifles, 80 rounds of ammunition, 20 sticks of dynamite issued to comrade E.

THIRD GROUP: At the Station. Leader, F.E.

5 volunteers (2 experts), 6 rifles, 1 revolver, 60 rounds of ammunition for rifle, 20 for revolver,

1,500 meters of insulated telephone wire issued to Comrade F.

FOURTH GROUP: (attacking party) H.Q. Basement of Town Hall, Leader G.

First Section: H.

4 volunteers, 4 rifles, 50 rounds of ammunition, 10 knives, 12 ropes.

Second Section: I.

4 volunteers, 4 rifles, 50 rounds of ammunition, 10 knives, 10 ropes. Special instructions.

SECOND GROUP: Blow up Railway and Fascist convoys.

THIRD GROUP: Link immediately Telephone Exchange P.O., Railway Station and Town Hall.

To ALL GROUPS: Save ammunition pending arrival of arms and ammunition from the cell at Rochefort.

First Group to commander all provisions, animals and fodder pending arrival of instructions from Rochefort for distribution. [8]

COMRADE PRESIDENT

Author's Comment

Recent history has proved that the instructions given by the Illuminati through Moscow for the subjugation of Spain have since been brought up to date, and carried out in all countries in Europe which have been subjugated since 1936. There is no reason to believe that the 5th Column in Canada, and the U.S.A., is less thoroughly organized. The 5th Column is ready to carry out the Illuminati's orders when those who direct the World Revolutionary movement consider the time opportune. There is ample evidence to prove that the members of the Communist party in Canada, and the U.S.A., have, since 1948, been practicing speedy evacuation from large cities and industrial areas so they could be in the country on picnics, and other reasonable excuses, during the initial stages of a Soviet bombing raid. They plan to return and take over while conditions are chaotic and the inhabitants are still in a state of panic.

While it is necessary to check Illuminism in Europe and Asia, it will be a tremendous, and costly, error if we fail to realize the full extent of the danger of their 5th Column. We must remove our internal danger or all our plans for civic emergency defense will be useless. We must deal with the enemy within first, then our defense plans, and other matters, will fit smoothly into gear unhampered by traitors and saboteurs. The fact to remember is that Communists are used to start the revolt. Those who lead the Communists then form a dictatorship of the Proletariat, which in turn is taken over by the agentur

151

of the Illuminati.

NOTES:

1 The details can be obtained by reading Arrara's Franco.

2 Reported in Gringoire issue February 11th, 1938.

3 The theft of this gold is still an international problem in 1955. Franco demands that the Soviets return the gold.

4 This order protected the bankers and capitalists who were working as agents of the Illuminati in exactly the same way in which similar order protected the Rothschilds in the French revolution.

5 In 1946 the author reported to the proper authorities that .303 rifles had been imported into Canada as scrap; in the same manner Canada's Cabinet Ministers permitted arms to be shipped to the Middle East as scrap in 1956.

6 This order also goes to show the Illuminati are the real leaders of a revolutionary effort. They are always in the top-levels of Governments, Society, Industry and the Armed Forces. The workers, the Mob, are simply the 'Pawns in the Game'. They are used and then subdued. Prove this to them and the Communist plot will fail.

7 It was after these orders had been issued that the date to revolt was changed to July 22nd.

8 The above information was made available to the 'Free Press of the World' by Free Lance writers and accredited correspondents as soon as it became available, but it was never published.

Chapter Fifteen

The Revolutionary Reign of Terror

Study of the methods employed by the Illuminati's agents in Spain, is of great value to those who would protect their country from the danger of similar tribulations. Revolutionary leaders have *Cells* occupy key positions in jails, prisons, and asylums. Their purpose is to control these institutions so they can release the anti-social elements under detention, and use them as shock troops during the revolt. *In every revolution to date the anti-social prisoners, and the criminally insane*, have been used to arouse the blood-lust in the mob and thus introduce the "Reign of Terror" which, the revolutionary leaders calculate, will cause the general public to surrender in the quickest possible time. [1]

The prison policy in Madrid was influenced greatly by the advice given the authorities in the Popular Front government by 'General' Kleber, the Canadian-Russian, who, after taking theoretical training in the Lenin Institute in Moscow, was sent to Spain to serve Stalin and obtain practical experience in revolutionary warfare.

As soon as the Popular Front government took office in March 1936, the extreme Leftist members insisted that an Amnesty Bill be passed, granting liberty to all those who had taken part in the Asturian rebellion. In addition to this small army of revolutionaries, 30,000 others, who had been arrested as Communists, were given their liberty. After July 17th, another 40,000 common criminals were released on condition they would bear arms in the Loyalist army. Revolutionary leaders liquidate most of the common criminals after they have served their purpose. By doing so, they convince a great many people that the atrocities committed during the revolution were the crimes of irresponsibles acting on their own initiative, and not in accordance with a pre-conceived plan of terrorism.

These were the conditions existing when General Franco decided he would try to save Spain from Communistic tyranny. Many books have been written telling how Franco, and a mere handful of Spanish generals, finally managed to defeat the Communist plot. It is an exciting story of courage, and fortitude, and great faith in their Christian Crusade. As soon as Franco issued his proclamation, the Red undersecretaries for army, navy, and air ordered the communist cells to liquidate all officers listed as enemies. This task was carried out with great thoroughness. Communist cells had been placed in the mechanical, communications, and signals branches of the services. This proved the organizers were sticking to the pattern laid down for the English, French, Russian, and German revolts.

Taken by surprise, nearly two-thirds of the officers were murdered cold-bloodedly during the initial stages of the attack. The mutineers tried to convince other ranks and ratings that they were carrying out the government's orders, and executing officers who had been convicted as enemies of the Popular Front government.

Many men would not believe what they were told. Before long it was not uncommon for one warship to be seen firing at a range of only a few yards into another. In one case, the fore-turret was manned by Reds and the after turret of the same ship manned by anti-reds. The massacres which started aboard the ships spread to the dock-yards and the cities in which they were located.

There might have been some excuse for the drastic action taken against the officers who could be expected to take sides with Franco, but it is impossible to excuse the terrorism which the Communists, acting as soldiers and police of the Popular Front government inflicted upon the unarmed and unsuspecting populace. The imposition of terrorism proved, at the cost of hundreds of thousands of innocent lives, that Lenin's policy had been accepted. He ruled that terrorism had to accompany every violent effort to overthrow a government because terrorism was the most economic method of subjugating the masses quickly and thoroughly.

It must be remembered that the leaders of a revolution don't consider the effort entirely wasted if it doesn't end in a proletarian dictatorship. Every revolt against constituted government and lawful authority is considered by those who plot and plan revolutionary efforts as a step in the right direction. If the effort falls short of success, that is bad but not hopeless. It doesn't matter how many people are killed. They are just pawns in the game. They are expendable. It is extraordinary how few of the top-level revolutionary leaders get killed during a rebellion. [2] It is accepted as good revolutionary technique, to sacrifice the masses and preserve the members of the Illuminati, for they are to govern the new order. Even in ordinary strikes the Reds usually stir up the trouble, and then sneak away. They leave the other workers to do the actual fighting with the police or militia.

The following facts are given to prove that during a revolution everyone who is not a party member or a fellow traveler may expect no mercy of any kind. Even Fellow Travelers are liquidated after they have been used to advantage.

Prior to July, 1936, the directors of the W.R.M. had literally flooded Madrid with agents. Moses Rosenberg arrived as Moscow's ambassador to Madrid. Anteneff Avseenko arrived in Barcelona. Dimitrov arrived to personally conduct the religious persecutions planned to follow the Communist Coup. During the Civil War Rosenberg ruled as tzar of Madrid. Avseenko assumed command of the Catalan Red Army. Rosenberg organized the Chekas in Spain and saw that they carried out their work of spying out more and more victims.

Moscow's agents organized "Purification Squads". Officially their duty was to seek out Fascists but secretly they liquidated all those who had been previously listed as reactionaries to the Illuminati's plan for subjugation of Spain. These lists had been compiled by Communist spies who had been worked into the Union of Concierges; (house and apartment janitors) the tax departments, the Postal Services, and other public offices. The lists of those to be liquidated were very complete because Moscow's spies, some disguised as scissors and knife grinders, had covered every district, street by street and house by house. All citizens were listed according to their political, labor, social, and religious standing and affiliations. When the order for the Reign of Terror to start was given, the Communists worked with the sureness, the ferocity, and the thoroughness, of starved brutes. Stalin had once stated: "It is better than a hundred innocent people die than one reactionary should escape." They obeyed this order with devilish persistency.

So others who live in countries not yet subjugated may understand what happens during a reign of terror, some actual atrocities will be described.

On July 17th, 1936, a group of Communists wearing the uniforms of government troops called at the Dominican Convent in Barcelona. The leader informed the Mother Superior that because mob violence was feared he had orders to escort the sisters to a place of safety. The sisters gathered together their few belongings and, unsuspectingly, accompanied the soldiers who took them to the suburbs where they murdered them all. The leader callously remarked afterwards, "We needed the building. We didn't want to muss it up before we occupied it. [3]

Señor Salvans was a known anti-Communist. Three times purification squads visited his home in Barcelona. When the third visit produced no information regarding his whereabouts, the Reds murdered the whole family of eight. That vile deed was performed in accordance with paragraphs 15 and 16 of the instructions already referred to.

One of the most senseless acts of violence ever committed in the name of "Liberty ... Equality ... Fraternity" was the murder of sixteen lay-brothers who worked voluntarily as male nurses in the largest hospital in Barcelona. Their only crime was that they belonged to a religious order. The fact that they nursed all who were sick, regardless of class, color, or creed, made no difference to those who ordered their "liquidation". E.M. Godden, who published *Conflict in Spain*, on page 72 reported: "The slaughter of the living was accompanied by derision for the dead. During the last week of July, 1936, the bodies of nuns were exhumed from their graves and propped up outside the walls of their convents. Obscene, and offensive, placards were attached to their bodies."

My cousin, Tom Carr, was a Mining Engineer in Spain from 1919 till 1938. He was married to the daughter of Mr. Allcock, the American Consul of Huelva. One of Caballero's 5th Columnists had been elected mayor of Huelva. When Moscow gave the word, he turned over the civic administration to the Communists. Their first act was to torture and then murder all the priests. The nuns were stripped naked and driven from the convents into the streets to provide sport for the revolutionaries. [4]

Godden also states that he interviewed two English women who only escaped molestation because they were foreigners. These two women told

Godden they had been forced to witness a mob of men and women act like fanatical dervishes. In the first instance the Reds tortured and mocked a priest before they finally hung his dismembered body and limbs from a statue of the Blessed Virgin. In the second instance the mob drilled a hole through the body of a young priest and then, while he was still living, transfixed him with a crucifix.

In September, 1936, Pere Van Rooy, famous French author, reported Dimitrov as saying: "We are reproached with destroying the churches and convents of Spain. What does the destruction of a few convents and churches matter? We are out to create a new world. [5]

A Committee, which officially investigated Communist atrocities in Spain in 1939, agreed that a conservative estimate placed 50,000 as the number of citizens *liquidated* in Barcelona as "reactionaries", between July, 1936, and December, 1937. In Valencia the number was set at 30,000. In Madrid they estimated that fully one tenth of the whole population was systematically murdered to make Spain into another totalitarian state. [6]

To illustrate what happened when the Reds took over control in Spain, I will quote some other independent witnesses. Marcel M. Dutrey, the famous French author, stated: "At Castre Urdiales the Communist Military commandant was an ex-municipal policeman who had been dismissed for theft. The new Chief of Police had previously made his living making and selling obscene postcards. The public prosecutor was the illegitimate son of a woman who had previously been a well-known streetwalker. He was nicknamed "Son-of-his-mother". The Red Tribunal was presided over by a miner who was assisted by two "Assessors" ... All these men were sadists. They glorified in carrying out the sentences they themselves imposed on their victims. They opened the stomach of Vincent Mura; they martyred Julie Yanko publicly in the market square; they dismembered Varez, the famous Spanish racing motorist, on the grounds that he refused to betray his friends into their hands."

Mr. Arthur Bryant, who wrote the preface to the fully evidenced, and authenticated, report on "Communist Atrocities in Spain" remarked on several occasions "Soviet agents obtained such a control of the communications systems that only reports favorable to their cause got into the majority of the world's newspapers, but, on the other hand, the most outrageous lies against the Franco forces were conjured up and given to the press of the world without let or hindrance." Bryant was so disgusted with what he saw that he wrote: "No university lecturer or anonymous B.B.C. commentator [7] has told the just, and compassionate, British people the truth about the women of San Martin de Valdeiglesias. For no greater crime than that they were found to possess some religious emblem, the women in San Martin de Valdeiglesias were condemned to be violated, and to satiate every vile passion, of twenty-five Red Militia men each. The fact that the fathers of some of the women had been imprisoned, and were under sentence of death, and that their mothers were forced to be present to witness the degradation of their daughters, was not sufficient to dissuade the Red Militia men from carrying out the sentence. The horrors of the hours suffered by these women had terrible effects on some of their minds. The survivors related how, again and again, they implored their executioners to kill them rather than submit them to such dreadful dishonor. The appalling cruelty of such atrocities can be realized by the fact that many of the condemned women were married, and when they were conducted between militiamen, before this pitiless tribunal, they carried children in their arms, and these children were witnesses of this culmination of the horror in the dishonor of their mothers." [8]

It is little wonder that the secret power directing the W.R.M. said: "Communists should not be required to carry out their plan of Terrorism in the localities in which they had lived with their families, but had to be used elsewhere."

Every Communist will declare that these atrocities were committed by "Uncontrollables" who were punished when they were caught. So that no person may be deceived by such lies I will again quote Lenin, the first canonized saint of the Illuminati totalitarian creed. Lenin said on various occasions: "There are no morals in politics, there is only expediency. A scoundrel may be of use to us just because he is a scoundrel."

On another occasion he said: "Young revolutionaries should start training for war immediately, by means of practical operations such as liquidating a traitor, killing a spy, blowing up a police station, or robbing a bank to provide funds for the uprising, etc... Do not shirk from these experimental attacks. They may of course degenerate into excesses, but that is a worry of the future". [9]

The Communist Krassikov was a libertine who squandered party funds on riotous living. Lenin, when ordering his liquidation said: "It does not matter that Comrade Krassikov has squandered party funds in a brothel, but it is scandalous that this should have disorganized the transportation of illegal literature". [10]

Communist training is designed to squeeze the last drop of human kindness out of the hearts of men and women who aspire to become high priests of the religion. Anna Pauker rose to dizzy heights in the Soviet hierarchy. She became Foreign Minister of Rumania. She proved she was loyal to Stalin when she rendered herself a widow by denouncing the father of her three children as a Trotskyite.

Communist terrorists encourage mere boys to become executioners of the enemies of the proletariat in order to harden them, and remove from their hearts every last vestige of human sentiment and sympathy. One such youth told how he had had a lot of fun with a priest. He said: "Night after night we took him out with the groups we had to kill, but always we put him last in the line. We made him wait while we killed all the others and then we took him back to the Bellas Artes again. (The Bellas Artes was the Building of Fine Arts which the Communists used as a prison). Each night he thought he was to die, but a quick death was too good for him. That 'Fraile' died seven deaths before we finally finished him."

Mr. Knoblaugh, on page 87 of his book *Correspondent in Spain*, tells of a horrible incident which confirms the contentions that the planners of World Revolution select potential leaders while they are very young and then train them until they are devoid of every trace of human sentiment and pity. Knoblaugh tells how two Communist youths boasted to a doctor, in his presence, that they had mutilated and murdered two young priests. They penetrated the disguise of these two religious men who, to escape detection and death, were working as coal-heavers. The two youths told how they made the two priests dig their graves with their coal shovels, then, in accordance with the Communist-designed Reign of Terror, they emasculated their two victims and forced the organs into their mouths. They stood by jeering while the priests died slow lingering deaths.

De Fonteriz, in *Red Terror in Madrid* pages 19-20 tells how the Chekas, organized by Dimitrov and Rosenberg tried to make a certain lady tell where her husband was hiding. The woman probably didn't know his whereabouts, but to make sure she didn't, the members of the Chekas made her sit and watch while they amused themselves piercing the breasts of eight women members of her household with long hat-pins.

To prove a previous statement, that those who design the pattern of the Reign of Terror used criminals and lunatics to stir up the blood-lust, I report what happened at Alcala on July 20th, 1936: The Reds released all the prisoners, both male and female, on condition that they would bear arms for the Communist Cause. They numbered one thousand men and two hundred women. They were formed into the Battalion of Alcala. They excelled themselves in the victorious attack on Madrid. As a reward they were sent to Siguenza. After taking over the town, they murdered two hundred citizens to break down the resistance of the others. This battalion of criminals occupied Siguenza for sixteen weeks. When they were driven out by Franco's forces, it was found that every female, from ten to fifty, had been violated. Many of them were pregnant and many diseased. Some were both. One girl, a waitress in a hotel, told how lucky she had been. She told how the criminals had murdered the bishop of Siguenza in a most horrible, barbarous, and unprintable manner. At a banquet held in the hotel that night, one of the battalion took a fancy to her and demanded that one of his comrades dress himself in the murdered bishop's vestments and marry them. The others thought this a great joke and carried out the mock ceremony. After the wedding the "Militiennes" performed the "Danse on Ventre" using the dining tables as a stage. After the orgy ended, the man claimed the girl as his own personal property. Relating this happening she remarked: "I was lucky. My man was an assassin, but it was better to belong to him than to be the plaything of all. I at least escaped disease."

Marcel M. Dutrey published the fact that in Ciempozuelos over one hundred religious brothers were bound to lunatics who were then furnished with knives. One can imagine the horror which followed. Moscow's army of trained propagandists told the world how Franco's troops had murdered the mayors of many small towns, but they didn't mention the fact that they had been tried by a properly constituted military court and proved to have been Communist agents of Largo Caballero who had plotted to turn Spain into a dictatorship.

If further proof is needed to substantiate the statement that the Secret Powers behind the World Revolutionary Movement use Communists throughout the world to further their totalitarian plans, the numerous desertions from the Communist party, all over the world, should provide that proof. Douglas Hyde, who for the preceding five years was news editor of the Daily Worker, Britain's leading Communist newspaper, in March 1948, announced his resignation from the Communist party. In a press release he stated: "I believe that the new 'line' of the Communist party, introduced after the formation of the Cominform last year (1947), if successful, will bring nothing but misery to the common people." Mr. Hyde went on to explain that since the end of World War II he had been worried regarding Moscow's foreign policy. He said he had finally become convinced that the Party Line as now determined by the Moscow Clique, was no longer in keeping with the ideals for which he had worked so long, and that the ultimate result would be to destroy the very freedoms and decencies for which Communists had been fighting for so long a time. He concluded with these words: "My growing disillusionment led me to seek some other answer to the problem of our day, and another way out of the world chaos."

Right on top of Mr. Hyde's resignation in London, England, came that of Mrs. Justina Krusenstern-Peters, a staff member of Soviet publications for the preceding twelve years. She announced her resignation in Shanghai, China. She said: "The strain of writing according to orders from Moscow became more than I could bear ... I am still a Soviet citizen. I am sure my feelings are shared by many of my colleagues in Russia, the only difference is that they are not able to protest against their enslavement."

Most Communists work to bring about an International of Soviet Socialist Republics. In other words, they feel that only by using revolutionary methods can they speedily destroy the stranglehold of selfish capitalism and place political power in the hands of the workers. Few party members realize they are working themselves into a state of slavery from which there is no hope of escape. [11]

NOTES:
1   Investigation of outbreaks in many prisons in both the U.S.A. and Canada indicate these revolt, were Communistically inspired. It took nearly twenty-three years to prove that some of the officials in Kingston Penitentiary, at the time Tim Buck was confined in the institution, were Communists. Evidence would indicate they helped him organize the Kingston Prison

Riots. I was a Free Lance writer at the time. I wrote that the whole thing smelt to high heaven as a plot to make a martyr of Tim Buck, in order to arouse public sympathy, in order to obtain his release. I declared it my opinion that guards, and other prison officials, were implicated. My story never appeared in print. In 1953 one of the officials I suspected in 1932 of having 'Red' affiliations contested the Federal election in British Columbia as the Labour Progressive Candidate. Between 1939 and 1944 this same man had charge of the training of personnel in the engineering branch of the Royal Canadian Navy. This information was given to the proper authorities. —Author.

2 It is an historical fact that ten times as many revolutionary leaders have died during Party Purges than died during the actual revolutionary ware.

3 Recorded in official reports "Communist Atrocities in Spain". Parts one, two and three. The investigations were conducted by a committee composed of men of different nationalities. The editing was done by Arthur Bryant, internationally known journalist and author.

4 This statement of my cousin's was confirmed an page 238 of the Spanish Arena, written by William Fees and Cecil Gerahty, and also by Arthur Bryant who investigated the Communist Atrocities in Spain.

5 See Catholic Herald, February 11th, 1938.

6 In case some people think that Communists hate only Roman Catholic, it is well to remember that the Secret Powers behind the world Revolutionary Movement are determined to ultimately turn this world into the despotism of Satan. That is the essence of Illuminism. In order to lull people, in countries not yet Sovietized, (sic) into a some of false security, they will try to convince them of their tolerance to religions other than Roman Catholic, but investigation shows that they are determined, when they have sufficient power, to wipe out all religions.

7 NOTE — Red agents had infiltrated onto the Staff of Britain's B.B.C. in 1938 and for nearly two years the policy was Pro-loyalist, i.e. Communistic. The present trend of the C.B.C. is much the same. The majority of programs are slanted sharply to the "left".

8 The details are on page six of the second report 'Communist Atrocities in Spain'.

9 Communist agents teach children, in all Free Nations the inversion of the Ten Commandments. Communism is therefore responsible for the increase in juvenile delinquency more than any other single cause. While professed atheists they serve the purpose of Illuminati and Satanism.

10 The magazine Time made reference to these views expressed by Lenin, November 17th, 1948.

11 Mr. Hyde, and others, who broke away from the communist party don't seem even yet to realize that they were only tools used to further the plans of the Illuminati.

✠ Chapter Sixteen

Events Leading up to WW2

It has been told how the international bankers enabled Germany to secretly re-arm, with the aid of Stalin, in spite of the restrictions imposed by the Treaty of Versailles. In order to understand what happened in Germany to bring Hitler into power, it is necessary to be familiar with the political intrigue which went on between 1924 and 1934. 'The Secret Powers' always have had their agents divide the population of countries. They plan to subjugate into many religious, economic, political, social, and labor groups. Their agents then divide the various groups into as many factions as possible. Their motto is 'United we stand. Divided they fall'.

Most German citizens, excepting only Communists, were agreed upon the following issues: That Germany had been winning the war when had she had first been betrayed and afterwards victimized. That the national money-lenders had used the so-called democracies of Britain, France, and the United States, to defeat Germany's armed forces. That the Jewish-led Communist Party assisted the international bankers by bringing about the chaotic conditions that preceded the signing of the Armistice and the revolution that followed. They agree that every patriotic German male and female should do his or her uttermost to build up post-war Germany, and break the economic and military stranglehold placed on their nation by the Treaty of Versailles.

Most political leaders, except Communists, were also agreed that in order to free themselves of the economic sanctions imposed upon the nation, it was necessary to break away from their dependence on the international bankers for financial assistance in the form of interest bearing loans. In other words, most German politicians, except Communists, were agreed that Germany should depart from the practice of financing the nation's business by incurring debts, a practice which had been imposed upon England in 1694, France in 1790, and the United States in 1791, by the International bankers. They realized that this system had resulted in astronomical National Debts, the principal and interest payments on which were guaranteed and secured by Direct Taxation of the people.

The Fascist leaders in Germany decided they were going to create their own money and use their national assets, such as the value of their real estate, their industrial potentials, their agricultural production, natural resources, and the nation's capacity to produce, as collateral.

The people of Germany found that, generally speaking, their views regarding future political and economic policy were shared by the people of Italy, Spain, and Japan, and thus came into being THE AXIS POWERS, and the Fascist Movement. Because of their dynamic personalities, Hitler, Mussolini and Franco became the chosen leaders. History proves that these three men did a great deal to help their countries recover from the effects of the preceding revolutions and wars. The industrial and agricultural developments were little short of miraculous. Their military rearmament was made possible by the secret assistance given by the agentur of the Illuminati who planned to bring the Fascist and Capitalistic countries into another World War.

When Hitler and Mussolini first rose to power they advocated the moderate Fascist policy which demanded that the wrongs done their countries be rectified; that they contain communism; and curb the powers of the Illuminati who controlled finance and industry. But as time went on, both Hitler and Mussolini came under the influence of the leaders of the hard core of Nazi War Lords who claimed the only way to establish a permanent peace in the world was by military conquest. The Nazi leaders sold the top-military leaders in Italy and Japan solidly on the theories and plans advocated by Karl Ritter in 1849. Franco in Spain refused to go along with their totalitarian plans. His religious beliefs convinced him that an ideology which denied the existence of an Almighty God was doing the work of the Devil.

The Totalitarian minded leaders in Germany, Italy, and Japan were determined to use Fascism to further their secret Long Range Plans in exactly the same way as their opponents, the international bankers, used Communism. The immediate plans of the War Lords were to first, defeat the Stalin-controlled Empire; second, wipe out Communism in Europe; third, consolidate the control of the Axis Powers on Continental Europe; fourth, invade Britain and France and subjugate the people, and fifth, to invade and conquer the United States by using two vast pincer movements. Japan was to land invading forces on the west coast of Mexico in the south and in the Northwest Territories in the north. Germany was to invade Canada by air in the North and the German-Italian forces were to jump the Atlantic from Africa, and attack the U. S.A. from South America and the Gulf of Mexico.

The Northern invading forces were scheduled to join together at a point in the vicinity of Chicago and push on down the Mississippi while the South-West and South-East invasion forces were to meet at New Orleans and push north up the Mississippi, thus dividing the country into two halves. [1]

With the conquest of Britain and the United States the Nazis planned to exterminate the Jews living in these two countries as they had exterminated those they located in Europe. The international bankers, and big capitalists controlled by them, were listed for immediate liquidation, together with confiscation of all their assets and estates.

While Hitler suffered imprisonment prior to 1934 because he was considered the personal enemy of the Nazi War Lords and the international bankers, he wrote Mein Kampf. On the very last page he stated: "The party (National-Socialist) as such stands for positive Christianity but does not bind itself in the matter of creed to any profession. It combats the Jewish materialistic spirit within and without us."

In 1933 Hitler also announced his policy in regard to Britain. He pointed out that Marx, Lenin, and Stalin had all repeatedly reiterated that before

162

International communism could reach its final objectives, Britain and her Empire had to be destroyed. Under these circumstances Hitler said: "I am willing to help defend the British Empire by force if called upon."

Of the Treaty of Versailles Hitler wrote: "It was not a British interest (intention) but, in the first place, a Jewish one to destroy Germany." He also wrote: "Even in England there is a continual struggle going on between the representatives of British States' interests and the Jewish World dictatorship. Whilst England is exhausting herself in maintaining her position in the world, the Jew today is a rebel in England and the struggle against the Jewish world menace will be started there also."

Hitler never wavered from his personal opinion that the survival of Germany as a great power depended upon an alliance with the British Empire. In 1936 he instituted proceedings to try to bring about this alliance. He arranged for unofficial conversations to take place between German and British diplomats, and after the meetings failed to produce the alliance he so greatly desired, he said: "No sacrifice would have been too great in order to gain England's alliance. It would have meant renunciation of our colonies; and importance as a sea power; and refraining from interference with British industry by competition."[2] He considered all these German concessions would have been worthwhile if only he had been able to bring about the German- British alliance. His failure to bring about the British Alliance caused him to weaken in his opposition to the totalitarian ideology as advocated by the extreme Nazi War Lords. The failure of the conference convinced Hitler that no moderate policy would ever break the control the international bankers had over British Foreign policy. He reluctantly began to concede that Karl Ritter had been right when he said: "The power the Jewish financiers hold over Communism must be destroyed, as well as of those who are members of the world revolutionary movement, before peace and economic freedom can be restored to the world."

The purpose of this book is to record the events in history which provided the 'Causes' which produced the 'Effects' we experience today. We are not concerned with the 'Rights' or 'Wrongs' of the decisions made by individuals, except to judge for ourselves whether the decisions furthered the Devil's Plan or were in accordance with the Plan of God. The only value of historical research is to obtain knowledge of how, and why, mistakes were made in the past so we can try to avoid making similar mistakes in the future.

The momentous meeting regarding the possibility of an alliance between Great Britain and Germany took place in January 1936. Lord Londonderry represented the British government and Goering, Herr Ribbentrop, and Hitler, Germany.

An authority on this phase of history informed me that Herr Goering and Herr Von Ribbentrop outlined the history of the World Revolutionary Movement to Lord Londonderry, explaining the detailed research work done by Professor Karl Ritter and others. They reasoned that the only successful way to

fight a totalitarian-minded conspiracy was to use Total War. They explained to Lord Londonderry their plan was to attack all Communist-controlled countries; liberate the people and execute all Communist traitors. They claimed the only way to wipe out Communism was the extermination of the whole Jewish Race.[3] They produced masses of documented evidence which, they claimed, was authentic, to prove Communism was organized, financed, and directed by powerful, wealthy and influential Jews, who also organized, financed and directed secret ambitions to bring about the Messianic Age.[4]

Hitler is said to have promised that he would continue to oppose the extreme totalitarian plans of the Nazi War Lords and confine his activities against Communism to Europe, providing the British government would enter into an alliance with Germany. When Lord Londonderry said he doubted if the British government would take part in a plan to abolish Communism, which called for 'Genocide,' Hitler compromised. He said Germany would undertake the task alone provided England would enter into an agreement that the two countries would under no circumstances war against each other for ten years. Hitler argued that the only way Britain, France, and Russia could shake off the unbearable and ruinous burden of ever-increasing national debts was to repudiate them and restore the issuing of money to the government where it originally and rightfully belonged.

Hitler is said to have pointed out that the purpose of his National-Socialist party ... call it Fascism ... was to put an end at once, and all time, to the power and influence the international money-lenders exerted on national and international affairs by reason of the fact that they were forcing every nation that still claimed to be independent, further and further into their debt. He is said to have quoted what Benjamin Disraeli made one of his characters say in his famous book Coningsby, "So you see, dear Coningsby, the world is governed by very different personages from what is imagined by those who are not behind the scenes." [5]

Goering is said to have backed up the Führer by pointing out that history had proved that the wealthy and influential Jews had obtained economic and political control of every country into which they had infiltrated by using illegal methods and corrupt practices.

Herr Von Ribbentrop is reported to have supported Goering's arguments by reminding Lord Londonderry that as recently as 1927-28 when he was in Canada, the Stevens Royal Commission into the Canadian Customs Service proved that the country was being robbed annually of over ONE HUNDRED MILLION DOLLARS by smuggling and other kinds of illegal traffic and trade organized and directed from an International Headquarters. He pointed out that

164

evidence placed before the Royal Commissioner had proved that in order to get away with gangsterism and licentiousness to 'Fix' thousands of public servants and hundreds of government officials, even as high as cabinet level. He pointed out that what had been absolutely proved to exist in Canada was ten times as bad in the United States of America. Ribbentrop reasoned that the only way to clean up the mess was to 'Get' the three hundred men at the top who were 'The Secret Power' master-minding the negative forces whose various evil influences, and criminal activities, all furthered the Long Range Plan of those who directed the World Revolutionary Movement. [6]

Goering is said to have reviewed once more the part the international bankers had played in bringing about, directing, and financing the Russian revolution in 1917, which had enabled them to bring into existence the adverse conditions being experienced throughout the world at that time. [7]

Hitler reminded Lord Londonderry of the millions of Christians who had been ruthlessly slaughtered in the Communized countries since October, 1917, and argued that the men responsible could not be considered as anything else than international gangsters.

The final item of discussion was the manner in which Stalin had been instructed to turn Spain into a Communist dictatorship. The whole pattern of international intrigue was laid bare. The manner in which Germany had been enabled to secretly re-arm: The way French politics were controlled by Grand Orient Freemasonry. [8] The manner in which Britain had been persuaded to disarm, while her potential enemies were being re-armed.

According to the Germans, it would be impossible for the world to enjoy peace and prosperity as long as those who directed the World Revolutionary Movement insisted on fomenting wars in order to create conditions favorable for revolutionary action. They argued both international Communism and political Zionism had to be stopped and the movements ended at once, or another war was inevitable, because the Secret Powers, pulling the strings, were determined they were going to reach their ultimate objectives.

Hitler was a great orator, and my informant claimed he ended the discussions with a plea that Lord Londonderry return to England and persuade the British government to join in the suggested alliance with Germany "because I am convinced that the British Empire and the Roman Catholic Church are both universal institutions, the continuance of which is absolutely essential as bulwarks for the preservation of law and order throughout the world in the future."

What has been said here of Hitler is so absolutely foreign to the general idea that the following historical facts and documents are quoted to support what has been said.

Lord Londonderry returned to London following the conference and made his report to the British cabinet. On February 21st, 1936, he wrote Herr Von

Ribbentrop. He referred to the conversations he had had. The letter reads in part:

"They (Hitler and Goering) forget that here (in England) we have not experienced the devastation of a revolution for several centuries... In relation to the Jews ... we do not like persecution, but in addition to this, there is the material feeling that you are taking on a tremendous force which is capable of having repercussions all over the world ... it is possible to trace their participation in most of these international disturbances which have created so much havoc in different countries, but on the other hand, one can find many Jews strongly ranged on the other side who have done their best, with the wealth at their disposal, and also by their influence, to counteract those malevolent and mischievous activities of fellow Jews." [9]

After Hitler realized his hopes to bring about an alliance between Germany and Britain had failed, he leaned further and further to the 'Right.' He became convinced that it was impossible for an individual, groups of individuals, or even a single nation to break the power and influence the international bankers exercised over the so-called democratic nations by reason of their financial control and the encumbrance of their national debts.

In July, 1936, the Spanish Civil War broke out and Hitler, Mussolini and Franco were drawn closer together. It was the fact that Franco had had to start a Civil War in Spain to prevent Spain from being Communized without a struggle. That caused Hitler to round out his boundaries and concentrate military power on his borders. He was determined to make sure that Stalin, who he knew was only the agent of the international bankers appointed to rule over Russia, would not extend his dictatorship over other European countries. Every step Hitler took in the direction was termed 'Acts of aggression' by the anti-Fascist press. Hitler explained such moves as 'preventive' wars or occupations. He stated that he was primarily concerned in 'preventing' Stalin establishing his sphere of influence on or about the 40th parallel of latitude in Europe. If he was allowed to, Germany, Britain, and other northern European countries would be entrapped like flies in a spider's web.

Hitler had not only failed to bring about the British alliance, but he had earned the enmity of the Nazi War Lords who advocated totalitarian methods for solving the very complicated and dangerous problem. They did not want an alliance with England. They did not want to see Christianity flourish. They did not agree with Hitler's "preventive" measures. They didn't agree with anything Hitler did to hinder their plans to wage 'Total War,' first against Russia, then against Britain and France. The 'hard core' of the pagan Nazi War Lords demanded that Hitler take offensive action, as the best defense against gradual encroachment by Communist underground and Stalin's armed forces. When Hitler refused to go all the way with them, they decided to get rid of him. The first attempt was made on his life. The Nazi War Lords next tried to weaken the control he had gained over the German people.

They launched a campaign to sell their Aryan Pagan ideology to the German people. They taught the superiority of the Aryan Race. They advocated war to establish the undisputed supremacy of the Aryan State. They made it a fundamental principle that all men and women of Aryan blood should give unlimited obedience to the Head of the Aryan State and acknowledge no mortal as above him. This campaign was attributed to Hitler, and the anti-Fascist press throughout the world cried to high heaven that Hitler was a pagan, and a Black-shirted totalitarian-minded Nazi War Lord. Thus started the clashes between both Catholic and Protestant clergy and the state. The clergy condemned the Nazi ideology on the grounds that those who preached it were preaching the deification of men.

The Nazi leaders charged that both Catholic and Protestant clergy were breaking the laws and defying the authority of the state. The Roman Catholic and Protestant bishops replied by stating the extreme Nazi doctrines were antagonistic and contrary to the Divine Plan of Creation. The Nazi leaders countered with the argument that the Church had no right to interfere in matters of state.

Hitler tried to pacify the clergy by banning the Grand Orient Lodges which were known to be the headquarters of the Aryan extremists throughout Germany. The Nazi leaders rendered this step abortive changing them over to "Orders of German Chivalry."

Hitler, in order to maintain a united front against Communism, tried to pacify the Nazis by issuing an edict that any clergyman preaching against the laws of the state, or questioning its supremacy, would be subjected to the full process of the law and, if found guilty, would suffer the penalties provided for such 'crimes'. This situation provides another example of how the forces of evil divided two powerful forces which were both combating a common enemy.

The anti-Fascist propaganda made the most of the disagreement between Hitler and the Pope. It is true Pope Pius XI denounced Nazism in no uncertain terms in the Encyclical of March 14th, 1937 "on the condition of the Church in Germany." He told Roman Catholics that he had weighed every word of the encyclical in the scales of truth and clarity. In reference to the Nazi conception of the superiority of the Aryan race and the supremacy of the state he said:

"While it is true that the race or the people; the state or a form of government; the representatives of a civil power, or other fundamental elements of human society have an essential and honorable place in the natural order, nevertheless, if anyone detaches them from this scale of earthly values and exalts them as the supreme form and standard of all things, even of religious values, deifying them with idolatrous worship, he perverts and falsifies the order of things created and constituted by God, and is far from true faith in God, and from a conception of life in conformity therewith...Our God is a personal God, transcendent, Almighty, Infinite, Perfect. One in the Trinity of Persons and three in the unity of the Divine Essence; creator of the universe;

Lord; King; and ultimate purpose of the history of the world; who does not suffer and can never suffer any other divinity besides Him ... Only superficial minds can fall into the error of speaking of a National God, of a National Religion, of foolishly attempting to restrict within the narrow confines of a single race that God, who is the Creator of the world, the King and Law-Giver of all peoples, before Whose greatness the nations are as small as drops of water in a bucket" (Isaias XL-15).

In a pastoral letter dated August 19th, 1938, the bishops of Germany struck out boldly against Nazi ideology. The letter says that the attitude of the Nazi towards the Christian religion in Germany is in open contradiction with the Fuehrer's assertions... [10] "What is aimed at is not merely the checking of the growth of the Catholic Church but the wiping out of Christianity and the setting up in its place of a religion which is utterly alien to the Christian belief in One True God." The letter goes on to point out that the Nazi attack on Dr. Sproll, the Protestant bishop of Rottenburg, clearly proved that the 'persecution' is directed not only against the Catholic Church but against the whole Christian idea as such... "An attempt is being made to get rid of the Christian God in order to replace Him with a "German God". What does a German God mean? Is He different from the God of other peoples? If so, then there must be a special God for each nation and for each people... This is the same as saying "There is no God."[11]

What happened in Germany in 1936 has happened in other countries since. The leaders of 'Black' Nazism joined forces with the leaders of 'Red' Communism in an attack on both the Christian religion and the British Empire. The totalitarian-minded Nazi War Lords initiated their followers into the German Grand Orient Lodges, using the ancient pagan rites and ritual handed down from the time the barbaric Aryan tribes and the Huns swept over Europe. The totalitarian-minded men who direct international Communism initiate their leaders into the Grand Orient Lodges of other countries using the ancient Cabalistic Rites of Illuminism. To understand this situation, it is necessary to recall that Jews have never, under any circumstances, been admitted into the German Grand Orient Lodges since 1785 when the papers found on the body of the Courier of the Illuminati, who was killed by lightning at Ratisbon, were handed over by the police to the Bavarian authorities, and proved that the Grand Orient Lodges in France were being used as the secret headquarters of the Jewish inspired revolutionary movement.

When complicated situations such as these develop, it can be understood why the Roman Catholic Church has taken such a definite stand against 'Black' Nazism, while tolerating the less extreme forms of Fascism, i.e. anti-Communism as practiced by Franco in Spain. It also explains why Cardinal Mindszenty collaborated with allegedly Fascist leaders who attempted to overthrow Communist domination in his country.

Franco has consistently refused to go off the deep end. He refused to support German Nazism in World War Two simply because the extreme Nazi Pagan War Lords had become all powerful in Germany. In Germany, Italy,

France, Spain, and Japan, millions of citizens, peaceful by inclination and charitable at heart, found themselves in the position of having to decide whether they became actively Pro-Fascist or Pro-Communist. They were given Hobson's Choice. They usually picked what they considered the lesser of two evils. They were immediately labeled accordingly.

By diabolical intrigue the nations of the world were being lined up for World War Two. The Russian dictatorship was secretly rearming the German armies. The Italian dictatorship, under Mussolini, was secretly building a huge navy of submarines to German specification and design. These submarines were tested out under conditions of actual warfare during the Spanish Civil War. These tests proved the German designed submarines were, in 1936, practically immune to British anti-submarine weapons including Asdic. The British government was informed in regard to this matter. Captain Max Morton, R.N., had emphasized the warnings being given by evading all the anti-submarine devices used for the protection of the British Mediterranean fleet while it was at anchor. He actually got into the guarded harbor and, in theory, sank half a dozen capital ships as they rode to their anchors. This act of Captain Max Morton brought him condemnation from the British Civil Sea Lords instead of praise and recognition. His promotion was held up, and he was silenced. He was not allowed to take a very active part in British naval affairs until 1940. When German U-boats threatened to starve Britain into submission he was asked to take over direction of the anti-submarine Battle of the Atlantic.

The British government was warned as early as 1930 that German-designed submarines had dived deeper than 500 feet, thus rendering obsolete all depth-charges then in use. They were warned that Asdic gear then in use was also obsolete. But they refused to heed the warnings. The Secret Powers were using their agents within the British government to weaken the British war potential, while they were secretly strengthening that of Germany. When the war broke out, Britain did not have one single modern anti-submarine ocean escort vessel in service. As a result she lost 75% of her merchant ships, and over 40,000 seamen, before the tide turned in her favor in April, 1943. [12]

Hitler antagonized the international bankers when he announced his financial policy and monetary reform program. He persuaded Italy, Spain, and Japan to back him in his determination to challenge the power of the Cartels and Monopolies financed and controlled by the international bankers, particularly their "Brain-child," the Bank of International Settlements. The German Reich abrogated the clause in the constitution which made Dr. Hans Luther, the president of the Reichsbank, a permanent fixture. Until the change was made, the president of the Reichsbank could not be removed without his own consent and a majority vote of the board of the Bank of International Settlements.

Since the Great War the international bankers had set up twenty-six central banks. They were modeled after the Federal Reserve Banks in the United States, which had been established in 1913 according to the theories of Mr.

Paul Warburg, the German who had gone to America in 1907 and become a partner in Kuhn-Loeb & Co. of New York.

Mr. Paul Warburg's creation of 1913 had been steadily attempting to set up a 'Central Banking Organization' which would acknowledge no authority on this planet as above it. Hitler knew that if Warburg and associates had their way, the Bank of International Settlements would become as autocratic as the bank of England is in regard to British National Affairs and Foreign Policy. Politicians and statesmen were being asked to believe this banker's dream would stabilize the banking system of the world. In this contention they were absolutely correct. The nigger-in-the-gold-pile is the fact, that with the realization of this dream, all hope of freedom and plenty for the individual and private industry would automatically disappear. The citizens of the world would have the same financial security as the criminal who enjoys social security behind bars. Against this process of reducing the people of the world to financial slavery Hitler decided to take a definite stand, and he refused to allow Germany to be merged into the league of Monopolist States, secretly controlled by agents of the Illuminati.

After Paul Warburg's Federal Reserve System had been in operation three years i.e. 1913 to 1916, President Woodrow summed up the economic situation in the United States of America as follows: "A great industrial nation is controlled by its system of credits. Our system of credit is concentrated. The growth of the nation, therefore, and all our activities are in the hands of a few men... We have come to be one of the worst ruled; one of the most completely controlled and dominated governments, in the civilized world... no longer a government by conviction and the free vote of the majority, but a government by the opinion and duress of small groups of dominant men." That is actually what modern so-called democracy really means. [13]

When the countries of the Western World were plunged into the economic depression of the 1930s, out of which only another war could lift them, President Franklin D. Roosevelt said: "Sixty families in America control the wealth of the nation... One-third of the nation's population is ill-housed, ill-fed, and ill-clad..." "Twenty per cent of the men working on W.P.A. projects are in such an advanced state of malnutrition that they cannot do a day's work... I intend to drive the money changers from the Temple." Roosevelt knew that unless he could drive the international bankers out of the modern temple of international finance only a full scale World War could relieve the chronic condition of financial constipation they had brought about on an international scale by withdrawing currency, restricting credits, and other financial manipulations. They grew richer while everyone outside their select circle grew steadily poorer. But soon Roosevelt was docile.

President Roosevelt found he couldn't break, or even curb, the power of the Illuminati. He was forced to lead his country into war against the only countries that held firm to the very policy he had so rashly announced soon after he was elected to office. And, after he had grown haggard and grey doing the bidding of the men whose money and influence had placed him in the office of president of the United States, he allegedly died in the home of the richest and most powerful man in the United States ... Bernard Baruch... A man above all others who, for the past forty years at least, has sat quietly in the background but was acknowledged the 'king' over all American bankers and undoubtedly one of the select few who, in our time, has been 'The Secret Power' behind the scenes of international affairs. If this were not so, why does Winston Churchill and his son visit him so often? Why did Winston Churchill make his momentous announcements regarding his attitude towards political Zionism and peaceful co-existence immediately after his visit to Bernard Baruch in 1954?

It is unfortunate, but true, that to-day 'democracy' is a very deceptive word. It is used to describe all countries which are in fact a money-lender's heaven. Today countries which are termed 'democratic' follow a monetary system devised by the international bankers, under which currency originates in debt to groups of private individuals who manipulate the price levels of different countries and use money as a stable value facilitating the exchange of REAL WEALTH. Britain, France, and the United States are termed 'democratic' countries only because they are linked together in debt to the international money-lenders. The Communist countries also call themselves 'democratic' republics and they are entitled to do so as long as they also are controlled by the same international financial groups.

When the Axis Powers in Europe refused to place themselves in usury to the international bankers, they placed themselves in exactly the same category as the small independent store keeper is in relation to the big chain-store organizations and business combines and monopolies. They were given the option of joining the big 'Happy Family' ... or else. In the case of an independent store keeper, if he refuses to 'see the light' he is put out of business by systematically applied pressure of unfair competition. In the case of nations who refuse to 'play- ball,' they are doomed to suffer war or revolution. There is no mercy shown to the nations whose leaders refuse to bow down and worship at the feet of Mammon. There is no consideration given to nations which refuse to place themselves in usury to the High Priests of the God of Mammon. All must pay the tribute demanded of them ... or else.

World War Two was started in order to enable the Illuminati to finally rid themselves of the barriers of caste and creed and prejudice. Their ideas regarding a new civilization had to be built through a world at war. In proof of the above statement a portion of the broadcast Sir Anthony Eden addressed to America on September 11th, 1939, is quoted. He said: "Can we finally rid Europe of the barriers of caste and creed and prejudice? ... Our new civilization must be built through a world at war. But our new civilization will be built just the same." What utter rot. Wars are destructive not constructive.

From 1930 onwards, informed and influential Britishers had been doing everything within their power to try to prevent England and her allies being inveigled into another war with Germany. As was to be expected, every one of these people was attacked by the anti-Fascist agencies as being 'black' totalitarian-minded Nazis.

Some of the British who opposed Communism — and also the continued subservience of the British government to the international bankers — openly declared themselves in favor of the Fascist principles as expounded by Franco and Hitler. This group was led by Sir Oswald Mosley. Others, mostly statesmen, retired admirals, and generals, worked quietly trying to inform politicians and members of the government regarding the purpose behind the international intrigue.

The anti-Semitic movement started in England early in 1921, after Mr. Victor E. Marsden returned from Russia where he had been imprisoned by the Bolsheviks. Mr. Marsden had been correspondent in Russia for the London Morning Post since before 1914. When Mr. Marsden returned to England he was in possession of the document which Professor Sergei Nilus had published in Russian in 1905 under the title Jewish Peril. Professor Nilus claimed the original documents had been obtained from a woman who had stolen them from a wealthy international Jew when he returned to her apartments after addressing top-level executives of the Grand Orient Lodges in Paris in 1901.

While Mr. Marsden was translating the documents he received a warning that if he persisted in publishing the book he would die. Mr. Marsden published his translation of the documents under the title Protocols of the Learned Elders of Zion and he did die under suspicious circumstances a few years afterwards.

Following the publication of the book by the Britons Publishing Society, Mr. Marsden was denounced internationally as a bare faced anti-Semitic liar. The book caused one of the greatest controversies the world has ever known. My own research work has caused me to believe that the documents published by professor Nilus in Russia in 1905 as Jewish Peril and by Mr. Marsden in England in 1921 as Protocols of the Learned Elders of Zion are the long range plans of the Illuminati which was explained by Amschel Rothschild to his associates in Frankfort in 1773. Rothschild was not addressing rabbis and elders. He was addressing bankers, industrialists, scientists, economists, etc. Therefore to charge this diabolical conspiracy as a crime against the whole Jewish people and their religious leaders is unjust. I am supported in this opinion by one of the highest ranking intelligence Officers in the British Service. He studied the matter in Russia, Germany, and England.

That the document which fell into the hands of Professor Nilus had been used as material for lectures to instruct leaders of the W.R.M. cannot be doubted because in addition to the original outline of the conspiracy there are additional remarks which explain how the plot had been put into effect; and how Darwinism, Marxism, and Neitzche-ism had been used since 1773. Mention is also made saying how it was intended to use political Zionism to service the purpose of the W.R.M. in the future ... the Illuminati.

172

The term Agentur contained in the document would seem to indicate an individual; a group; a race; a nation; a creed; or any other agency that could be used as a tool or an instrument to further the Long Range Plan of the Illuminati for ultimate world domination.

Regardless of its origin, no person who has read it can deny that the trend of world events has followed the program suggested in the document from 1773 to date. No one can be otherwise than amazed at the deadly accuracy of the forecast made in the document.

To give only one glaring instance of many. the document outlines how Zionism shall be aided to reach its objectives. Theodore Herzl was the founder of the Zionist Movement. He is recorded as saying: "From the first moment I entered the Zionist movement my eyes were directed towards England, because I saw by reason of the general conditions there the Archimedean point where the lever could be applied." Then again: "When we sink (the we referring to Zionists) we become a revolutionary proletariat; the subordinate officers of the revolutionary party; when we rise, there rises also our terrible power of the purse." [14]

More amazing still, and getting back to near the time the document came into professor Nilus's possession, Max Nordeu, addressing the Zionist Congress held in Basel, Switzerland, August 1903, is quoted as saying : "Let me tell you the following words as if I were showing you the rungs of a ladder leading upward and upward... The Zionist Congress: The English Uganda proposition: The future World War: The Peace Conference where, with the help of England, a free and Jewish Palestine will be created." The fact to remember is this — these men who were outstanding leaders of the Zionist Movement probably spoke in all sincerity. History proves, however, that the small select group, who have in the past, and still do, comprise 'The Secret Power' behind the World Revolutionary Movement, have used both Communism and Zionism to further their own selfish totalitarian ambitions.

The contents of the document translated by Mr. Marsden detail the "Party Line" as followed by the Bolshevik revolutionary leaders under the leadership of Lenin and Stalin, just as it details the policy followed by the leaders of the Zionist movement. Lord Sydenham read the document and then remarked: "The most striking characteristic ... is knowledge of a rare kind, embracing the widest field ... knowledge upon which prophesies now fulfilled are based."

Henry Ford studied this document. He had many outstanding and learned men study it also. He published a book of amazing disclosures, all of which add up to the sum total that the document details the plan by which a small group of international financiers have used, and still use, Communism, Zionism, and all other agencies they can control, regardless of whether they be Jewish or Gentile, to further their own secret totalitarian ambitions.

Mr. Henry Ford was interviewed in regard to the document by a reporter of the New York World. His comments were published February 17th, 1921. He said: "The only statement I care to make about the Protocols is that they fit in with what is going on. They are sixteen years old, and they have fitted the world situation up to this time. They fit it now."

Mr. Ford made his statement thirty-four years ago and what he said then is equally applicable to- day. This should prove to any unbiased person that the document is a genuine copy of the originally conceived plan which has been put into practice. It has almost achieved the purpose for which it was intended.

One may well ask "How long are the people going to stand for such a state of affairs?" Revolution is not the answer. Revolution only plays into the hands of the powers of evil. Only the indignant voice of the masses of all free nations can insist that their elected representatives end the totalitarian plans of the money-lenders before they reach their goal.

From 1921 to 1927 Mr. Marsden remained in the employ of the *Morning Post*. He had many friends but he had made powerful enemies. In 1927 he was chosen to accompany the Prince of Wales on his 'Tour of the Empire'. It is very unlikely that Mr. Marsden failed to avail himself of this opportunity to inform His Royal Highness in regard to the document and the manner in which international financiers were involved in international intrigue and the Communist and Zionist movements. When the Prince of Wales returned from his tour of the Empire he was a very changed man. He was no longer 'A gay young blade'. He was much more matured and had assumed the serious role of 'Good Will Ambassador of the British Empire'. It may be pure coincidence, but Mr. Marsden, whose health had improved greatly during his travels abroad, took suddenly ill the day after he arrived back in England and died a few days later. It reminds one of what Mr. E. Scudder wrote regarding the death of Mirabeau in his book *The Diamond Necklace*. "King Louis of France was not ignorant of the fact that Mirabeau had been poisoned." Mirabeau died because he had told the king of France who the real instigators of the French Revolution were.

Everyone who has had the privilege of knowing the present Duke of Windsor knows how deeply he was affected by his experiences at 'The Front' during the 1914-1918 war. He insisted on spending a great deal of time in the Front Lines cheering and encouraging the troops. He won their admiration and loyalty, and in return he loved and respected his future subjects who fought so well and died so bravely.

After the tour of the Empire, His Royal Highness took a great interest in social and economic problems. He visited the coal mining districts and entered the miners' homes. He chatted with miners and their families regarding their problems. He wanted to dispense with many of the frills which encumber royal ceremonial proceedings. He had the audacity to disagree when statesmen and politicians tendered him advice he knew was unsound. He dared to express his opinions in regard to Foreign Affairs. He was alert and opposed to any proposed government policy which might play into the hands of 'The Secret Powers' and lead the country into another war.

174

After he was proclaimed king, January 20th, 1936, he took his responsibilities even more seriously. He didn't intend to be just 'another king' on the international chess-board, to be moved here and there at the will of the Powers-behind-the-throne, until he had been maneuvered into a position of stalemate or checkmate. It became quite evident he had a mind and a will of his own. A king with his knowledge and characteristics can be a serious obstacle to the men who are determined to have affairs of State managed according to their plans. He had to be got rid of.

From the time he became associated with Mr. Marsden be had been subjected to a modern version of "L'Infamie". A whispering campaign of slander hinted that he was 'wild' and inclined to licentious conduct. He was accused of leaning to the 'Right' and being associated with Sir Oswald Mosley's Fascist movement. [15]

When his friendship with Mrs. Wally Simpson was discovered, the full power of the 'leftist' press was turned loose on them and, regardless of his position, the vilest insinuations were made, and the worst possible construction placed on their relationship. This was exactly the kind of situation his enemies could use to further their own unscrupulous plan. The Prime Minister of Great Britain was given his orders. In 1936 Mr. Baldwin carried out their mandate in regard to King Edward VIII's abdication in exactly the same way Messrs Lloyd George, Churchill and Balfour had carried out their mandate in regard to the Palestine Mandate in 1919.

King Edward was maneuvered into a position in which he either had to make Mrs. Simpson his 'Morganatic' wife, and lose the love and affection of his subjects, or he had to abdicate and marry her. He took the only course a gentleman could take under the circumstances.

The reader may wonder why the document over which there is so much controversy cropped up in 1901. The answer is to be found in the fact that the artificially created depression in 1893 brought about conditions favorable to war. The international bankers met in London to consolidate their position, and work out the details for the Boer War. They considered this war necessary in order to obtain control of the African gold fields and diamond mines. The Jameson Raid took place as scheduled January 1st, 1896. This led to the most unjustifiable war the British have ever fought. Winston Churchill hot-footed it to Africa to act as observer. Officially he was a war correspondent. A great deal regarding this period of history remains to be written.

The details leading to the Spanish-American War had to be worked out. This war gave the American bankers control over sugar production in Cuba. More important still was the business that had to be transacted in regard to the war scheduled to take place between Russia and Japan in 1904. This business was very complicated. Matters had to be so arranged, that while the Rothschilds financed the Russians, Kuhn-Loeb and Co. of New York financed the Japanese, an understanding had to be reached by which both groups made money while the Russian Empire was weakened, and made ready for the Menshevist revolution scheduled to take place in 1905.

While the international bankers met in the financial district of London, the leaders of the World Revolutionary Movement met in the slum-district of the same city. Lenin received his orders. He was told how he should manage the various revolutionary groups so that independent action on their part would not seriously interfere with the overall plans of those who directed the W.R. M. It has been proved that the Directors of the W.R.M. used the heads of the Grand Orient Lodges in France, and other countries, to further their revolutionary plans, therefore it is reasonable to suppose that an agent was sent from London to Paris in 1900 or 1901 to instruct the top-level executives of the Grand Orient Lodges in regard to the part they were to play to bring about the program of wars and revolutions agreed upon, in exactly the same way they had sent the agent who was killed in Ratisbon, from Frankfort to Paris in 1785. It is just another illustration of how and why history repeats itself.

NOTES:

1 This military plan had been in existence since before 1914 and was reported to the Allied Governments fighting World War One by intelligence officers of both the British and American armed forces. The plan is explained in detail in *Hell's Angels of the Deep* and *Check Mate in the North* by W.G. Carr.

2 This statement and others of a similar nature prove that Hitler never had accepted or agreed with the extreme Nazi War-Lords' Long Range Plan for World domination by Military conquest.

3 Once again rabid anti-Semitism shows itself and yet history proves that the International conspirators have used every race and creed to serve their own secret and selfish ambitions.

4 Most of this evidence is reproduced in The Palestine Plot by B. Jensen, printed by John McKinley, 11-15 King Street, Perth, Scotland.

5 The book *Coningsby* was published in 1844 just before Karl Marx published "The Communist Manifesto". At that time several revolutions were being planned and took place immediately after Karl Marx's book appeared in print.

6 Ribbentrop was evidently quoting from an article Weiner Freie Presse published December 14th, 1912 by the late Walter Rathenau in which he said, "Three hundred men, each of whom is known to all the others, govern the fate of the European Continent and they elect their successors from their own entourage." These are the Illuminati.

7 Most countries of the world were mired deep in economic depression.

8 Hitler closed all Grand Orient Lodges in Germany.

9 Quoted from the Evening Standard, London, dated April 28, 1936. For further particulars regarding Lord Londonderry's conversations with Hitler, Goering, and Von Ribbentrop read *Ourselves and Germany* published by Lord Londonderry.

10 For the full text of these letters read, The Rulers of Russia by Rev. Fr. Fahey pp. 64-70.

11 The opening paragraph of this letter confirmed the opinion reached by the author i.e. the extreme Nazi plan was at variance with Hitler's plan.

12 The author personally informed both the Canadian Chief of Naval Staff, the First Lord of the Admiralty and other government officials regarding this sorry state of affairs.

13 For further particulars regarding international finance read Wealth, Virtual Wealth and Debt by Professor Soddy, pp. 290 and on.

14 Theodore Herzl in A Jewish State (Judenstaat) re-quoted from p. 45 of The Palestine Plot by B. Jensen.

15 As recently as November 1954, this old slander regarding the Duke of Window's connection with Fascism was revived. He was accused in the Press of having given secret information to German officials regarding allied defenses and plans in 1936. This he vigorously denied.

⊙ Chapter Seventeen

World War Two Breaks Out

After King Edward VIII abdicated, many well-educated Britishers, including members of parliament and retired naval and military officers of high rank carried on a strenuous campaign to try to convince the leaders of the British government of the truth regarding "The International Bankers' Conspiracy". Amongst these were Capt. A.H.M. Ramsay and Admiral Sir Barry Domvile, K.B.E., C.B., C.M.G. Captain Ramsay was educated at Eton College and Sandhurst Military College. He served with His Majesty's Guards in France from 1914 to 1916 when he was seriously wounded. He was appointed to Regimental H.Q. after recovering from his wounds. Later he was transferred to the British War Office. He served with the British War Mission in Paris until the war ended. He was elected to parliament in 1931 as member for Midlothian-Peeblesshire and served in that capacity until 1945.

Admiral Sir Barry Domvile had a brilliant naval career. He earned the reputation of being one of Britain's better Gunnery Officers. He started his naval service 1894 as a midshipman in sail and steam driven warships. Because of ability, he received accelerated promotion and was made lieutenant in 1898. In 1906 he was awarded the gold medal of the Royal United Services Institution. He was placed in command of destroyers in 1910. When World War I appeared unavoidable he was appointed assistant secretary to the Committee of Imperial Defense. After hostilities started he was appointed to the Harwich Striking Force consisting of light Cruisers and destroyers under Admiral Sir Reginald Tyrwhitt. He commanded seven destroyers and light cruisers all of which earned an enviable reputation as "Fighting Ships". He was made "Flag Captain to Admiral Tyrwhitt in 1917 and served in that capacity until the end of the war.[1] His postwar service included Director of Naval Intelligence; president of the Royal Naval College, Greenwich; and vice-admiral commanding the War College. He retired in 1936 with the rank of full Admiral.

During the years 1920-1923, because of his special ability and varied war experience, he was first, assistant director, and subsequently, director of the Plan (Policy) Division of the Admiralty Naval Staff. In this capacity he attended a number of conferences at Paris, Brussels, Spa, San Remo, and the Washington Naval Conference.

Both these ex-officers, one army — the other navy, suspected the Bolshevik revolution in Russia had been plotted and planned, financed and directed, by men who considered the liquidation of the British Empire was essential before they could achieve undisputed control of the wealth, natural resources, and manpower of the entire world.

Both these gentlemen have been frank to admit that until 1935 they had failed to identify those who constituted the "Secret Power" behind the world revolutionary movement and international affairs.

In 1933, by reason of their studies and research, they reached a decision that the leaders of World Jewry, headed by the international Jewish bankers, were the "Secret Power" behind the World Revolutionary Movement. They became convinced that these men used the wealth they possessed to purchase sufficient power to influence international affairs in such a manner as to bring nations into conflict with each other. They also reached the conclusion that the motive behind the Long Range Plan was to establish the Messianic Age, so that International Jewry, with a central government in Palestine, could enforce their totalitarian ideology upon the peoples of the entire world. With this latter conclusion I agree. As the reader knows, I admit going through the same period i.e., 1907 to 1933 in doubt and uncertainty, but in 1939 I became convinced, after the way the Jews had been "purged" by Stalin in Russia, and used to start abortive revolutions in other countries, and then abandoned to their fate, that the men who constitute the "Secret Power" behind national and international affairs were the Illuminati who used Zionism and anti-Semitism; Communism and Fascism; Socialism and selfish Capitalism to further their secret plans to bring about a One World Government which they intended to control in exactly the same way as they had controlled Russia, in the person of Lenin, after October 1917. A worldwide dictatorship is the only type of government which could, by police rule, enforce their edicts upon the people, and thus assure peace. If there is only ONE STATE governed by ONE DICTATOR, there can't be any wars. This is pure logic, because to have a dispute — a quarrel — a fight — a revolution — or a war, there must of necessity be two individuals, holding opposing ideas and opinions which they intend to make the other party accept by force of arms if argument and negotiation fail. Furthermore, my studies and research convinced me that from the time of Christ right down to the present day, the men who have been the "Secret Power" behind national and international intrigue have always used their wealth illegally to obtain the power and influence to put their secret plots and plans into effect. They have used usury, bribery, corruption, graft, illegal methods of traffic and trade, slavery, assassinations, wars, revolutions, prostitution, drugs, liquor, and any and every other form of licentiousness and vice to bribe, blackmail, or in other ways force unwilling humans to do their bidding. These "tools", be they Jew or Gentile, Freemason or otherwise, have been, without exception, liquidated by one method or another if, after serving their purpose, they were considered to know too much.

Considering these facts, I became convinced that the top conspirators did not belong to any one race or nation; they were "Agents of Satan", doing his will, and serving his purpose, here on earth. The one and only purpose of the Devil is to win the souls of men away from Almighty God. The men who plot and plan wars and revolutions have done a great deal to bring about a Godless world. This reasoning enabled me to understand the evil genius of these men. They could not move nearer to their totalitarian-materialistic goal without

179

fomenting wars and revolutions. They must of necessity destroy the civilization founded in accordance with the Divine Plan of Creation before they could impose their evil totalitarian ideology upon the peoples of the world.

Both Captain Ramsay and Admiral Domvile tried from 1936 to 1939 to prevent Britain becoming engaged in war with Germany, because they considered "international Jewry" intended to arrange a war in which the German and British Empires would destroy each other. The people who survived could be easily subjugated by Communism afterwards in exactly tile same way Russia had been communized.

I agree that World War II was engineered by the Illuminati who used anti-Communism, anti-Fascism, anti-Semitism and anti-everything else to further their evil Long Range Plans and secret totalitarian ambitions. I arrived at the conclusion that it was a fatal mistake to be anti-anything but anti-evil. I believe the only way to defeat the diabolical international conspiracy is to educate as many people as possible in regard to tile truth and convince them that they have been used as "Pawns in the Game" by these evil men.

Captain Ramsay tried hard to Convince Mr. Neville Chamberlain that it was against the best interests of tile British Empire to allow the international conspirators to involve Britain in war with Germany. He was right. He did not convince the British Prime Minister, but he at least impressed him sufficiently so that when he went to Munich he compromised with Hitler and returned to England waving exuberantly his famous umbrella, and a paper which he said was an agreement "Guaranteeing Peace in Our Time".

Immediately this announcement was made, the Press, controlled by the international bankers, started an anti-Fascist campaign of hate. The controlled Press damned Chamberlain as "An old woman willing to buy Peace at any price." They lampooned him with his umbrella. They accused him of being Pro-Fascist. Their agents in Moscow burned Chamberlain in effigy in the public squares. The British public was never allowed to know the difference between Pagan Aryan Nazism, and Christian Anti-Communistic Fascism. According to the Press, German and Italian Fascism are both black-pagan atheistic ideologies and totalitarian in purpose. Few people understand the difference between Nazism and Fascism and Communism and Socialism.

Space does not permit recording all the details of the intrigue put into effect by the evil group who were determined to bring about way between Britain and Germany. In my opinion, Hitler's anti-Semitic policy was wrong, but throwing Britain and Germany at each other's throats wasn't going to save the Jews residing in Germany, Poland, and other countries from persecution and death. Forcing the countries into a war enabled the anti-Semitic hatreds of the Nazis to be vented on the Jews by direct action on a tremendous scale, with a hideous ferocity only witnessed previously during a revolutionary "Reign of Terror". If those who claim the way was brought about by the international Jews, and not the Illuminati, (who don't give a damn for the Jews or anybody else for that matter) would stop and think, they will realize that by fomenting World War II those responsible condemned a great many innocent Jewish people to death, while most of the Jewish revolutionary Communists escaped death by going "underground" and later obtained illegal entrance into Palestine, the U.S.A., Canada, and other countries. If peace had continued, the German anti-Semitic feelings could never have reached the extremes they reached during the war. A peaceful solution could have been found for the problem. But NO! The Long Range Plan of the International Illuminati called for the destruction of the British, the German Empires, and the Jews who were not actively Communistic and therefore not their "Tools".

Captain Ramsay had promised Mr. Neville Chamberlain that he would produce documentary evidence to prove a conspiracy existed to force Britain into declaring war on Germany. This evidence consisted of secret coded cables which had passed between Mr. Winston Churchill and President Roosevelt, unknown to Mr. Chamberlain, the then Prime Minister. Captain Ramsay offered to obtain copies of these documents to prove that the International Bankers were determined to bring about World War II for the purpose of bringing the rest of the European nations under Communist control. The Illuminati control both.

Tyler Kent was the coding officer who had coded and decoded these secret documents in the American Embassy in London. Anna Wolkoff was his assistant. Like Gouzenko they felt sick at the thought of the world being plunged into another Global War to further the ambitions of a few totalitarian-minded men whose wealth compelled even presidents and top-level statesmen to do their will. The same conditions existed in 1938 as existed in Paris in 1919, prior to the signing of the Treaty of Versailles.

Captain Ramsay in 1944

Tyler Kent, like many other people, knew Captain Ramsay was suspicious of "An international Jewish conspiracy". He knew Captain Ramsay was trying to prevent the war. When Captain Ramsay told him Mr. Chamberlain would prevent such a conspiracy from being put into effect if he was given authentic documentary evidence to prove such an international conspiracy did actually exist, Tyler Kent offered to show Captain Ramsay the damning documents in his flat at 47 Gloucester Place, London.

The international conspirators had, however, been busy. In March, 1939 they had tricked Mr. Chamberlain into signing a guarantee to protect Poland from German aggression by presenting him with a false report to the effect that a 48-hour ultimatum had been delivered by Germany to the Poles. The facts are that the German government did not issue any 48-hour ultimatum. The German note set forth reasonable suggestions for a "peaceful" solution of the problems created by the Treaty of Versailles in regard to the Polish Corridor and Danzig.

History will prove that the only reason the Polish government ignored the German note was because agents of the international conspirators advised its leading statesmen that the British guarantee assured them against German aggression.

Month after month went by and still Poland ignored the German note completely. Meanwhile the anti-German Press speeded up its torrents of abuse against Hitler because he had dared to defy the power of the international Money-Barons. Hitler had earned their hatred by his independent financial policy and monetary reforms. The public was made to believe, and at that time I was also made to believe, that Hitler's word couldn't be trusted. The public was told after his "Putsch" into Sudetenland, that Hitler had said he "intended to make no further demands." It was made to appear by the press that the German note to Poland suggesting a "peaceful" solution to the problems created by the Treaty of Versailles was "another demand", and therefore, "a broken promise".

History proves it was no such thing. What Hitler had said was that he would make no further demands AFTER he had rectified the injustices inflicted upon the German people by those who had dictated the terms and conditions incorporated into the Treaty of Versailles. That is a horse of a very different color. It is a typical example of how a half-truth is far more dangerous than a direct lie.

Hitler's promise was qualified. He promised he would make no further demands after the problems involving Sudetenland, part of Czechoslovakia, the Polish Corridor and Danzig, had been solved.

The German grievances were real and justified. By the Treaty of Versailles the Polish Corridor had separated East Prussia from the rest of Germany. Danzig, a purely German city, had been isolated; the Germans who had remained in the territory which became known as Czechoslovakia, had been persecuted; the expressed wish of the Austrian people to unite with Germany, for their own protection against Communist aggression, had been denied. Generally speaking, public opinion in the Western World has been molded to blame France and the nations which formed the 'Little Entente' for insisting on this policy towards Germany. It cannot be denied that the post-war policy of the Allied Powers towards Germany was in direct contradiction to the principles of "Self-Determination" which had been accepted by the governments involved on behalf of the people who had elected them to manage their affairs.

Each succeeding German democratic chancellor had tried by diplomatic negotiation to obtain redress and had failed. It was their failure to obtain justice by peaceful means that influenced the German people when they swept Hitler to power. Winston Churchill labeled Hitler "That Monstrous Abortion of lies and deceits", but it cannot truthfully be denied that in 1939 Hitler was trying once again to arrange a peaceful solution of the problems created by the Polish Corridor, and Danzig, when the agents of the international conspirators deceived Prime Minister Chamberlain into believing that Hitler had issued an 'Ultimatum' to the Polish government and had moved in his armies to back up his demands. It was this act of deception that caused Mr. Chamberlain to reluctantly advise His Majesty's government to declare war on Germany.

This is a grave accusation to make, but its truth and justification is proved by the fact that exactly the same thing happened all over again towards the end of, and immediately after the end of, World War II.

It would be ridiculous to suppose that sincere, Christian statesmen could repeat, and compound, such injustices as those perpetrated by the Treaty of Versailles. But these injustices were repeated by the Allied Powers by the adoption of the policy of unconditional surrender; by the adoption of the Stalin-White-Morgenthau Economic Plan; by the partitioning of Germany; by the evil motives behind the German re-armament plan; by the post-war crisis with France; and (as will be explained in another chapter) by the dangerous game that has been played between the international financial interests, and the Soviet and Chinese dictators, since the war with Japan ended. Any unbiased person must admit that it is not the common people of the democracies who demand that their governments carry out such a policy of hatred and injustice against the German people. It is not the elected representatives of the people who conceive these diabolical programs of persecution and irritation. It is the evil powers behind the scenes of government who are responsible. Their evil policy is based on devilish cunning. They know that a house divided against itself must surely fall. That nations divided against each other must surely be subjugated also. The more human beings are forced to fight each other, the stronger grow those who sit back and push them into the wars. By allowing this secret scheming, plotting, and planning to continue we are allowing the forces of evil to make us commit national and racial suicide.

When Hitler tired of waiting for Poland's reply, and of being insulted by the Allied Press, he moved his armies into Poland. Britain then declared war in accordance with her agreement. The criminal nature of the advice given Poland can be realized by the fact that although Britain declared war on Germany she was powerless to give Poland any direct aid, either naval, military, or with air-power.

No lesser an authority than Lord Lothian, who was in recent years British Ambassador to the United States, stated in the last speech he made at Chatham House: "If the principles of self- determination had been applied in Germany's favor, as it was applied against her, it would have meant the return of Sudetenland, Czechoslovakia, parts of Poland, the Polish Corridor, and Danzig to the Reich."

It is safe to assume that had the British people been permitted to be correctly informed regarding these matters they would never have permitted war to have been declared. But it was "War", not Truth or Justice, upon which the international conspirators were determined.

Even though Britain had declared war, Hitler refused to depart from the policy he had set forth in Mein Kampf regarding Britain and her Empire. He ordered the generals, in command of the famous Panzer Corps, to halt on May 22nd, 1940, when they could easily have driven the British armies into the sea or made them surrender. Captain Liddell Hart in his book *The Other Side of the Hill* quotes Hitler's telegram to General Von Kleist:

"The armored divisions are to remain at medium artillery range from Dunkirk. Permission is only granted for reconnaissance and protective movements."

General Von Kleist was one of the Germans who didn't agree with Hitler's policy towards Britain. He decided to ignore the order. Captain Hart quotes Von Kleist as telling him after the event.

"Then came a more emphatic order. I was ordered to withdraw behind the canal. My tanks were kept halted there for three days." [2]

Captain Hart next quotes a conversation which took place between Hitler, Marshall Von Runstedt, and two members of his staff. According to Marshal Von Runstedt "Hitler then astonished us by speaking with admiration of the British Empire; of the necessity of its existence, and of the civilization that Britain had brought into the world ... He compared the British Empire with the Catholic Church — saying they were both essential elements of stability in the world. He said all he wanted from Britain was that she should acknowledge Germany's position on the continent; the return of Germany's lost colonies would be desirable but not essential; and he would even support Britain with troops if she should be involved in difficulties anywhere. He concluded by saying that his aim was to make peace with Britain on a basis that she would regard compatible with her honor."

Thus it was that Britain was given time to organize her evacuation forces and get her soldiers back home from Dunkirk.

It will be recalled that for the first few months of the Second World War Hitler did not bomb Britain. While Neville Chamberlain remained Prime Minister, Britain did not bomb Germany. The controlled press called it "A Phony War".

It is quite obvious that two great empires cannot destroy each other if they will not fight. Chamberlain would not initiate the offensive because he was almost convinced that he had been the victim of international intrigue. Mr. Winston Churchill had been given full powers and responsibilities regarding all naval, military, and air operations. He decided he would take the initiative.

Churchill conceived the idea of "The Norway Gamble". This poorly planned, and executed, "combined operations" involved Britain's army, navy, and air force. It was doomed to failure before those involved ever got into action. Even a person with only an elementary knowledge of military strategy would have realized that such an operation could not possibly succeed unless the invading forces had control of the Kattegat and Skagerrack. Churchill had this fact pointed out to him by competent naval authorities. Churchill is not a fool, but he went ahead with his project in opposition to his naval and military advisers, exactly as he had done when he sent the Naval Divisions to save Antwerp in 1914; and when he insisted upon the invasion of Gallipoli in 1915. The results in all three of "Churchill's Gambles" were the same. No gains, severe reverses, exceptionally heavy casualties, and loss of valuable equipment and materials. The fiasco of "The Norway Gamble" was not blamed on Churchill, however. His friends, "The international Money-Barons" used their controlled press to release their full powers of hatred, criticism, invective, censure, sarcasm, and satire against the Prime Minister, Mr. Chamberlain. They wanted Chamberlain out of the way so they could put Winston Churchill in his place and turn the "Phony War" into a "Shooting War".

This propaganda campaign forced Chamberlain to resign, exactly as Mr. Asquith had been forced to resign in 1915. Thus, once again, history repeats itself. In May, 1940, Churchill again joined hands with the Socialists to form a new government.

Mr. J.M. Spaight, C.B., C.B.E., was the principal assistant secretary to the British Air Ministry during World War II. In his book *Bombing Vindicated*, published in 1944, he reveals that the ruthless bombing of German cities started on May 11th, 1940, the evening of the day Winston Churchill became Prime Minister. Britain started the bombing and, as was to be expected, Germany retaliated. Thus the war was placed on a destructive basis.

Mr. Spaight also reveals that on September 2nd, 1939, when Mr. Chamberlain was still in office, a declaration had been made by the British and French governments that "Only strictly Military objectives, in the narrowest sense of the word, would be bombarded." Churchill's policy to bomb open towns and cities has been defended but it never can be justified.

There is another point, not generally known, that needs to be mentioned. It has been recorded that many German generals did not agree with Hitler's policies. The Nazi War Lords knew they had to get Hitler out of the way, and subjugate the Communist Dictatorships controlled by Stalin, before they could carry out their Long Range Plan for world domination. The all-out- war against Britain was not in keeping with their program. Russian Communism, and the Jews, had to be subjugated and destroyed before they could launch their attack westward and subjugate Britain and the United States. This was the Nazi Plan, not the Fascist policy. The Nazi plan was international in scope. The Fascist cause was national.

A secret meeting of Nazi War Lords was held in May, 1941. They decided they would use Herr Hitler's friendly policy towards Britain to try to get Britain to call off the war against Germany. Rudolf Hess was instructed to fly to

Scotland and contact Lord Hamilton and Churchill, so he could try to influence the British government to sign a Peace Treaty.

Hess was instructed to tell the British government that if they would sign a Peace Treaty the German generals would get rid of Hitler and then concentrate all their military power on the destruction of Communism in Russia and other European countries. Hitler knew nothing of this plan.

Hess flew to Scotland, but Churchill refused to agree to the offer made by Hess. The German generals then persuaded Hitler to undertake an all-out offensive against Russia, pointing out that until Russia was defeated they could not extend their military operations outside of Germany without undertaking the serious risk of being stabbed in the back by Stalin when he considered the moment opportune.

On June 22nd, 1941, German Forces invaded Russia. Immediately they took action to crush the Communist menace Britain and the United States of America pooled their resources to aid Stalin defeat the German armed forces. Convoys of ships were organized to carry munitions of war to Russia via Murmansk and the Persian Gulf. [3]

During the Irish Rebellion, a security regulation 18-B had been passed by Order in Council to enable the English police to detain and interrogate people they "suspected" might be members of the Irish Republican Army intent on committing acts of annoyance or sabotage. In 1940 the practice had been discontinued for many years.

On May 23rd, 1940, during the first two weeks of Mr. Churchill's Premiership, he used this obsolete regulation to arrest all the prominent people who had tried to prevent Britain from being dragged into a war with Germany, prior to September, 1939, and those who had opposed his policy to turn the Phony War into a Fighting War.

Many hundreds of British subjects were arrested without any charge being made against them. They were thrown into prison without trial under Regulation 18-B which deprived them of the rights and privileges of the Habeas Corpus Act. Magna Carta was ignored and ridiculed.

These wholesale arrests were made by the police on the unsupported statement of Mr. Herbert Morrison that he, as Secretary of State, "had reasonable cause to believe the said persons had been recently concerned in acts prejudicial to the public safety, in defense of the realm, or in the preparation or instigation of such acts, and that by reason thereof, it was necessary to exercise control over them."

Captain Ramsay, Admiral Sir Barry Domvile, their wives and friends, and hundreds of other citizens were thrown into Brixton prison. Some of them were detained until September, 1944. [4] They were treated like criminals, and far worse than prisoners on remand.

Just prior to this outrageous action on the part of those who did the bidding of the international bankers, the press controlled by the Money-Barons had conducted an hysterical propaganda campaign claiming Germany had a strong and well-organized 5th Column in Great Britain ready to give aid to invading German troops the moment they landed.

Subsequent investigation proved that the very competent British Intelligence Service never produced at the time, or since, even the flimsiest evidence that any of those arrested were ever engaged in any conspiracy.

There is plenty of evidence to prove that the newly formed British government, under Churchill, was ordered to take this unjust action against all prominent and influential people in Britain who had voiced their opinion that "International Jewry" had promoted the war between Britain and Germany.

Just before the wholesale arrests were made, Mrs. Nicholson, the wife of Admiral Nicholson, another very distinguished British naval officer, had been arrested as a result of a "Smear" campaign. She had stated publicly she thought the plot to involve Britain in war with Germany was the work of the international Jewish bankers. Four charges were actually 'framed' against Mrs. Nicholson. She was tried by a judge and jury. She was acquitted on all counts. This action on the part of the judge and jury did not suit those who were determined to persecute people who objected to the international bankers in Britain, France, and America running the affairs of the nation so as to inveigle them into another Global War. So the antiquated Regulation 18-B was used to put them out of the way. The Phony War became a fighting war. The British and German Empires weakened, as those who started the wars strengthened their positions. The Illuminati laughed up their sleeve.

Notwithstanding the fact that Mrs. Nicholson had been exonerated of all guilt and blame regarding the charges laid against her, she was among those arrested and imprisoned under Regulation in 18-B in May, 1940.

Captain Ramsay tells the whole story of the events that led up to his arrest and imprisonment in his book The Nameless War. Admiral Sir Barry Domvile tells of his experiences in his book From Admiral to Cabin Boy. These are books which should be read by every person interested in the continuance of freedom. [5]

Mr. Neville Chamberlain died in 1940. He was worn out in body and soul fighting "The Secret Powers" who govern from behind the scenes. So also had died Mr. William Pitt. But those who swim with the tide of Illuminism, and do as they are told, usually live to a "Ripe Old Age". They are showered with earthly honor and worldly wealth. One thing is certain: they can't take wealth and honors with them when they die — and after death will come the judgment.

NOTES:

1　The author published the story of the Harwich Striking Force in 1934, under title Brass Hats and Bell-Bottomed Trousers.

2　The review of The Manstein Memoirs in the Globe and Mail, Toronto in 1955 confirms this statement.

3　I was one of Canada's Naval Control Officers at this time. I felt it my duty to protest the policy which diverted ships that were sorely needed to take supplies to England, and send them to Murmansk. My protest was ignored. The battle to save International Communism had started.

4　Mr. Herbert Morrison visited Canada in November 1954. He was Chief Speaker at a meeting held in Toronto to raise funds for the support of 'Political Zionism'. The author is informed that the U.S.A. Government agreed that the British authorities arrest and detain Tyler Kent. This action was against all the accepted principles governing personnel attached to Embassies in foreign countries. This matter was brought up again in the U.S.A. as recently as 1954 but nothing seems to have come of it.

5　While revising and editing this M.S.S. October, 1954, I received a later from the head of Publishing Firm in England who had dared publish Admiral Domviles' book. The letter said in part : "The 'Evil Powers', regarding which you are so well informed, made things so difficult that I was 'forced' to go out of business after more than 50 years."

 # Chapter Eighteen

The Present Dangers

By studying history it is possible to predict future trends with a certain degree of assurance. History repeats itself because those who direct the W.R.M. do not CHANGE their Long Range Plans — they simply adapt their policies to suit modern conditions and adjust their plans to take full advantage of the advancement of modern science.

In order to understand the international situation as it is to-day, we must recall what has happened since Lenin established the totalitarian dictatorship in Russia in 1918. It has been proved that the dictatorship was established to provide the Western Internationalists with the opportunity to put their totalitarian ideas and theories for a universal dictatorship into effect. They wished to iron out any wrinkles by the process of trial and error.

When Lenin died Stalin took over. At first he was ruthlessly obedient to the dictates of the international bankers. He appointed Béla Kun to put their ideas for the collectivization of farms into effect in the Ukraine. When the farmers refused to obey the edict, five million were systematically starved to death when their grain was taken from them forcibly. This grain was dumped on the markets of the world to aggravate the artificially created depression. Another five million farmers and peasants were sent to forced labor to teach the rest of the subjugated people that the STATE was supreme and the Head of the STATE their God, whose edicts must be obeyed.

It was not until Stalin began to purge a great number of Jewish Communist leaders, who were undoubtedly Marxists that Trotsky and other revolutionary leaders knew for certain that he had abandoned the Illuminati and developed imperialistic ambitions.

Stalin's conduct of the revolution in Spain perturbed the Western Internationalists still more, particularly when Serges and Maurin proved Stalin was using international Communism to further his own secret plans and imperialistic ambitions.

After Franco won the Civil War, Stalin's conduct was very difficult to understand. Revolutionary leaders in Canada and America just couldn't follow the drastic changes in the Party Line as they had been taught it during their indoctrination into the Marxian theories. When Stalin signed the non-aggression pact with Hitler, after the British and German Empires had been plunged into World War Two, it appeared as if Stalin wanted to do everything within his power to aid Hitler overrun Western Europe and destroy the power of the international bankers.

The situation looked so grave from the international bankers' point of view that they decided they had to try to persuade Stalin to abandon his imperialistic ambitions and go along with them in a spirit of peaceful co-existence. They tried to persuade Stalin that it was quite feasible that he should rule the Eastern World by Communism, while they ruled the Western World under a super-government. Stalin asked for proof of their sincerity. This was the beginning of the now much talked about theory of peaceful co-existence. But peaceful co-existence between two internationalist groups; or between people who believe in God and those who believe in the devil, is impossible.

By secret communications between Churchill and Roosevelt, which Tyler Kent exposed, it was agreed that Chamberlain should be removed as Prime Minister so that Churchill could assume office and turn the 'Phony' war into a 'Hot', and shooting war. They considered this act would convince Stalin of the sincerity of their intentions.

History reveals that Mr. Chamberlain was ousted as Prime Minister in May 1940 in much the same way Asquith was ousted in 1913. Churchill assumed office as Prime Minister May 11th, 1940. He ordered the R.A.F. to start bombing German cities and towns that same night. Mr. J. M. Spaight, C.B., C.B.E., was principal assistant secretary at the Air Ministry at that time. After the war he wrote a book Bombing Vindicated. In it he justifies Churchill's policy to bomb German cities and towns on the grounds that it was done to 'Save civilization'. The author admits however that Churchill's order was a breach of the agreement entered into by Britain and France on September 2nd, 1939. On that day the Prime Minister of Britain and the President of the French Republic agreed that war must be declared on Germany because of Hitler's invasion of Poland. They also agreed they would NOT bomb German cities and towns, and make the German people suffer for the sins of one man. The leaders of the two governments solemnly agreed that bombing should be restricted to strictly military objectives in the narrowest sense of the word.

Since the war it has been proved that the real reason Churchill bombed German cities, contrary to the agreement, was because the Western international bankers wished to give Stalin a definite assurance that they were sincere in their desire to carry out their suggested policy of peaceful co-existence between Eastern Communism and Western Illuminism.

The bombing of Germany brought about immediate retaliation and the people of Britain were subjected to an ordeal the like of which had never been experienced since the dawn of creation.

It is difficult for the average citizen to appreciate the depths to which those involved in international intrigue can sink. It will be proved that the Illuminati had no intention of keeping faith with Stalin. It will be proved Stalin had no intention to keep faith with them. It will also be proved that the Nazi War Lords, while secretly determined to crush both international Communism and international capitalism, actually tried to deceive Churchill into believing they did not have secret plans for world domination by military conquest.

In the Spring of 1941 the Nazi War Lords, unknown to Hitler, ordered Hess to fly to Britain and tell Churchill that if he would agree to end the war against

Germany they would guarantee to get rid of Hitler and then destroy Stalin and international Communism. After consultation with Roosevelt, Churchill turned down the offer made by Hess.

The Nazi War Lords then tried to convince the Western internationalists of the sincerity of their intentions by ordering Hitler's assassination. The plot failed and Hitler escaped with his life. When this act failed to charge the minds of those who were secretly instructing Churchill and Roosevelt, the Nazi War Lords decided they must first attack Russia and defeat Stalin, and then turn their military forces against Britain and the Americas. They launched their attack against Russia June 22nd, 1941. Immediately, this happened, both Churchill and Roosevelt announced publicly that they pledged their respective governments to support Stalin to the limit of their resources. Churchill, ever dramatic, said he would shake hands with the Devil himself if he promised to help him destroy German Fascism. He referred to Hitler as "That monstrous abortion of lies and deceits", and yet Churchill must have known that Hitler, for all his faults, was not an internationalist.

This action was calculated to remove from Stalin's mind any doubt he might still have regarding the honesty of the intentions of the Western internationalists to divide the world into two halves and then live in peaceful co-existence. Roosevelt and Churchill then proceeded to provide Stalin with unlimited aid. They borrowed astronomical sums from the international bankers and paid them interest on the loans. They then charged the principal and interest to the National debts of their two countries so that the tax payers paid for, and fought, the war fomented by the Illuminati while the bankers sat back and made hundreds of millions of dollars out of the deal. This extraordinary generosity with the people's blood and money paved the way for the meetings which 'THE BIG THREE' subsequently held in Tehran, Yalta, and Potsdam.

Stalin played a very cunning game at Tehran. He made it clear that he still suspected the Western internationalists might be deceptive rather than sincere. He played at being difficult to persuade, and very hard to get. He made outrageous demands. He demanded unreasonable concessions. He implied that in making these demands he was only testing out the sincerity of the men he knew only too well, from long experience, were the directors of the international conspiracy. Roosevelt had been well briefed. He gave Stalin everything he asked for. Churchill had to go along or lose the financial backing of the international money-lenders and the military support of the United States.

Then came Yalta. Stalin changed his attitude. He pretended he had been won over. He became the perfect host. Churchill and Roosevelt were dined and wined. Stalin dissolved the Comintern. The Comintern was the executive body which had plotted and planned revolutions in every country. Stalin, Roosevelt, and Churchill drank damnation to the Germans. Roosevelt assured Stalin that after they were through there wouldn't be enough German left to worry about, he is reported to have advocated shooting 50,000 German officers without trial. The controlled press has never stopped harping upon the Nazi policy of genocide against the Jews, but it has been singularly silent in regard to Roosevelt's policy of genocide against the Germans. In return for the dissolution of the Comintern, Roosevelt gave Stalin more concessions. Six hundred million human beings east of Berlin were handed over into Communist bondage.

Churchill acquiesced in everything Roosevelt and Stalin did. History will prove that at the Yalta meeting Stalin and Roosevelt had several secret meetings after Churchill had been dined and wined too well to allow him to keep his wits alert. Roosevelt pretended to be friendly with Churchill but, on the evidence of his own son, he often said things, and suggested policies, which showed, that secretly, he looked upon him with contempt.

Only Churchill can explain WHY he had to sit and listen to Roosevelt's suggestions that Hong Kong be given to Communist China to bribe Mao-Tse-Tung to play along with the Western internationalists. How could Churchill profess publicly, such a close and sincere friendship for Roosevelt when Roosevelt was constantly repeating that he considered the dissolution of the British Commonwealth necessary to the future welfare of the human race? Hitler thought just the opposite.

But Stalin was nobody's fool. He had been associated with the agents of the international bankers so long that he could read their most secret thoughts like an open book. He knew better than any man alive that they had used Communism to further their totalitarian ideas, so he played them at their own game. During the final stages of the war he forced the Allied Armies to halt and wait until his armies occupied Berlin.

The above statements are proved by the existence of a secret order issued by Stalin to the General Officers of the Soviet Armies to explain his policy. The order is dated February 16th, 1943. It reads:

"The Bourgeois Governments of the Western Democracies, with whom we have entered into an alliance, may believe that we consider it our sole task to throw the Fascists out of our land. We Bolsheviks, and with us the Bolsheviks of the whole world, know that our real task will only begin after the second phase of the war is ended. Then will begin for us the Third phase which for us is the last and the decisive one ... the phase of the destruction of world capitalism. OUR SOLE GOAL IS, AND IT REMAINS, THE WORLD REVOLUTION: THE DICTATORSHIP OF THE PROLETARIAT. We have engaged in alliances because this was necessary, to reach the third phase, but our ways part where our present allies will stand in our way in the achievement of our ultimate aim."

Stalin did not show his true colors until after he had captured Berlin and occupied Eastern Germany. Then he broke every promise he had made. This turn in events was kept out of the Press because neither Roosevelt nor Churchill wished the public to know how Stalin, the bank robber; the murderer; the international counterfeiter had put it over them like a blanket.

The Western internationalists just had to bide their time. They realized that if Stalin and Mao-Tse-Tung joined forces, the Communist hordes could sweep over the western world like a plague of locusts. They reasoned that Stalin was getting old. They knew he hadn't too long to live. It was better to curry favor with him rather than have him spill the beans and expose the whole diabolical conspiracy.

The Western capitalists considered Stalin's open defiance a serious matter, but they had a trump card up their sleeves. Before playing this card, they instructed Roosevelt to make one more effort to bring Stalin back into line again. Roosevelt offered to grant anything Stalin demanded, as far as the Far East was concerned, if only he would play along with the Western capitalists. The controlled press would have persistently reported that Roosevelt gave Stalin the concessions he did in the Far East because his military advisers had told him it would require two full years of heavy fighting, after the collapse of Germany, before Japan could be brought to her knees. This lie is so apparent that it was really unnecessary for General MacArthur to give Roosevelt the lie direct. The American generals knew that Japan had been trying to negotiate a peace for a considerable time before Roosevelt made the concessions he did to Stalin.

Once again Stalin took all he could grab in Manchuria. He again reneged on his promises and renewed his defiant attitude. This time the powers behind the White House administration were really angry. They must have made some suggestion of such a diabolical nature that it even shocked Roosevelt, for he sickened and died. It has been said that he died in the house of Bernard Baruch. The Advisers of the United States government then decided to play their trump card ... the atomic bomb. The atomic bombs were dropped on Hiroshima and Nagasaki to indicate to Stalin what was in store for Russia unless he toed the line. The fact that America had atomic bombs had been kept secret. Japan was already defeated when they were dropped. Surrender was only a few days off. Over one hundred thousand human beings were sacrificed, and twice that number injured in Japan, to demonstrate to Stalin that the United States actually did have atomic bombs. Thus it is seen that Churchill ordered the unrestricted bombing of Germany to try to fool Stalin into believing the international capitalists wanted to be friends, and then the U.S.A. bombed Japan with atomic bombs to warn him that he better play along and do as he was told ... or else.

Molotov was the one man best able to judge what was going on in Stalin's brain. During the post-war period Molotov was the Soviet's Foreign Minister. He represented the Kremlin at the United Nations for many years. Molotov married the daughter of Sam Karp of Bridgeport, Connecticut. Thus, Molotov became the connecting link between the Kremlin and the international financiers of the

Western World. It has been reliably reported that immediately after Stalin withdrew Molotov from the United Nations he sent Molotov's wife into exile in Siberia. These acts alone strongly indicate that Stalin had broken with the Western capitalists who had helped put him in power in Russia.

The fact that Tito broke with Stalin after the war ended is further proof that Stalin had determined to go ahead with his imperialistic program. Tito has always been subservient to the western Financiers who supplied him with all the money he required to establish himself in his present position in central Europe. Churchill's son risked his life on more than one occasion during World War Two by parachuting into Tito's territories to confer with him on behalf of the western powers.

Finally Stalin died, or was disposed of. He left this world with his lips sealed like any other gangster. The agents of the Western internationalists, located in Moscow, struck as soon as Stalin died. Beria, and Stalin's other trusted lieutenants, were done away with. Stalin's son disappeared without a trace.

In order that what was happening in Russia would not appear too obvious, it was arranged that Malenkov should take over temporarily after Stalin's death. He was ordered to decry the Great Stalin and, for a time, he did deflate him in the eyes of the people. Then he changed his tactics. He renewed friendly relations with the Chinese Dictator; he started to make friends with the Russian people; he sponsored the development of a spirit of national pride. By doing so he sealed his own fate.

The Western internationalists countered with a demand that Western Germany be immediately rearmed. France was the stumbling block. Mendes-France was placed in power long enough to have France ratify the agreement to rearm Germany. Having served his purpose he was placed amongst the discards as so many others have been.

The situation in the Far East has deliberately been confused but it is not difficult to explain. The Western internationalists had friends in China, just as they had in Russia, but Mao-Tse-Tung cannot be considered one of them. He and Stalin had very similar ideas in regard to the Western internationalists. But both the Eastern and Western totalitarian-minded groups had one thing in common ... They wished to get rid of Chiang-Kai-Shek.

The Western capitalists started a propaganda campaign against Chiang-Kai-Shek just as soon as the Japanese war ended. This action had a two-fold purpose. They wanted to prove to Mao-Tse-Tung that co-existence with them was feasible and, at the same time, they wished to eliminate the nationalist leader. The press charged that the nationalist government was corrupt; that the nationalist generals were lax, and did not maintain discipline amongst their troops; that the nationalist troops committed pillage and publicly performed rapes. It is only right to admit that many of the charges made against the nationalists were true.

The fact that many officials in the nationalist government in China were proved to be corrupt was used to justify Great Britain's policy to recognize the Communist regime. It was also used by certain United States advisers as the grounds on which they advocated that America withdraw support from Chiang-Kai-Shek. What the general public has not been told is the fact that, after the Communists took over in China, it was proved that most of the high officials who had brought Chiang-Kai-Shek and his nationalist government into disrepute were Communist cells who had infiltrated into the nationalist government for the purpose of wrecking it from within. This statement is substantiated by the fact that many of the nationalist government officials, who came under criticism for corrupt practices, were absorbed into the Communist regime, and given favored positions and accelerated promotions. The Rev. Leslie Millin of Toronto, who was a missionary in China during this period, will vouch for the truth of the above statements.

The way international affairs developed after 1946 would indicate that Stalin did not have atomic weapons at the time of his death. Had he possessed atomic weapons he could have knocked the principal cities of Canada and the United States into a cocked hat.

Churchill has served their purpose as far as the international bankers are concerned. He is growing old and a bit troublesome. He has to be relegated into the discard also. But Churchill has been built up by the propaganda of the western Capitalists as a GREAT man. He is the people's national hero. He couldn't very well be disposed of by a campaign of L'Infamie. He couldn't be ridiculed out of office. With rare cunning the Western internationalists disguised their intentions by ordering the Press to organize the greatest tribute a man ever had. On Churchill's eightieth birthday they showered him with gifts and honor. They convinced the vast majority of people that Churchill didn't have an enemy in the world.

Events indicate that both the Communist dictators and the Western internationalists were agreed that Churchill could be an obstacle to the furtherance of their plans. The Communist dictators decided they would use Aneurin Bevan to grease the skids under Churchill. They indicated this to Communists throughout the entire world when the Chinese dictator Mao-Tse-Tung entertained Attlee and Bevan at a banquet when they visited China in 1954. The international press published pictures taken at this banquet.

It is unlikely that one person in a million, other than a Communist, understands the significance of that picture. Attlee was shown as sitting at the head table. Bevan was shown as having been placed at the bottom nearest the door. The general impression was that Attlee was the guest of honor; and that Bevan was considered of very little significance as far as the Communist regime in China, and the Soviets, were concerned. But this is how the public is confused and deceived. In China it is customary to seat the Guest of honor nearest to the door.

In view of the events recorded it is reasonably safe to predict that in the near future the following events will take place.

One. With or without his knowledge the Communist dictators will use Aneurin Bevan to help oust Churchill by attacking his foreign policy in the House of Commons.

Two. That the Western internationalists will use Bevan's attacks on Churchill as a lever to get Bevan out of the British Labor party and parliament. At the same time they will get rid of Churchill by casting doubts into the minds of the people regarding his ability to carry on top level secret negotiations now he is past eighty. It is possible the Western internationalists may lift the screen from secret diplomacy just sufficient to justify those chosen to lead the attack. By doing so the threat would be implied that if he didn't step down gracefully they would make known all that went on behind the scenes at Tehran, Yalta, Potsdam, etc.

Three. It is safe to predict Churchill will step down immediately pressure is brought to bear on him. It is equally safe to predict that Bevan will not step down. The chances are a hundred to one that Attlee and Deakin will leave, or be removed, from the Labor party in Britain and that Bevan will lead the party against Sir Anthony Eden when he decides to contest a general election after taking over from Churchill. [1]

Four. The fact that Roosevelt's son has given a glimpse of the fact that Churchill had to play along with his father; and had to do as he was told, and even had to profess publicly his friendship for the president after the president had so rudely told him that he favored the dissolution of the British Commonwealth of nations, is a clear indication as to the line of attack the Western internationalists will take to get rid of, what so many people consider, 'The Grand Old Man of British Politics'.

The point to remember is this, the Nazi internationalists have, for all intents and purposes, been eliminated from the game. Two totalitarian-minded groups of men remain ... the communist dictators of Russia and China; and the Western capitalists or internationalists, whichever one wishes to name them.

Just as long as both groups are satisfied to live in peaceful coexistence, with the world practically divided between them, there will be an uneasy peace. But if the leaders of either side decide that coexistence is too frail a structure upon which to build their respective New Orders there will be war.

World War Three, if started by the Eastern Communist dictators will begin without any preliminary warning. An international general strike will be called in all capitalistic countries. This action is calculated to produce the paralysis previously referred to. The Communist planes will bomb all industrial centers to knock out the war potential of the United States and Canada and kill as many of the population as possible in order to bring about speedy surrender and subjugation. Britain will likely get the same treatment. Nerve Gas may be used on industrial areas the enemy does not wish to destroy. Soviet forces will occupy the mining districts of northern Canada from coast to coast. The occupied areas will be used as bases of operation against the southern objectives. The international general strike will tie up shipping in every port in the world making it impossible for supplies to reach the people of Great Britain. A blockade of the British Isles by Soviet submarines will stop any leaks. The people of Britain will be starved into submission four weeks after the outbreak of hostilities. The members of the Communist underground in all cities in the western world will evacuate target areas immediately before the attacks. The underground armies will return and take over the devastated areas as soon as the "All-Clear" has been given. The Communist 5th Column will round up and liquidate all people whose names are on the black list. Thus will the directors of the Western internationalists be got rid of in much quicker time than they got rid of their Nazi opponents by means of the Nuremberg Trials.

On the other hand, if the Western internationalists become convinced that an attack is to be made upon them by the Communist dictators, then they will force the western democracies into another World War in order that they may get in the first blow. As a prelude to their attack the public will be made aware of the dangers of international Communism. The danger to Christian democracy will be emphasized. The atheistic-materialists, who have the western world in economic bondage, will call for a Christian Crusade. They will justify their atomic attacks upon Russia and China as Churchill justified his attack on Germany. They will say it was necessary to save our civilization. But don't let this fool ourselves. Regardless of how the case may be presented to the public the fact will remain that if World War Three is allowed to take place it will be fought to decide whether Eastern Communism takes over the entire world or whether the Western capitalists will continue to rule the international roost.

If World War Three is permitted to take place, the devastation will be so extensive that internationalists will continue to justify their contentions that ONLY a world government, backed up by an international police force, can solve the various national and international problems without resorting to further wars. This argument will appear very logical to many people who overlook the fact that both the Eastern Communist leaders, and the Western capitalist leaders, intend to ultimately bring into effect, THEIR ideas for an atheistic-totalitarian dictatorship.

People who wish to remain FREE can follow only one plan of action. They must support Christianity against ALL forms of atheism and secularism. They must support private responsible enterprise against cartels and combines. They must support those who advocate 'The New Economy' against those who would continue with the old.

When a person is in doubt regarding the right and wrong of anything, all he or she needs to do to solve his or her uncertainty is recite the first half of the Lord's Prayer SLOWLY and contemplate on the meaning of those wonderful words of wisdom. "Our Father ... Who art in heaven... hallowed be Thy name ... Thy kingdom come ... Thy will be done ... in earth as it is in heaven." It doesn't require more than a few minutes to decide if any act to be performed individually, or collectively is in accordance with the Will of God, or furthering the machinations of the Devil.

If we intend to save the future generations, from the fate being prepared for them by the forces of evil, we must take IMMEDIATE ACTION ... THERE IS NO TIME TO LOSE. The reader may well ask: "But what action must we take?"

That is a very good question. If the answer wasn't provided there would be no justification for the publication of this book. Far too many men spend a great deal of time damning this and damning that. They are anti this and anti that. But very few speakers or writers who condemn an idea, an organization, or a movement, offer practical solutions to the problems, or make suggestions to bring to an end the evils exposed.

FIRST: We must as individuals recognize the spiritual issues involved. Once again the Scriptures advise us how to accomplish this purpose. Ephesians 6th chapter 10th to 17th verses tells us: "Brethren be strengthened in the Lord and in the whole of His power. Put on the armor of God that you may be able to stand against the wiles of the devil. For our wrestling is not against flesh and blood, but against Principalities and the Powers, against the world rulers of this darkness, against the spiritual forces of wickedness on high. Therefore take up the armor of God that you may be able to resist the evil day, and stand in all things perfect. Stand therefore, having girded your loins with TRUTH, and having put on the breast-plate of justice, and having your feet shod with the readiness of the Gospel of peace, in all things taking up the shield of Faith, with which you may be able to quench all the fiery darts of the most wicked one. And take unto you the helmet of salvation, and the sword of the spirit, that is, THE WORD OF GOD."

SECOND: We must take practical steps and use constitutional means to counteract the threat of both international Communism and international capitalism, and any other subversive ideologies which may try to destroy TRUE Christian democracy. In order to carry out the mandate in the above Gospel we must do the following things:

A. Demand monetary reforms : Because selfishness and greed, and the desire for power, are the roots from which all evil grows, it is only logical that constitutional means be instituted to take away the wealth, and curb the powers, of the leader, of all atheistic-materialistic groups who, in the first place, usurped it from the governments of the people. This being the TRUTH the tax-payers have a legal right to demand that their elected governments redress the wrongs committed against them; put an end to all forms of usury; and reimburse their treasury departments to the extent of the loans floated during the last century to fight wars fomented to further the interests of those who loaned the money and charged interest on these loans. If this advice is followed the proletariat will have restored true democracy mid the Soviet and Chinese dictators would have no excuse to disguise their imperialistic ambitions under the cloak of anti-capitalism.

B. Monetary controls: The electors must insist that the issue of money, and the control thereof, be placed back in the hands of the government where it rightfully belongs. By government is meant the top-level executive body chosen from the elected representatives because of their qualifications to conduct the affairs of the nation in an efficient and business- like manner, basing their decisions on democratic justice and Christian charity.

C. Punitive action: The electorate can justifiably demand that heavy penalties be imposed on all those found guilty of corruption and graft because these two evil practices are the principal means used by the agents of all revolutionary organizations to subvert, or force, others into doing their will. All subversive organizations must be outlawed and all people, proved to be members, must be made liable to punishment provided by the law. Those who advocate the violent overthrow of constitutional government do so in order that they may usurp wealth and power without having to work for it. Their punishment should therefore consist of performing manual labor and/or public services. Their hours should be extended 25 per cent beyond the union limits, and their pay should be 25 per cent below the union rates. The period of their detention should be decided by the way they improve from their negative attitude towards society and religion.

D. Diplomatic negotiations: Because the agents of the international conspiracy always work behind the scenes of government, and always use SECRET meetings and diplomacy to further their own plans and ambitions, secret negotiation should not be allowed under any circumstances. If government is to be "Of the people; by the people; for the people"; then the people have every right to know every detail of what is going on.

E. Christian Crusade: Laymen of all Christian denominations should unite in the Name of God to put an end to bigotry and misunderstanding which enables anti-Christian ideologies to keep Christians divided and at logger-heads. The house divided within itself must fall. The Crusade should be organized for the purpose of educating the public in regard to the methods need by those who direct atheistic-materialistic ideologies. Special attention should be given to interesting the youth of our nations in the movement in order that they may be protected from the subversive actions of the agents of the conspirators. The Crusaders should be trained to take a POSITIVE approach when dealing with those who have joined subversive organizations either willingly or because of ignorance. To abuse, to knock, and condemn persons only increases their resistance and makes them more anti-social.

By first gaining their confidence the Crusader is in position to prove to them that the heads of all atheistic-materialistic ideologies only use others as "Pawns in the Game" to further their secret plans and ambitions. Once a person is convinced he or she will be thrown into the discard just as soon as the directors of their movement consider they have outgrown their usefulness, this will hurt their pride and cause them to reflect upon the wisdom of their behavior. Having once created doubt in their minds it is then possible to convince them by supplying them with suitable literature on the subject. It was to supply this need that Pawns In The Game was published. A religious revival amongst the members of all Christian denominations is essential in order to change men's thinking in regard to the values and importance they place on worldly possessions. The hearts of men must be turned towards love of Almighty God. We must learn once again to take a real delight in rendering Him service and in performing His Holy Will. The National Federation of Christian Laymen has been organized to put this idea into action.

F. United Nations: Because the constitution of the United Nations comes up for revision this year, possible changes may be recommended. It is important, therefore, that all those who oppose internationalism in any form organize political pressure groups in all parties to urge that the delegates of the Christian-democratic nations do not lend themselves in any way to suggestions favoring the trial of a World Government, regardless of whether it is called a super- nationalist government or disguised in any other way. Churchill's suggestions for a United States of Europe was only a move in the direction of internationalism. Only he can say whether it was intended to help the Eastern Communists or the Western capitalists.

G. Illegal traffic and trade: Because the subversive 5th columns, and undergrounds, are organized, hidden, and subsist in the underworlds of large cities, and because no revolutionary effort can hope to succeed without the full co-operation of a well-organized, properly trained, fully equipped, and well-disciplined 5th column, or underground organization, it is necessary that public opinion be organized to demand that all those engaged in illegal traffic and trade, or criminally connected with the underworld, shall be arrested and brought to trial regardless of what their political affiliations may be, or what position they hold in society. The public must be organized to give support to all honest police officers and law administrators. Public opinion expressed on the floor of the Houses of Parliament must insist that the underworlds be CLEANED up, and not just raided and scattered. The policy of raiding and scattering the underworld characters has only resulted in creating a hundred dens of iniquity where only one existed before. Those convicted should be treated as recommended in subsection 'C'.

H. Publicity: Christian laymen must be organized to counteract the propaganda of those who advocate internationalism and the atheistic materialistic ideologies. Local branches should be organized to insist that subversive propaganda be eliminated from the press, the air, and T.V. programs. They should demand that time and space be made available so the Christian democratic way of life may be presented to the people. It is unfortunately TRUE that it is several centuries since Christian democracy functioned properly.

I. Defeatism: Every effort must be made to counteract the efforts of those who preach defeatism. They usually argue that there is nothing that can be done to correct the existing conditions. They suggest that since the pending fate is inevitable it is no use worrying. The attitude of the Defeatist is like that of the professional rapist who advises his intended victim that, because her fate is inevitable, she might as well relax and enjoy it. Those who claim there is nothing we can do to escape totalitarianism ignore the fact that God exists and is interested in the destiny of man. People who get discouraged must be reminded that the only way they can save their immortal souls is to keep on fighting against the Forces of Evil, thus giving service to God. They must be made to realize that they won't be judged according to their achievements and victories, but solely on the merits of the effort they put into the Crusade.

J. Brotherly Love: Because God has provided mankind with all he requires for this earthly existence there is no logical reason why some of his creatures should live in opulence while others starve to death. The theories of the new economists should be tried out to devise better methods for the more equitable distribution of the necessities of life. Once these have been assured to all human beings it will be a comparatively simple matter to persuade those who have too much to share it with those who have decidedly less and a greater need. To share what we have with others in need provides the greatest happiness it is possible to enjoy on this earth. By living in accordance with the plan of God, economic conditions would improve to such an extent that the establishment of homes, and the raising of families, could be undertaken in reasonable security. Conditions of 'Fear' and 'Uncertainty' would be abolished.

K. Military Preparedness: Military preparedness is absolutely necessary just as long as the conditions exposed in this book are allowed to continue. Everyone who accepts the hospitality of a country, and enjoys the privileges of citizenship, should be prepared to defend that country from aggressors, be they external foes or the enemy within. The only justification for fighting a war is to prevent subjugation by the enemy on the rational argument that as long as we have some resemblance of freedom left there is still hope that we can overcome the forces of evil and re-establish true Christian democracy.

L. Internal Security: The best way to strengthen the internal security of any nation is to build up a strong and efficient Civil Defense organization. To permit of rapid development Civil Defense should be made part and parcel of the national internal security, system. As such, it should be a Federal project and responsibility. This suggestion is particularly applicable to Canada because the Minister of Justice supported by the Royal Canadian Mounted Police, is charged with the responsibility for the nation's internal security. Civil Defense is the organizing and training of the civilian population into auxiliary units to augment the regular departments which render public service during normal conditions.

Civil Defense workers are trained how, to protect themselves and the communities in which they live, in the event of attack by an enemy. Because our only potential enemies use their 5th Column and underground organizations to overthrow the constituted government by revolutionary action, and subjugate the population by means of terrorism, it stands to common sense that Civil Defense should be organized as a counter-revolutionary organization. The Civil Defense special police, and intelligence units, should therefore be trained under the supervision of the R.C.M.P. so they could co-operate with them to ensure our internal security during any emergency.

M. Action. There is no time to lose: In reading this book you have faced the challenge and your response to the action outlined, undertaken with a strong faith in God, will determine the future of humanity and bring about the overthrow of the forces of evil which plot to destroy our Christian democratic way of life. The task is not beyond our capabilities. We must remember that the Devil's important nucleus of evil in this world at the present time is centered in no more than about three hundred master-minds.

N. Faith, Hope and Charity: We must never forget that the Christian religion is based on Faith, Hope and Charity, while all atheistic ideologies are based on doubt, hatred, and despair. Almighty God has permitted us to GRADUALLY solve many of the mysteries of NATURE in order that we would use rather than abuse these extra-ordinary benefits. We can now use or misuse atomic energy. If we allow it to be misused the powers of evil undoubtedly hill off one half the human race and cripple most of the others. We can rest assured that amongst those who survive will be the agents of the powers of evil. Almighty God has provided the human race with all we need to live. He has provided for our comfort and reasonable pleasures. It is our duty to see that all members of the human race share equally in the bounties and blessing provided by Almighty God. There should never be a time when the granaries of the western world are bursting at the seams, while the people of the Far East are dying by the millions from starvation. We must share freely and generously with others what we have above our own requirements, because it is certain we cannot take anything with us when we die.

O. The Christian Crusade: It is suggested that 'THE CROSS AND THE FLAG' be the slogan for the Christian Crusade. It is also suggested that the following anthem should be used to open or close all public meetings held in connection with the crusade.

"THE CROSS AND THE FLAG"
The Cross and The Flag our emblems shall be,
Our purpose in life to serve only Thee,
Thy Will shall be done ... Thy Kingdom shall come
On earth as in Heaven Eternally.

1.
The powers of Satan
Our God may deny.
And claim there's no heaven
For us when we die
All tyrants and despots
Our Faith may decry
Their torments and terrors
We'll always defy.

2.
We'll march into battle
Upholding Thy Name
No worldly enchantments
Our 'Cause' shall defame
No evil enslavements
Shall swerve from their goal
Thy militant Legions
Till they reach Thy Fold.

3.
What doth a man profit
To gain the whole world
By serving 'neath banners
Hell's agents unfurled?
We'll hold to Thy promise.
"Hell shall not prevail."
O Lord give us wisdom
Vile plots to curtail.

4.
Men seek greater riches
Use wealth to gain power.
But Lord, we all need Thee.
Life's span's but an hour.
Through darkness to daylight
Sustain us with grace.
We'll fight on to glory,
We'll run the Good Race. [2]

NOTES:

1   This was written prior to March 1955

2   Since writing the above Dr. Joseph Roff set it to music. It has been published in two editions by The Neil A. Kjos Music Co. of Chicago, Illinois. One edition is for four voices while a 'Special Edition' is for Choirs and community singing. Download a free copy at www.dauphinpublications.com/pawns.html

"The National Federation of Christian Laymen"

The National Federation of Christian Laymen is now being organized and a charter is being applied for. Our purpose is to try and unite all existing Christian Laymen's organizations to combat all forms of atheistic materialism and internationalism. The N.F.C.L. will be kept strictly non-partisan and non-denominational. It is not intended to interfere with the autonomy of any existing Christian organizations. Our purpose is educational.

PAWNS IN THE GAME was published to find out how many citizens are interested in taking constitutional action to end the international conspiracy as exposed in this book, and to take legal action to break the economic stranglehold a few internationalists have obtained on the Governments and peoples of the so called Free Nations by their practice of systematically applied usury. The response has been remarkable and justified the printing of this edition.

It is suggested that interested persons organize branches of the N.F.C.L. in their cities and towns and farming communities. Each group should provide itself with a library chosen from the books listed on another page. The material in the books will provide matter for thought and subjects for discussion at study groups. When local branches have been organized it is intended to send speakers, well qualified to explain the various angles of international affairs, to address public meetings sponsored by the local branches of the N.F.C.L.

Our Policy

1. We advocate Christianity and oppose illuminism and atheistic-materialism. We hold out the hand of friendship to ALL who worship God and oppose Satanism.

2. We support Nationalism and oppose Internationalism of any kind.

3. We advocate responsible private industry and oppose cartels and combines.

4. We advocate Loyalty to the Constitution and oppose all kinds of subversive activities.

5. We support lawful authority and oppose organized crime.

6. We advocate the practice of ethics in trade and commerce and oppose all forms of illegal traffic and trade.

7. We recommend brotherly love amongst all God-fearing people and oppose bigotry in any form.

8. We stand for Liberty and oppose licentiousness.

9. We stand for Freedom as opposed to Dictatorships and tyranny.

10. We advocate justice for all and favors for none.

11. We recommend that punishment should be made to fit the crime.

12. We advocate National Preparedness against internal and external foes.

13. We advocate active interest and participation in political, economic, health and educational matters as opposed to apathy, indifference, and despair.

14. We work so that Almighty God's plan for creation may be put into practice in this earth.

Join Our Crusade

The Federation of Christian Laymen is non-partisan and nondenominational. Our purpose is to help people who have been deceived into joining a subversive movement by telling them the TRUTH, and to inform others regarding their danger from those who plot, plan, finance, and direct ALL phases of the international conspiracy. We hope to finance our work by selling the literature we publish. If you agree with what we have to say then help us make the facts known. Send copies of our publication to your elected representatives and tell them how you wish them to act on your behalf. This is very important. Send copies to your friends and acquaintances, and to people you feel should be informed about these all important matters. Ask them to do the same. This is our only means of obtaining circulation as the TRUTHS we are trying to make known are being given the 'SILENT TREATMENT' by the controlled press. We work to retain our national form of government; to protect the Christian religion, to uphold private responsible enterprise; and to preserve our God-given rights and prerogatives.

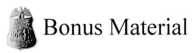 # Bonus Material

FBI Files

In an effort to create awareness and expose the International Conspiracy, William Guy Carr sent copies of his book to FBI's J. Edgard Hoover. Many other readers from around the United States, shocked with disbelief after reading the book, and concerned for it's contents, also sent letters to the FBI.

The following pages are unclassified documents, thanks to the Freedom of Information Act. The bureau responds to the author, readers' letters, and forms its own erroneous opinion about the book.

b6
b7C

62 Talbot Road,
WILLOWDALE, Ontario

Dear Fellow Citizen:

"Pawns In The Game" has been sent to you by a friend who believes you will be interested in helping to solve the political and economic problems which the author explains have been in the past, and still are today, the "CAUSES" which produce the adverse "EFFECTS" which have so seriously affected all our lives during the past half century.

If you agree with the proposals made in Chapter 18 to remedy the situation and preserve our heritage for our children and generations still unborn, then help us in our work by sending copies of this book to your friends. If you wish, we will mail them to the addresses you submit with a copy of this letter enclosed.

We realize only too well that you may have good reasons for not wishing to take an active and open part in our "Crusade". If this is so, we will be only too pleased to keep your name strictly confidential.

The MSS of "Pawns In The Game" was submitted to recognized authorities on Geopolitical Science, Political Economy, Education, Organized Labour, Industry, Religion, Politics, and those responsible for our Internal and External security BEFORE publication. It was the consensus of opinion that the book should be published in the public interest. Copies of the book have been filed with the R.C.M.P., The F.B.I., and sent to over five hundred other citizens we consider are like yourself, interested in the future welfare of our countries and our civilization.

The National Federation of Christian Laymen (N.F.C.L.) is strictly non-political and non-denominational. Our purpose is to unite the efforts of all sincere Christians and their organizations, so that we may direct the full force of our combined energies and united efforts against the men who secretly direct the world Revolutionary Movement from behind the scenes, rather than continue to permit them to divide us and conquer by the simple expedient of making us fight each other.

Yours faithfully,

William Guy Carr

ENCL. ENCLO. BEHIND FILE

INDEXED-61
RECORDED-61

SE 8

WILLIAM GUY CARR,
Publications Chairman,
National Federation of
Christian Laymen.

64 JUN 15 1955

2 JUN 9 1955

The following message appears on page
3 of the foreword of the attached book:
"Dear Mr. Hoover, Please let me know
what you think of this book.

                    /s/ William Guy Carr
                         May 30th 1955"
***

No record located in Bureau files on
William Guy Carr or the National
Federation of Christian Laymen.

STANDARD FORM NO. 64

Office Memorandum · UNITED STATES GOVERNMENT

TO : Mr. Nichols   DATE: June 3, 1955

FROM : M. A. Jones

SUBJECT: WILLIAM GUY CARR
NATIONAL FEDERATION OF CHRISTIAN LAYMEN
WILLOWDALE, ONTARIO, CANADA

        Bureau has received a form letter from captioned
individual in which he is described as Publications Chairman
of above organization. Bufiles contain no record of Carr
or his organization. He enclosed a book entitled "Pawns in
the Game" which he wrote and noted in pen "Dear Mr. Hoover
Please let me know what you think of this book." The book
has been rapidly reviewed in the Crime Records Section and
appears to be an interpretation of the world revolutionary
movement, traced through history and appears to be outspokenly
anti-semitic in its concept.

RECOMMENDATIONS:

        (1) In view of anti-semitic undertones of book
and lack of background information in Bureau files on Carr,
it is recommended that receipt of this book not be acknowledged
at the Bureau.

        ALL INFORMATION CONTAINED
HEREIN IS UNCLASSIFIED
DATE 5-31-02 BY SP4BTA/DFW
0 455251

        (2) It is recommended that the book be forwarded
to the Central Research Desk for review.

cc - Mr. W. C. Sullivan
    Room 7630A

RECORDED-01

105 - 38603 - 2

2 JUN 9 1955

JUN 15 1955
RGE:bs
(3)

Office Memorandum • UNITED STATES GOVERNMENT

TO : MR. A. H. BELMONT   DATE: June 7, 1955

FROM : W. C. Sullivan

ALL INFORMATION CONTAINED
HEREIN IS UNCLASSIFIED
DATE 5-31-02 BY SP4 BJA/DFW
I 95525I

SUBJECT: WILLIAM GUY CARR
NATIONAL FEDERATION OF CHRISTIAN LAYMEN
WILLOWDALE, ONTARIO, CANADA

A review of the explanatory information regarding the National Federation
of Christian Laymen set forth at the conclusion of the enclosed book does not
indicate that a review of the book would be of any value to the Central Research
Section. Since this group is now being organized in Canada, its activities may
possibly be of interest to the Espionage Section.

RECOMMENDATION:

It is recommended that the enclosed book be forwarded to the Espionage
Section to determine whether or not the activities of the National Federation of
Christian Laymen are of any interest from an investigative standpoint.

Enclosure

JFC:mjh
(4)
1 - Mr. Belmont
1 - Mr. Branigan
1 - Section tickler

RECORDED-61   38603-3

EX-121   2 JUN 9 1955

Lot E-15 New Ranch Trailer Park.
2291 Gulf to Bay Blvd.
Clearwater.Fla. USA.
April.17th.1958

Mr.J.Edgar Hoover   ALL INFORMATION CONTAINED
Director F.B.I.   HEREIN IS UNCLASSIFIED
Washington. D.C.   DATE 5-31-82 BY SP4BJA/DFW
                         II 955251

Dear Mr Hoover:- *National Association Christian Laymen*

Because I published the exposure of how those who control the
'Illuminati',and the New and Reformed Palladian Ribe,also organized Nazism,
Communism,and Political Zionism so these international movements could be used
to further their own secret plans and diabolical ambitions,I have been flooded
with requests to comment on your recently published book "Masters Of Deceit"
"News Behind The New"
I have studied ALL aspects of the World Revolutionary Movement since 1911 in
almost ALL countries of the world. I have had access to the archives of many
governments and universities.I have had the help and cooperation of for men who
at one time or another were Directors of British and Canadian Naval Intelligence.
When I published what my research and investigations have discovered in 1954
I did so because I had proved it was utterly impossible to persuade the HEADS
of Church and State to accept the TRUTH because it became obviousthat to-day,
as in the days of Christ,those who further the Luciferian ideology,as diametrically
opposed to God's plan for the Rule of the Universe ,control ALL those in High
Places.
I sent youl the Head of the R.C.M.P.,(I worked with [   ]during 1944-46)
and British and Canadian Directors of Intelligence copies of "Pawns In The Rame"
and "The Red Fog Over America" .Copies were also sent to a great many elected
representatives of the people in Britain,Canada,and the U.S.A. It was the exposure
that Prime Minister MacKenzie King had been educated and trained to serve the
interests of the Illuminati (One Worlders) from his boyhood days,and had furthered
the interests of the Rockeffelers to the extent that he had secretly agreed the
British Empire should be disolved in the interests of a One World Government,
that caused the defeat of the Liberal Party in the recent election.The TRUTH
that King and the MAJORITY of those he had picked as his cabinet were secretly
One Worlders was made known to a few honest and sincere Christians in nearly
every community in Canada and the United States between June 1955 and election
day 1957.When we saw the effect we redoubled our efforts with the result that
those who had comprised the Cabinet under the Liberal regeáme 'Hit the Dust'.
Our task now is to educate the newly elected M.Ps into what goes on BEHIND the
scenes of government,and who constitute the Secret Power.
               EX-135   REC-91 100

     I have received a vast amount of additional information since I published
my books and I have kept my readers located in almost every city and town throughout
the world this side of the Iron and Bamboo Curtains) informed regarding the
way the international conspiracy is being advanced to its final goal by publishing
"News Behind The News" monthly. I send copies to the F.B.I. every month but never
receive an acknowledgement: I must have hit on the TRUTH because those who control ALL subversive organizations and international movements have ordered that I
be given 'The Silent Treatment'.   CRIME 820

          EX-135   I will look forward to hearing from you. I had a letter form a Director
of Naval Intelligence, who had read my books, and he said he was 58 years of age
before he became convinced that 'A SECRET POWER' controlled the policies of ALL
National Governments but he admitted he had not identified WHO comprised
the Secret Power until he had read my books.
                              Sincerely William Guy Carr.

P/S Please excuse the hurried note that personally
I am away from my home in Canada.

Office Men **** um • UNITED ST **** GOVERNMENT

TO : Mr. Nease

FROM : M. A. Jones

SUBJECT: MR. WILLIAM GUY CARR
EDITOR *National*
NATIONAL FEDERATION CHRISTIAN LAYMEN
77 OTTER CRESCENT
TORONTO 12, ONTARIO, CANADA

DATE April 22, 1958

W. J. G. Carr

By letter dated April 17, 1958, the captioned
individual wrote the Director enclosing a 14-page pamphlet entitled
"News Behind the News" which was mailed from Clearwater, Florida,
where Carr states he is in residence for the month of May, 1958. He
enclosed a stamped self-addressed envelope for the Director's reply
to his temporary address in Clearwater.

Carr is not identifiable in Bufiles insofar as background
or biographical data is concerned. He has previously submitted similar
pamphlets bearing the same title which were not acknowledged because
they were anti-Semitic in nature and of no interest to this Bureau.
105-36603

The present issue of his publication being volume two
number six dated April, 1958, bears the caption "The Conspiracy to
Destroy all Existing Governments and Religions." It is of no particular
interest to the Bureau and from examination appears to be devoted more
to sex than any other topic. The last page of this issue makes known the
fact that Carr is available for lectures in the United States during the
month of May and while there is no charge for his services, he requests
the kind cooperation of those inviting him to guarantee his expenses at a
minimum of $50 plus accommodations. His subject will be "The
International Conspiracy."

RECOMMENDATION:
That the letter from William Guy Carr of 4-17-58 not be
acknowledged.

JK:pv
(2)

MCT

16 3 105—36603

EX-135

8 APR 24 1958

53 APR 29 1958

CRIME REC

OFFICE OF DIRECTOR
FEDERAL BUREAU OF INVESTIGAT
UNITED STATES DEPARTMENT OF JUSTICE

Mr. Tolson ____
Mr. Boardman ____
Mr. Belmont ____
Mr. Mohr ____
Mr. Nease ____
Mr. Parsons ____
Mr. Rosen ____
Mr. Tamm ____
Mr. Trotter ____
Mr. Jones ____
Mr. Clayton ____
Tele. Room ____
Mr. Holloman ____
Miss Holmes ____
Miss Gandy ____

Dear Sir:

I have considered you as one of
the greatest Americans of our era.
I have read your "Masters of Deceit,"
and also I have read two other books dealing with
conspiracy in America.

If you have the time (if, I receive no answer, I'll
understand) would you give me your opinion on these
two books.' "Red Fog Over America"
Pawns In The Game   by Wm. Guy Carr

Sincerely,

COPY:bak

REC-56 /05-38603-7X

EX-101

May 19, 1958

5-31-02 per letter dated 12-18-02 SP/BJA/DFW
1-16-03
CLASSIFIED BY NLS/BJA/DFW-60267-AMC
DECLASSIFY ON: 25X 6
E955251

        Your letter of May 12, 1958, has been received and the interest which prompted you to communicate with me is certainly appreciated.

        It was indeed thoughtful of you to comment as you did, and I am pleased to learn that you have read my book, "Masters of Deceit."

        In response to your inquiry concerning the books, "Red Fog Over America" and "Pawns in the Game" by William Guy Carr, while I would like to be of assistance, I must point out that this Bureau in its capacity as a fact-gathering agency does not make evaluations or draw conclusions relative to the integrity or character of organizations, publications, or individuals. I am sure that you will appreciate the factors which preclude my assisting you, and no inference should be made either that we do or that we do not have the information which you requested.

MAILED 9
MAY 20 1958
COMM-FBI

        Sincerely yours,

        L. Edgar Hoover

REC'D-READING ROOM
FBI
MAY 19 3 52 PM '58

NOTE: There is no record of correspondent in Bufiles. William Guy Carr on 5-30-55 sent to the Director a copy of his book "Pawns in the Game," requesting the Director's opinion. He later wrote to various individuals from Ontario, Canada, indicating that copies of the book had been filed with the RCMP and the FBI. A review of the book, sponsored by the National Federation of Christian Laymen, indicated that it had strong anti-semitic overtones and in view of lack of background info concerning Carr, receipt of the book was not acknowledged.

Tolson
Boardman
Belmont
Mohr
Nease
Parsons
Rosen
Tamm
Trotter
Clayton
Tele. Room
Holloman
Gandy

CFM:wgl

5-2 JUN 4 1958

(Note continued next page)

Mr. Chester Kotlarz

On 4-17-58 Carr wrote to the Director enclosing a 14-page pamphlet
"News Behind the News" from Clearwater, Fla. The pamphlet bore
the caption "The Conspiracy to Destroy all Existing Govt. and
Religions," was found to be of no particular interest to the Bureau
and was devoted more to sex than any other topic. Carr's letter
was not acknowledged.

His (S)

anti-semitic ideas and basic fascist theories are expressed also
in "Red Fog over America." (S)(4)

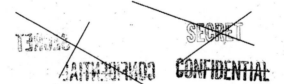

(NOTE)   Bufiles contain no information identifiable with
William Guy Carr sent the Director a copy of his book, "Pawns in the Game,"
on 5-30-55, requesting the Director's opinion. Carr later wrote to various
individuals from Ontario, Canada, indicating that copies of the book had been
filed at the RCMP and FBI. A review of the book, sponsored by the National
Federation of Christian Laymen, indicated that it had strong anti-Semitic
overtones and in view of the lack of background information concerning
Carr, receipt of the book was not acknowledged.

His (S)

anti-Semitic ideas and facists theories are also expressed in "Red Fog
Over America." (S)(u)

Ontario, Canada, is the subject of Bufile 105-38603. This group has not
been investigated by the Bureau; however, its official publication, "News
Behind the News," has been brought to the Bureau's attention previously.
This publication is largely anti-Semitic in nature. The editor of this
publication, William Guy Carr, has furnished us with copies of this official
publication and asked for comments concerning it. His letters have not
been acknowledged. "The Canadian Intelligence Service," published at
Flesherton, Ontario, Canada, formerly at Walters Falls, Ontario, is

- 2 -

WORTHINGTON-JEFFERSON
CONSOLIDATED SCHOOL CORPORATION

WORTHINGTON, INDIANA

October 1, 1962

Office of the Director
Federal Bureau of Investigation
Justice Department
Washington, D.C.

ALL INFORMATION CONTAINED
HEREIN IS UNCLASSIFIED
DATE 5-31-02 BY SP/BJA/DFW
C955251

Dear Sir,

    I am a social studies teacher at a small high school in Indiana and in the performance of my duties I asked a question and got some rather surprising comment from one of my better students. Upon inquiry as to her source she bought to me a book that would be considered rather ridiculous if it were not for the seriousness of the situation and the villification of some of our leading figures.

    I am writing to ask if you have any information concerning the book, its author or the organisation which publishes it.

    The book is titled Pawns in the Game by Wm. Guy Carr and published by the National Federation of Christian Laymen, 77 Otter Crescent, Toronto, Ontario, Canada.

    It was quite astonishing to find affiliation with such an organisation in a small community like this and I am quite interested in finding out more about this outfit. I know that if you can help me in any way I will be very grateful.

        Thank you for your trouble and I am
        sincerely yours

Worthington-Jefferson High School
Worthington, Indiana

REC- 30   105-38603- 13

9 OCT 8 1952

REC-30

105 - 38603 - 13

October 5, 1962

Worthington-Jefferson High School
Worthington, Indiana

ALL INFORMATION CONTAINED
HEREIN IS UNCLASSIFIED
EXCEPT WHERE SHOWN
OTHERWISE

Your letter of October 1, 1962, has been received.

Although I would like to be of service, the FBI
being an investigative agency of the Federal Government neither
makes evaluations nor draws conclusions as to the character
or integrity of any organization, publication or individual. I
regret that I am unable to help you and hope you will not infer
in this connection either that we do or do not have data in our
files relating to the subjects of your inquiries.

Enclosed is some literature which I hope will
be of interest.

Sincerely yours,

E. Edgar Hoover

John Edgar Hoover
Director

Enclosures (5)
The Courage of Free Men 2-22-62
4-17-62 Internal Security Statement
Your People Can Help Defeat Communism
FBI Jurisdiction Does Not Cover Making Evaluations
My Answer to Communism and Crime
SEE NOTE NEXT PAGE
EFT:js (3)

Tolson
Belmont
Mohr
Casper
Callahan
Conrad
DeLoach
Evans
Malone
Rosen
Sullivan
Tavel
Trotter
Tele. Room
Holmes
Gandy

MAIL ROOM ☐ TELETYPE UNIT ☐

CLASSIFIED BY NES/BJA/DKW-60367 RAG
DECLASSIFY ON: 25X

TRUE COPY

July 31, 1965

Dear Mr. Hoover,

on   Would you please tell me if you have any information
of the National Federation of Christian Laymen. Are they a subversive
organization? Have they ever been investigated?

Also, do you write a monthly law enforcement paper?
If so, how could one obtain them?

Thank you for sparing your valuable time.

                              Sincerely,

                    s/

REC- 57 105-38603-15

TO AUG 9 1965

EX-101

CORRESPONDENCE

17C 8/5/65 dlw
ash 8/6/65
DFc/dlw

August 6, 1965

REC- 57

EX-101

I received your letter of July 31st and want to thank you for your interest in writing.

With respect to your inquiry, information contained in our files must be maintained as confidential in accordance with regulations of the Department of Justice. I trust you will understand the necessary reasons for this policy and why I cannot comment as you suggested.

This Bureau does prepare an FBI Law Enforcement Bulletin; however, it is restricted in distribution and I am unable to furnish you copies. I regret I cannot be of help in this instance.

Enclosed is other material I hope you enjoy reading.

Sincerely yours,

J. Edgar Hoover

Enclosures (2)
"Our Heritage of Greatness"
Communism and The Knowledge To Combat It!
NOTE: We have had one prior outgoing to [   ] dated 7/6/65
in which she was furnished the list of organizations cited as subversive
by the Department of Justice.
DFC:dls (3)

Tolson ____
Belmont ____
Mohr ____
DeLoach ____
Casper ____
Callahan ____
Conrad ____
Felt ____
Gale ____
Rosen ____
Sullivan ____
Tavel ____
Trotter ____
Tele. Room ____
Holmes ____
Gandy ____

AUG 10 1965   MAIL ROOM ☐   TELETYPE UNIT ☐

CPSIA information can be obtained at www.ICGtesting.com
Printed in the USA
BVOW02s1643131016

464951BV00002B/115/P